AngloArabia

AngloArabia
Why Gulf Wealth Matters to Britain

David Wearing

polity

First published in 2018 by Polity Press
Reprinted 2019

Polity Press
65 Bridge Street
Cambridge CB2 1UR, UK

Polity Press
101 Station Landing
Suite 300
Medford, MA 02155, USA

ISBN-13: 978-1-5095-3203-2
ISBN-13: 978-1-5095-3204-9 (pb)

A catalogue record for this book is available from the British Library.

Typeset in 10 on 16.5 Utopia Std by Servis Filmsetting Ltd, Stockport, Cheshire
Printed and bound in the UK by CPI Group (UK) Ltd, Croydon

The publisher has used its best endeavours to ensure that the URLs for external websites referred to in this book are correct and active at the time of going to press. However, the publisher has no responsibility for the websites and can make no guarantee that a site will remain live or that the content is or will remain appropriate.

Every effort has been made to trace all copyright holders, but if any have been inadvertently overlooked the publisher will be pleased to include any necessary credits in any subsequent reprint or edition.

For further information on Polity, visit our website:
politybooks.com

Contents

Acknowledgements

While responsibility for any errors – grammatical, factual or analytical – is entirely my own, I owe a debt of gratitude to many whose help was crucial in carrying out this research.

Gilbert Achcar has been an invaluable mentor and a formative intellectual influence. I am very grateful to him, and to Adam Hanieh and Alfredo Saad Filho, for their guidance and advice on the doctoral thesis that formed the basis of this book. In general, the academic community at the University of London's School of Oriental and African Studies – both staff and students – provided the perfect environment in which to develop and sharpen my understanding of this complex topic.

The Lipman–Miliband Trust was kind enough to award me a small grant from the Peter Gowan Prize fund to support my endeavours. Campaign Against Arms Trade kindly provided access to their meticulously curated archives and to their considerable collective knowledge and expertise. Rosemary Hollis and Tony Norfield were both very generous with their time, and I learned a great deal from our conversations. In attempting to turn my thesis into a manuscript that retained its academic rigour while becoming accessible and engaging for a general audience, I am indebted to the patience and professionalism of Louise Knight and Nekane Tanaka Galdos at Polity, and to the wisdom of a very kind and constructive academic reviewer. Thanks must also go to David Gee, Caroline Richmond and everyone involved in the production of the book, which has benefited significantly from their input.

For a mixture of helpful chats, support and good company, heartfelt thanks go to Mike Walton, Rachel Shabi, Nithya Natarajan, Maya Goodfellow, Niheer Dasandi, Sarah Crook and Clare Clark. For their unique insights and their inspiration to me, I am deeply grateful to Ala'a Shehabi, Maryam al-Khawaja, Iona Craig, Rasha Mohamed and Sayed Alwadaei.

Above all, this work is dedicated to my family and to the fond memory of my grandparents, with much love.

Tables and Figures

Introduction

The Gulf Arab monarchies, and Saudi Arabia in particular, are among Britain's most important allies in the world – arguably more important than any other states in the global south. Investment from the Gulf is becoming highly visible in the UK economy, and controversy over British arms sales in the region – in the context of the Arab uprisings or the war in Yemen – is rarely far from the news. At the time of writing, a major humanitarian catastrophe is unfolding in Yemen, in large part as a result of a military intervention led by Saudi Arabia in which British-supplied arms have played a very significant role. Yet, until now, no detailed and comprehensive study of Britain's relationships with the Gulf states has been produced in the modern era.

This book attempts to map the deep, material structures of Britain's relations with the states of the Gulf Cooperation Council (the GCC), a grouping of Arab monarchies comprising Saudi Arabia, Kuwait, Bahrain, Qatar, the United Arab Emirates (UAE) and Oman. It will trace the historical background to these relationships, the arms that have been sold, the investments that have been made, the real significance of oil, and the balance of power between the two sides. What emerges is a unique Anglo-Arabian nexus of power and interests holding major importance for British capitalism and foreign relations. The reader will hopefully come away with a rich and detailed sense of why the Gulf Arab monarchies matter to the UK, and why the UK matters to them.

The key arguments of the book can be summarised as follows. First, UK–GCC relations in the modern era are the product of historical processes, particularly relating to the century and a half when the British Empire was the dominant power in the Gulf. Second, British power has been an important factor (among others) in the promotion and preservation of monarchical rule in the region. Third, the UK's current interest in Gulf oil and gas is less about direct energy supply and more about strategic, geopolitical and commercial interests. Fourth, the current forms of capitalism that exist in the UK and in the GCC area have come to complement each other in a series of important ways. Fifth, and relatedly, the GCC area is as important to British capitalism as – and, in some crucial senses, more important than – any other part of the global south. Sixth, UK arms exports to the Gulf Arab monarchies are less about commercial profit and more about their strategic value to British military power, which value is highly significant and growing. Seventh, the British government has in recent years played a key enabling role in supporting both the authoritarian backlash against the 'Arab Spring' in the Gulf and the disastrous Saudi-led intervention in the war in Yemen.

The primary focus of this book is the period following the end of the Cold War up until the present day. This is a distinct epoch in the modern history of international relations, part of the broader era of neoliberal 'globalisation' in international political economy. The period after 1991, the fall of the USSR and the end of the Gulf War to expel Iraqi forces from Kuwait is also a specific historical chapter in the international relations of the Middle East.

AngloArabia situates UK–GCC relations within the global structures that define this historical moment, treating capitalism as an analytically indispensable dimension of interstate relations. The position of a state such as the UK within the international system is defined as much by its status as a capitalist power as by, say, its military strength. The decisions made by individual politicians at specific times are important but must ultimately be understood within these wider structural contexts. It is this deep background to the news headlines that this book attempts to provide.

Britain's modern relationship with the Gulf Arab monarchies is a product of the history of empire. Chapter 1 will show how the Anglo-Arabian relationship was born and subsequently evolved: through the rise and decline of British imperial power in the Middle East; the emergence of oil as a key strategic resource; the establishment of the regional state system under imperial domination; the challenge posed by local nationalist forces and the rising power of the United States; and the seminal shift in UK–Gulf relations that occurred when the oil-producer states seized full control of their energy industries and started to maximise the economic benefits flowing to them. It is through the sweep of this historical narrative that we learn how Gulf wealth came to matter to Britain in the way it does today.

Gulf oil and gas are best understood, first, as a source of geostrategic power; second, as a source of energy; third, as a site of capital accumulation for the world's energy firms; and, fourth, as a generator of sizeable revenues ('petrodollars') for the producer states, which can be recycled back into the global economy to the advantage of major capitalist powers such as the UK. The last of these factors is addressed in chapters 3 to 5. Chapter 2 addresses the first three. It examines the importance of the Gulf states to UK energy consumption; the wider geostrategic value of Gulf hydrocarbons to the United States (the UK's main strategic ally) and to the UK itself; and the value of Gulf energy to the major British and Anglo-Dutch corporations, BP and Royal Dutch Shell.

Petrodollars represent a vital opportunity for British capitalism in a number of ways. Chapter 3 shows how the economies of both the

UK and the Gulf have developed in such a way as to complement each other, with Britain's need to attract financial inflows and secure lucrative export markets matched by the Gulf states' considerable capital surpluses and growing domestic demand. Chapter 4 details the various dimensions of Anglo-Arabian trade and investment today and attempts to ascertain precisely how much Gulf wealth matters to British capitalism.

Gulf wealth does not simply matter to Britain in a narrow economic sense. Chapter 5 explains the role that major petrodollar-funded arms contracts play in supporting the UK's military industry, an indispensable component of its enduring status as a global military power. The chapter also shows how the importance of the Gulf monarchies has led London to establish a relationship of close military cooperation with them, committing itself to projecting power into the Gulf and maintaining the coercive security apparatus of the conservative regional order.

Chapter 6 takes a closer look at how these military ties work in practice by examining two of the most significant episodes in the history of UK–GCC relations: the Arab uprisings and the war in Yemen. It details the British response to both these events, showing how the UK moved to support its local allies, including with increased arms sales and closer military cooperation, in instances where they were threatened by popular calls for democracy, and when they were involved in a conflict that degenerated into a humanitarian disaster. The Conclusion ties these various strands together, sizing up the UK–GCC relationship as a whole and touching on a few analytical, ethical and policy implications.

Before we continue, it is worth confronting and clearing away a few common misconceptions about the relationship between the UK and the Gulf monarchies which might obscure the picture and impede our understanding of the issues. In one of the most important and influential books in Middle Eastern studies, *Orientalism*, Edward Said argued that European colonial rule had been enabled and justified by the specific ways in which the region was represented in academic and cultural texts and in the thoughts, speech and actions of imperial policy-makers. Within this dominant discourse, Said argued, West and East were portrayed in a simple, juxtaposed binary: the West was progressive, dynamic, rational and morally upstanding, while the East was by turns backward, stagnant, superstitious, irrational, dishonest, lazy, sensual and exotic. This discourse was continually produced and reproduced until it became an all-pervasive common sense – one which flattered the West by comparison with its inferior Eastern 'other' and justified the projection of imperial power on ostensibly enlightened grounds. Moreover, this common sense evolved and survived in various forms through the twentieth and into the twenty-first century, influencing many attitudes towards the Middle East that remain prevalent in the West today.[1]

Echoes of this juxtaposition can sometimes be heard when British ministers and officials are challenged on the UK's relationship with the GCC states. When questioned by the House of Commons Foreign Affairs Select Committee about Britain's support for Saudi Arabia and Bahrain during the Arab uprisings, the Foreign Office minister Alistair Burt said that '[t]he values of these countries will never completely mirror ours and we cannot expect that',[2] while Sir Tom Phillips, who was British ambassador to Saudi Arabia at the time of the uprisings, affirmed the need to 'work with the grain of particular societies to advance UK values'.[3] Under questioning from another parliamentary select committee in 2016 on the UK's support for the Saudi-led intervention in Yemen, Sir Simon Mayall, a former Middle East adviser to the Ministry of Defence (MoD), said that '[w]e are a values-based society. They are a values-based society. It is a different set of values.'[4]

Within the prevailing Western discourse regarding the Middle East, these familiar allusions do not need to be elaborated upon in order to be understood. 'UK values' are, it goes without saying, those of liberal democracy, in contradistinction to those of the Arabian Gulf. The picture then is one of a liberal democratic Britain encountering monarchies that have emerged from a fundamentally different culture and conducting necessary international relations as best it can in these challenging circumstances. The reality, however, is considerably more complex.

The political and cultural present in both the UK and the GCC states is the result of dynamic processes of social contestation that have unfolded over a long period of time. People in the Gulf, like people in the UK and everywhere else in the world, have disagreed vigorously and across a spectrum of opinion (a spectrum that includes democrats and human rights defenders)[5] about the ways their societies should be run. The outcomes of this contestation are not predetermined by culture but, rather, are contingent on a number of factors. As we will see later on in this book, British power played an important role in the early decades of state formation in the Gulf and has been one important factor among others that has favoured the continued authoritarian rule of the region's elites. UK-GCC relations are best analysed not as a clash of cultures but as a multidimensional and evolving interaction of state, class and economic interests.

In general, it helps if we think about states and the relations between them – not entirely, but to a significant degree – with reference to the context of modern capitalism. Taking a longer historical view, the international political economy of the present day – particularly in terms of relations between states of the global north such as the UK and states of the global south such as the Gulf Arab monarchies – is the product and legacy of the earlier age of formal empire. The hierarchical structures originally laid down by the imperial powers have changed and evolved considerably in recent decades, but the hierarchy itself endures in fundamental disparities of power and economic capacity. The more 'developed' and powerful states reside at the core of the system, while the states of the global south populate the periphery. At the top of this hierarchy sits a hegemonic power – the United States – which polices the system and plays the leading role in managing and reproducing it.[6]

The Middle East was brought into this system primarily by Britain and France during the nineteenth and early twentieth centuries. The economic role of the emerging regional states was then to transmit primary goods (such as oil) and capital surpluses to the core, while local ruling elites suppressed any popular challenges to the system. Today, these states are no longer the imperial subjects of global north powers such as Britain, nor are they literally subordinate to the hegemonic United States. They are independent, sovereign and more powerful than they once were. Rather, the relationship is one we might describe as 'asymmetric interdependence'. Both the Gulf monarchies and their allies in the global north need each other, but the power balance is skewed in favour of the latter, and the hegemon above all.[7]

As for the British state, it should be understood as representing not so much a general 'national interest' as primarily the interests of those socio-economic classes and concentrations of wealth and power best able to penetrate, influence and shape it.[8] Essentially, the state works to manage and reproduce a socio-economic system that benefits those powerful and privileged interests above all.[9] The leading states of the global north perform this role both domestically and at an international level, which is important to bear in mind when we attempt to analyse their foreign relations.

Bob Jessop, a leading theorist on this subject, puts it in the following way. First, states establish and secure those conditions required for capital accumulation that private interests cannot secure by themselves. Second, they organise the collective interests of capital, as opposed to 'the one-sided pursuit of any single set of capitalist interests'. Third, the state manages 'the many and varied repercussions of economic exploitation within the wider society' in so far as this is required to ensure that the conditions necessary for capital accumulation are maintained. The importance of these roles make 'the large territorial national state ... irreplaceable', including in the current context of globalisation.[10]

Different major powers fit into and attempt to shape the global economic system in different ways, depending on their own specific circumstances and balance of interests.[11] Whereas China and Germany, for example, have pursued 'neo-mercantilist' approaches to world market integration, given the importance of different kinds of manufacturing to their economies, the US and the UK have been leading proponents of the neoliberal approach. This preference can be understood in light of the fact that neoliberal globalisation has strengthened international finance and New York and London are the world's two leading financial centres.[12] This alignment of economic interests provides part of the explanation for Britain's commitment to Washington's continuing status as the hegemonic power in the world system.

The hierarchical international order described here constitutes a form of neo-imperialism: a structure of political-economic relations wherein the core capitalist states of the global north have the power both to create and maintain opportunities for capital accumulation to serve their own interests and to exert their state power (through military or political means) to that end. This is distinct from the narrower phenomenon of colonial empire, which refers to the acquisition of control over territory. Therefore, although the British Empire is long since defunct, Britain as a second-tier global power, alongside the likes of France, can still be seen as acting in an imperialistic way. As the number one imperial power, the United States belongs in a separate category, with its immense structural power in the world system granting it the status of hegemon, at least up until now.

The oil riches of the Gulf have a crucial role in this system. As the Lebanese specialist on the political economy of the Middle East Gilbert Achcar puts it, '[c]ontrolling access to oil, especially the biggest reserves in the Arab-Iranian Gulf, gives the United States a decisive strategic advantage in the battle for world hegemony, putting it in a position of dominance vis-à-vis both its greatest potential rival, China, and also its traditional vassals, Western Europe and Japan, all heavily dependent on oil imports from the region.' In addition, the UK and the US are able to use their status to turn the wealth of the Gulf producer states to their advantage in the form of arms purchases and capital flows to their financial centres. Securing access to Gulf oil and gas for direct energy needs or supply to the world economy is only one part of the picture.[13] As the historian Mark Curtis notes,

Oil is, of course, the fundamental Anglo-American interest in the Middle East, and was described by British planners in 1947 as 'a vital prize for any power interested in world influence or domination'. 'We must at all costs maintain control of this oil', British foreign secretary Selwyn Lloyd noted in 1956. . . . Oil is designated to be controlled by Western allies in the Middle East to ensure that industry profits accrue to Western companies and are invested in Western economies. A traditional threat in the past has been that the nationalist regimes would use oil wealth primarily to benefit local populations and to build up independent sources of power to challenge US domination over the region. Traditionally, such regimes have been overthrown or prevented from arising by British and US power.[14]

This brief sketch of the relevant actors, relationships, interests and structures provides us with a rough map to aid our exploration of UK–GCC relations and helps us to pinpoint the various and complex ways in which Gulf wealth matters to Britain. It indicates that we should look into the historical development of the UK's involvement in the Gulf, from the age of empire to the present era. It reminds us of the importance of Gulf hydrocarbons in both strategic and commercial terms, and it suggests that any evaluation of UK–GCC trade and investment should be conducted with particular attention to the precise character and current state of British and Gulf capitalism in the context of the wider global economy. Finally, it points us towards the importance of military and coercive power at all levels of the relationship. This then is the route that the following analysis will take.

1

Empire's Legacy

For over a hundred years British imperial power dominated the Gulf, overseeing the creation of the regional state system that we see today and the emergence of Gulf oil as perhaps the greatest strategic and material prize in the world. Britain's current relationship with the Gulf Arab monarchies is best understood, in the first instance, as the product of historical processes unfolding through this period and into the decades immediately after the end of its formal empire. Global capitalism, and the nature and place of British capitalism within it, changed significantly over this time. Britain's power in the international system declined in both relative and absolute terms. And the landscape of alliances and rivalries within which British power operated shifted from one historical epoch to the next. This chapter will outline the evolution of the UK's position in the Gulf from the turn of the eighteenth and nineteenth centuries to the end of the Cold War in the context of these wider changes.

Throughout the period under discussion, London worked to advance the interests of British capital, to maintain and extend the scope of the wider international capitalist system, and to maintain, enhance or at least defend the global prestige and power of the British state. As this applies to policy with respect to the Gulf, set in the context of the wider Middle East, we can identify a few key themes. These include the strategic importance of the region's geopolitical location;

the value of oil as a source of power, wealth and energy; London's view of local nationalisms and even democracy as a threat to its relationships with the Gulf elites; and the importance of the means of violence and physical coercion in maintaining these relationships, in terms of internal repression, military intervention and arms exports. These themes have broadly persisted into the post-Cold War period.

The history of Britain's relationship with the Gulf Arab monarchies can be divided into three distinct phases. First, between the end of the eighteenth century and the conclusion of the Second World War, Britain established itself as an imperial hegemon and power-broker in the Gulf, bringing the local elites under its protection and securing a major stake in the region's newly discovered oil reserves. Second, from the start of the Cold War until 1971, London was forced to come to terms with and manage imperial decline in the face of its diminished economic strength, the rise of the United States, and the emergence of local nationalist movements. Third, in the period up until the present day, Britain adjusted to its new status, working to ensure that its financial and industrial sectors (particularly arms exporters) benefited from the increased wealth of the Gulf monarchies and, to that end, providing those monarchies with the arms and protection necessary to ensure their survival.

In each of these periods, the Gulf region has been of vital strategic interest. As the leading expert on UK foreign policy in the Middle East, Rosemary Hollis, puts it, 'the energy resources of Iran and later of various Arab states maintained British naval power in the early twentieth century and fuelled the British economy thereafter. Following nationalisation, the oil wealth of the Arab Gulf states has also sustained the British defence industry, buttressed the financial sector and provided a lucrative market for other corporate interests.'[1] These benefits accrued from Anglo-Arabian relationships that were born and developed in the context of empire.

Britain's Arabian empire takes shape

The French invasion of Egypt in July 1798 lent the Gulf region its first genuine significance for the British Empire, with a hostile European power now emerging on India's western horizon.[2] Britain's first Arabian treaty – with the Sultan of Muscat in 1798 – was designed to close the Gulf to French naval forces, and the British authorities in India now tasked themselves with securing the region.[3]

The historian Peter Sluglett describes how, 'between 1800 and 1914, in addition to the annexation of Aden [in what is now Yemen] and the arrangements with the rulers of the smaller Persian Gulf sheikhdoms – the Trucial States – and Muscat and Oman ... Britain established unequal treaties with the rulers of Afghanistan, Bahrain, Iran and Kuwait (and rather later with Qatar).'[4] The overall strategic aim in establishing these relationships was to create a cordon sanitaire around the Indian jewel in the British imperial crown.[5]

The construction of this system in the Gulf began with an initial, time-bound truce signed with a few of the coastal sheikhs in 1835, with Britain set up in the role of naval policeman and adjudicator in the case of any disputes, marking the commencement in earnest of its role as imperial power-broker. These temporary arrangements were subsequently upgraded to a ten-year truce, signed with what had become known as the Trucial Sheikhs in 1842. In 1853, the truce was made permanent.[6]

In 1880, Bahrain signed an agreement with Britain which barred the ruler and his successors from establishing relations with any other state without Britain's consent, thus becoming effectively a British dependency. Similar exclusive agreements were signed with the Trucial Sheikhs in 1887 and 1892 and with the dominions of Muscat and Oman in 1891, in the latter case to block a French attempt to set up a coal depot there and so gain a strategic foothold in the Gulf. In 1899, an exclusive agreement was signed with the Emir of Kuwait in response to plans for the construction of a railway from Asia Minor to the Gulf, a project attracting interest from Russia and Germany. A similar agreement was signed with Qatar in 1916. A 1906 treaty with Russia dividing Persia up into spheres of influence explicitly recognised British supremacy in the Gulf.[7]

By the end of the nineteenth century, the Gulf was firmly under British control, with the British resident (London's chief regional diplomat) able to call in naval support from the Royal Indian Marine, under the overall command of the Bombay government, or from the Royal Navy itself.[8] The principle was now established in British policy that no rival power's presence would be tolerated in the Gulf.[9] British interests in the broader Middle East were also expanding, with Cyprus occupied, Egypt and Sudan brought under imperial control, and Whitehall purchasing nearly half the shares in the Suez Canal Company.[10]

In 1914 the British government bought a 51 per cent stake in the Anglo Persian Oil Company (APOC – the firm which later became British Petroleum, or BP), an early indication of the growing strategic importance of oil. In anticipation of a coming war with Germany, the First Lord of the Admiralty, Winston Churchill, decided on grounds of efficiency to switch the Royal Navy's fuel source from coal to oil. The Admiralty bought its stake in APOC on terms that guaranteed it a secure supply at a predictable and affordable price.[11]

The commencement of the First World War prompted an immediate tightening of British control, established through further treaties of loyalty and cooperation with the local sheikhs. Churchill dispatched three ships to protect the APOC oil refinery at Abadan, and a costly three-year military campaign was fought (by troops from Britain's Indian army) to secure control over Mesopotamia, which was deemed essential to protect Britain's position in the Gulf. By the end of the war, that position was even more secure. Germany was defeated, the Ottoman Empire was no more, and the Soviet Union, as the successor state to the Russian Empire, was entirely preoccupied with internal developments.[12]

Britain now benefited from the carve-up of the former Ottoman Empire, gaining custodianship through League of Nations mandates of a number of territories in the Middle East and, alongside the French, drawing borders that would form the basis of the modern state system.[13] The region was now an important communications link connecting Britain to its empire in Asia. In addition to its control of the Suez Canal, it now had Cairo as an air transport hub, while bases in Palestine, Iraq and along the Gulf coast together comprised a strategically vital air route to India.[14]

British-controlled Iraq included the Middle East's biggest economic prize at that time: the oil reserves of Mosul province. The First World War had demonstrated the strategic value of oil, and it was now widely recognised among the Western powers as an indispensable asset. London moved to secure the region by constructing an informal empire, paid for largely by Middle Eastern taxpayers and operating behind a façade of dependent local elites, with British power on hand to suppress dissenters and troublemakers by force where necessary.[15] Meanwhile, a new presence was emerging from the heart of the Arabian peninsula.

The origins of modern Saudi Arabia can be traced back to the mid-eighteenth century and the alliance between Muhammad ibn Abd al-Wahhab and Muhammad ibn Saud, one the founder of a fundamentalist religious movement, the other a central Arabian tribal chief.[16] The alliance between militantly puritanical Wahhabism and the political and military power of the House of Saud remains the foundation of the modern Saudi state.

Britain achieved victory in the Middle Eastern theatre of the First World War in large part by cultivating alliances with local rulers against the Ottomans. Its policy of staying out of the affairs of central Arabia came to an end at this point, as it sought to secure the cooperation of the Saudis in the centre and east of the peninsula and the Hashemites in the west. It was the Hashemites who went on to lead the Arab revolt, but, though the Saudi role was more passive, the Anglo-Saudi treaty of 1915 – similar to those signed previously with the Gulf elites – had great significance in terms of Britain's developing position in the region.[17]

A decade later, Saudi–Hashemite rivalry escalated into all-out war. When Saudi forces conquered the west of the Arabian peninsula, seizing Mecca and Medina and expelling the Hashemites, Britain recognised their victory as a fait accompli, with Sharif Hussein's crucial assistance in the First World War now effectively counting for nothing. Under the new Anglo-Saudi treaty of 1927, Britain recognised the 'absolute independence' of Saudi Arabia, and its king, Ibn Saud, undertook to respect Britain's informal empire in the Gulf. During a subsequent internal rebellion, Britain provided Ibn Saud with military assistance, including the deployment of air power, which Daniel Silverfarb argues 'probably provided his narrow margin of victory and preserved the rule of his dynasty'. Britain played a role in the creation and shaping of Saudi Arabia in another sense, in that its presence in the Gulf protected those lands from the Saudi expansionist push of that period.[18]

Today's Saudi kingdom, in other words, did not emerge smoothly as an inevitable expression of the essential culture of the Arabian peninsula. Rather, like the status quo in any other part of the world, it is the relatively recent product of processes of social contestation, contingent upon a number of factors. One of those factors was the role of British power, which would continue to be a factor working in favour of monarchical rule across the Gulf over the next hundred years.

That being said, the Saudi kingdom was not to have the same dependent relationship with the British as the smaller monarchies of the Gulf coast, instead allying itself more closely with the United States. The American challenge to British regional influence had started even before the Second World War. Saudi oil production began in 1938 under the auspices of the Arabian American Oil Company – ARAMCO. By 1943, the US government had decided that the defence of Saudi Arabia was a vital strategic interest. Lend-lease aid began to flow, as did training to the Saudi military, while the US built a large airbase at Dhahran, close to the oil wells. The alliance was sealed when President Roosevelt met Ibn Saud in 1945 and the latter declared war on the Axis powers.[19]

The Second World War was fought by highly mechanised armies that relied on oil to function, and it was therefore vital to exclude the Axis powers from the Middle East, both to deny them access to the region's reserves and to secure a key lifeline for Western support to the USSR. Saudi Arabia occupied a vital position along the shore of the Red Sea – the key route between Britain and its Indian empire – while its oilfields, further south than those in Iraq and Iran, were easier to defend from the Axis powers. Britain therefore pledged to defend the kingdom, providing arms and financial assistance. Meanwhile, fuel from Iran's Abadan refinery was critical in supporting the Soviets during their drive westwards to Berlin. The key German defeats on the Eastern Front, in North Africa, and at the Battle of the Bulge were in large part the result of inadequate access to fuel. Overall, the experience of the two world wars had put the strategic importance of oil beyond any serious doubt.[20]

By the end of the Second World War, extensive oil discoveries in Bahrain (1932), Kuwait (1938) and Qatar (1940) had given the region an entirely new strategic significance, but, with the increased presence of US oil companies and with Saudi Arabia now placed firmly in the American camp, London felt its position was gradually being usurped by its American allies.[21] In 1928, British, French and American oil firms had brokered the 'Red Line Agreement', carving up the reserves of the Arabian peninsula, the Levant, Turkey and Iraq between themselves, but the commercial treaty was increasingly seen as an inconvenience by the Americans, and by the end of the war it had broken down.[22] Britain's undisputed hegemony in the Gulf was now increasingly subject to inter-imperialist competition with its Western allies.

The long retreat: the Second World War to 1971

Even before the war had ended, it was becoming clear to US policy-makers that Britain's status as a leading global power was now firmly on a downward trajectory, creating an historic opportunity for Washington.[23] Imperial decline and the American succession were to become the defining strategic realities for Britain's post-war Middle East policy.

After the war, the European colonial powers sought to exploit their imperial possessions for their own reconstruction. Those colonies could serve as markets for exports and investment and as suppliers of raw materials, while also earning, through their own exports, the foreign exchange (particularly dollars) that was desperately needed to purchase food and goods. This approach was tolerated by the United States in the interests of shoring up Western Europe in the context of the early Cold War.[24]

London recognised that, if it were voluntarily to relinquish any of its imperial domains, it would not only lose its economic advantages in those areas but also risk undermining both its prestige in other parts of the world and the strength of the Western powers more generally.[25] This last factor should be emphasised. The capitalist democracies now saw their interests as mutually interdependent to a far greater extent than had previously been the case, albeit the interests of individual states were still pursued with great vigour.

Britain now sought to maximise its position within the new American-led global capitalist order. In regions where it retained key military and commercial interests, London had to secure Washington's support for its position rather than allow itself to be usurped by the United States in those areas. However, the historian Mark Curtis notes that. 'in the Middle East, . . . the US had already started to encroach on the British position before the war, with control of oil as the key prize. Active collaboration between London and Washington . . . took place alongside an uneasy rivalry as the two aimed to reshape the region to their interests.'[26]

Notwithstanding its own imperial aspirations, the US recognised that it had a stake in ensuring that Britain continued to play a role in defending the Middle East in the common interests of the West.[27] From the British point of view, performing this role would help demonstrate to the US London's continued capacity to play an important part in the new global order, as well as shoring up Britain's wider international credibility in the face of growing Soviet power and the loss of India. In the event of a third world war, the region would not only need to be defended but could also be used as a base to attack Russian oilfields and industry. In addition, with the money to be made from the booming Gulf oil industry, the Middle East's strategic and economic value was very clear.[28]

Britain and the US therefore had clear mutual interests in the Middle East, including unfettered access to the Suez Canal, the retention of the region within the global capitalist system and the denial of the Gulf's resources to the communist bloc.[29] Britain's region-wide network of air bases and military installations therefore constituted key strategic assets, particularly vital to London's ability to project power into the heart of the Arab world now that it could no longer draw upon an imperial army in India.[30]

British planners now recognised Middle Eastern oil as a vital strategic prize, bringing enormous influence to whoever was able to exert control over it. Domination of the Gulf therefore had to be maintained at all costs. Their counterparts in Washington agreed, perceiving a joint interest, at least for the time being, in Anglo-American cooperation over controlling Middle Eastern oil, albeit each side would clearly aim to maximise its own benefit within these parameters.[31]

The increasing dependence of the industrial societies on oil was the reason for its status as a source of strategic vulnerability and therefore, by the same token, power to those who controlled it. Anthony Sampson, in his history of the oil industry, notes that 'between 1950 and 1965 the share of oil in providing energy for the six Common Market countries went up from 10 per cent to 45 per cent.' In the immediate post-war period the Gulf supplied Britain with 80 per cent of its oil needs.[32] For most of the twentieth century, until the discovery and bringing online of North Sea oil, London was highly conscious of its vulnerable position given that the UK had no reserves of its own and therefore relied on imports from distant parts of the world.[33]

Oil and sterling

Another major consideration for London was that revenue from the oil fields of the Gulf region, under the control of British companies, was critical to the UK's balance of payments, not least because Britain's protectorates in the Gulf were part of the sterling area (whose states traded in sterling and kept their reserves in London, thus supporting the pound). However, these benefits were offset by the drain on resources represented by the British commitment to defending the region militarily.[34]

As Steven Galpern details in an important study, maintaining the strength of the pound sterling was an absolute strategic priority for British policy-makers in the post-war era, and Britain's interests in Gulf oil were crucial to London's success in this regard. A strong pound benefited Britain's financial services sector (then even more important given the destruction of British industry during wartime) and was a key symbol of Britain's enduring prestige. Middle Eastern oil, as produced and sold by British oil majors – the Anglo-Iranian Oil Company (AIOC, formerly Anglo-Persian), in which the government had a 51 per cent share, and Royal Dutch Shell, in which British capital had a major stake – was indispensable for two reasons. First, taxes from AIOC and Shell and oil supplies via those firms from states within the sterling area such as Kuwait and Iran helped Britain to maintain a healthy balance of payments. Second, AIOC's and Shell's sales to states outside the sterling area helped earn precious foreign exchange, which could purchase essential imports or be held in reserve to defend the pound in times of crisis.[35]

AIOC's monopoly of Iranian production and major stakes in the Kuwaiti and Iraqi oil industries allowed Britain to save dollars by importing oil from the sterling area, while Shell earned dollars by exporting to dollar markets. The two firms thereby contributed hundreds of millions of pounds a year to the balance of payments.[36] Control of Gulf oil, its secure passage through the Suez Canal, and the sterling reserves of the producer states were therefore vital to the strength and prestige of the pound in those precarious post-war years.

The question of the pound was central to the nature of British capitalism, given London's role as a global financial centre, whose external investments extended even more widely than the boundaries of Britain's formal empire.[37] Alexander Anievas describes, during the early part of the twentieth century, 'the formation of a City–Treasury–Bank [of England] relationship constituting the "core institutional nexus" within British state and society, which came to be the chief proponent of a liberal-internationalist hegemonic project and capital accumulation strategy based on free trade and a London-centred Gold Standard.'[38] Close ties existed between the City of London, the Bank of England, the political class and the wider establishment in a phenomenon the historians Peter Cain and Anthony Hopkins describe as 'gentlemanly capitalism'. Here, the term 'gentlemanly' refers to the governing layer of a highly stratified class system, growing out of the public schools and Oxford and Cambridge universities and dominated by the City of London, which extended its reach into British industry in the decades after the war.[39] British foreign and economic policy tended to serve primarily these interests rather than a general 'national interest'.

'[A] central preoccupation of British policy', Cain and Hopkins wrote, 'was the preservation of sterling's role in financing international trade and investment, and with it the maintenance of the earning power of the City of London.'[40] In the view of the gentlemanly capitalists, the Gulf oil helping to prop up the pound belonged to those with the power to exploit it.[41] Many of those in whose countries the oil was to be found, unsurprisingly, took a different view, and the political movements arising from their opposition now constituted the principal threat to British power in the Middle East.

The threat of nationalism

In 1953, Albert Hourani, the great historian of the Arab world, articulated the nationalist perspective that was gaining in prominence across the Middle East, describing a 'deep and almost universal feeling against Britain and the West'. Imperial rule was exercised 'behind a façade of indigenous government',[42] and 'even where direct Western control has been relaxed and ended, and even in countries where it has never existed, there has been for the last few generations an indirect, concealed but none the less effective Western hegemony.'[43] Under these conditions there had emerged 'a close bond of feeling between the different Arab countries, and what happened in one country had immediate effects upon the others. Thus in each country Britain was faced . . . with the discontent [not only] of that country alone, but of all.'[44] Indeed, a persistent theme on Cairo's 'Voice of the Arabs' radio, broadcast into the Gulf region, was that British imperialism was attempting to separate the Gulf from its rightful position within the greater Arab nation.[45]

Given the British state and capitalist interests that Arab (and Iranian) nationalism now threatened, it was unsurprising that an anti-nationalist worldview (often articulated as anti-communism) now emerged as a legitimating ideology among Britain's governing elite.[46] The fear was that independence and popular self-determination would result in the expulsion of British advisers from the governments of local regimes, the expropriation of British assets, and cooperation with anti-Western states and powers in the United Nations. Nationalist movements were therefore deemed unacceptable whether they were revolutionary or reformist, and, since the prevailing popular mood rendered democracy out of the question, British imperial power committed itself to shoring up and defending the autocratic regional order it had helped to establish.[47]

The crisis in Iran that culminated in the coup of 1953 was a defining nationalist-imperialist clash over British oil interests in the Gulf region. The causes lay in the iniquities of Britain's dominance of the Iranian oil industry. Operating the largest refinery in the world in Abadan, AIOC made £33 million in profit and paid £50 million in taxes to the British exchequer in 1950, while impoverished Iran received a mere £16 million in royalties. British attempts to placate growing nationalist feeling came too late to stop the rise of Prime Minister Mohammad Mossadeq, who nationalised the company in 1951.[48]

The balance of payments crisis that Britain experienced that summer served further to concentrate minds in Whitehall, with the outgoing Labour and the incoming Conservative administration sharing the fear of Treasury officials that the loss of Iranian oil could devastate the pound. London therefore responded strongly, effectively working to shut down the Iranian oil industry. When a Panamanian ship tried to export oil out of Abadan, RAF planes forced it into Aden harbour, where its cargo was impounded. AIOC secured the agreement of the other six oil majors not to buy Iranian oil. The effect on Iran's oil-dependent economy was severe, and London understood that this could destabilise Mossadeq's government. Meanwhile, AIOC used its position in Kuwait to ramp up production there and stabilise the market.[49]

Ultimately, the US and Britain collaborated in the 1953 overthrow of Mossadeq, with the CIA leading the operation. Most accounts of the coup mention the West's fear of communist subversion, but in reality the Iranian communist party Tudeh had not been a significant actor in the movement behind Mossadeq.[50] The issue was not communism but the democratic expression of nationalism, which the coup swept aside in favour of the dictatorial rule of the shah, who reigned with British and American arms and assistance until the revolution of 1978-9.

The price for Washington coming to London's aid against Mossadeq was a reduced (though still significant) stake for AIOC in Iranian oil, with Shell and a number of US firms moving in. Of paramount importance to the British in the post-coup negotiations was that Iranian oil would continue to be traded in sterling, with success on this score making the loss of monopoly somewhat easier to bear.[51] But it was clear that the challenge of growing US power in the region would be at least as hard to resist as that from nationalist local forces.

This jostling for position within the US–UK alliance also manifested itself in the clash between Saudi Arabia and Oman over the oasis of Buraimi, where ARAMCO was prospecting for oil. The oasis, which lay across the territory of both Abu Dhabi and Oman, was occupied by Saudi troops in 1952 with the tacit support of the Americans. Britain strenuously objected to the Saudi move, seeing it as a serious challenge to its regional authority, while also being mindful of the potential value of oil to be found at the oasis itself. Such was Britain's determination to defend its interests that the Foreign Office threatened that any Americans found in the disputed area would be killed.

The dispute was put to arbitration, and the Saudis eventually left in August 1954. But considerable ill-feeling remained. The Saudis broke off diplomatic relations with Britain for eight years, and tensions increased temporarily between Washington and London as well.[52]

Like the events in Iran, the Suez crisis of 1956 exemplified the challenges a declining Britain was facing in the Middle East. What is not commonly understood is that, from the British Empire's point of view, it was the role of the Suez Canal in transporting oil from the Arab Gulf states that lent the crisis its almost existential nature.

Britain had agreed a military withdrawal from Egypt with the new nationalist president Gamal Abdul Nasser, while simultaneously creating the 'Baghdad Pact' alliance system with Iran, Iraq, Pakistan and Turkey to shore up its regional position. But Nasser's nationalisation of the Anglo-French Suez Canal Company on 26 July 1956 was a step too far for London.[53] At the time of the crisis, three-quarters of Britain's oil imports came from the Middle East, and the canal carried two-thirds of Britain's sterling oil to Western Europe. There had been another run on the pound in the summer of 1955, and the loss of the canal threatened to further damage confidence in sterling. In September 1956, Britain's dollar and gold reserves were nearing the US$2 billion mark, the minimum required, according to the Bank and the Treasury's estimate, to keep the sterling area afloat.[54]

Whitehall feared that if the crisis forced a second devaluation in less than a decade it would spell the end for sterling's international reserve role. In addition, if Nasser were successfully to nationalise the canal (and resist any Western countermeasures), he would be in a position to turn the oil producers of the Middle East against Britain.[55] The forcefulness of London's actions during the crisis can be attributed to the fact that it viewed Nasser's move as nothing less than an existential threat to the British Empire.

In response, the British, French and Israelis agreed a secret pact whereby Israel would attack Egypt, and then Britain and France would intervene to separate the warring parties and, in the process, occupy the canal zone. However, fearing that this virtually naked display of imperialist aggression would play into the hands of nationalists and discredit its own attempts to dominate the region, Washington exerted intense pressure on Britain to cease its actions, including, crucially, a refusal to provide dollar support for the falling pound, which amounted to a threat of bankruptcy. The subsequent ceasefire and withdrawal was a humiliation for the UK. Nasser was elevated to the status of a regional hero, Anthony Eden's premiership was destroyed, and the limits of British power and independence - both regionally and globally - had been dramatically exposed.[56]

The reported American preference for a coup against Nasser (if one could successfully be carried out), rather than military intervention,[57] shows that the Anglo-European differences over Suez were tactical rather than strategic (much less on any serious point of principle), but this does not diminish their importance. There was also a realisation in Washington that Britain's decline was severely undermining its ability to serve wider Western interests in the Middle East. After the crisis, President Eisenhower and Eden's successor, Harold Macmillan, moved quickly to restore amicable Anglo-American relations, with Britain effectively conceding hegemony over the Middle East to the United States while preserving its dominance in the Gulf region.[58]

The unravelling of British power in the wider Middle East was nevertheless a threat to its position in the Gulf. The 1953 evacuation of the Suez garrison had raised a serious question - especially given the loss of India - over where Britain might draw military reserve power from to defend its key Gulf interests. Hopes of using Iraqi airfields to compensate partially for the loss of the Suez garrison were ended by the 1958 coup in Baghdad.[59] The strategic losses were now coming in steady succession.

The port of Aden now became the chief British garrison between Cyprus and Singapore and the basis of its projection of military power into the Indian Ocean and the Persian Gulf. In 1961, nationalist officers overthrew the monarchy in Yemen, and civil war ensued. The US wanted to contain the conflict, given its potential to exacerbate the nationalist-conservative division in the wider Arab world, but Egypt and Saudi Arabia took sides. Britain joined the latter camp, leading to anti-imperialist protests in Aden and then to a full-scale revolt, which the British found impossible to quell. In the end, London agreed that the South Arabian Federation, including Yemen, would become independent by 1968, although British access to the Aden base would continue.[60]

Meanwhile, in Oman, a left-nationalist rebellion in the Dhofar region (discussed further below) also threatened British control, and these combined problems were giving cause in Whitehall for a deeper rethink of Britain's commitments in the region. By 1966, the Labour government had decided both to withdraw from Aden by 1968 and to cancel or cut back on orders for weapons systems such as aircraft carriers and long-range bombers whose function would have been to project power into the Gulf. An eventual withdrawal from the Gulf itself was now being contemplated – perhaps to be effected during the mid-1970s – but announcing this as well would have been to hand too big a propaganda victory to the Nasserist forces.[61]

One positive development for British power amid the more general picture of decline was a rapprochement with Riyadh. The Buraimi crisis was set aside and UK–Saudi diplomatic relations were restored to meet the threat from the new revolutionary republic of North Yemen. The British helped to establish and train the new Saudi National Guard and also secured what was then the largest arms export deal in its history, providing £120 million of jets, air defences and associated training.[62] In 1964 Britain played a key role in supporting a palace coup that replaced King Saud – who had proved unwilling or unable to enact reforms that would shore up the regime against challenges from below – with his more pragmatic brother Faisal. British advisers to the National Guard drew up plans for the force to protect and support Faisal during the coup.[63]

When it came in 1961, Kuwaiti independence was, from the point of view of both the ruling al-Sabah family and the British, primarily about defusing the threat of Arab nationalism. The assurances of support given in 1899 were renewed, although Kuwait would now be at liberty to conduct relations with other states at its own discretion. In general, the Gulf rulers were torn between their need for British protection and the domestic political costs of their client status, while Britain tried to calculate the correct balance in the relationship that would allow their allies to claim to be independent of empire while at the same time preserving the fundamentals of British influence.[64]

The greatest threat to the Kuwaiti monarchy that British officials perceived was internal subversion rather than external aggression. Kuwaiti security forces had violently dispersed pro-Nasser demonstrations during the Suez crisis.[65] Uzi Rabi argues that '[t]he reason why Britain went along with Kuwait's requests [for independence] was that Kuwait was willing to maintain economic and military links with Britain and to continue to invest her oil revenues in London',[66] which continuity necessitated a policy of domestic repression.

Almost immediately after independence in 1961, Kuwait was threatened by the revolutionary government in Baghdad. During Ottoman times, the province of Basra had been responsible for the governance of Kuwait, and a view persisted in Baghdad that the emirate was rightfully a part of Iraq. The fact that Kuwait was also the Gulf region's largest oil producer in the early 1960s was clearly also of relevance to the Iraqi government, as it was for the UK, since Kuwait provided 40 per cent of Britain's oil needs at the time. In the end, a show of British military force appears to have been sufficient to see off the Iraqi threat.[67] Historians disagree about the extent to which the British were justified in treating this 'threat' as anything more than rhetoric on Baghdad's part, but London's desire to demonstrate the continuing relevance of its military power is clear in any event.[68]

Grassroots challenges to monarchical rule were gaining new strength across the Gulf. Adam Hanieh, an expert on the political economy of the region, notes that, in Bahrain, 'militant labor struggles occurred through the 1960s [culminating] in a three-month uprising in March 1965 ... led by Communist and nationalist leaders who fused agitation against the ongoing British presence in the Gulf with demands around worker and social issues.' This groundswell 'drew support from wide layers of society', while '[w]orker actions and nationalist-inspired movements were also widespread in Saudi Arabia, Kuwait and the smaller Gulf emirates.' The House of Saud 'faced the rise of revolutionary and nationalist movements during the 1950s and 1960s, which were severely repressed with the open support of US and British advisors.'[69]

From London's point of view, any development and reform in the Gulf were means to imperial ends rather than ends in themselves, valued to the extent that they helped to shore up British influence.[70] Modest political reforms together with gradual economic modernisation could undermine the appeal of nationalist forces without threatening the status quo.[71] It follows then that there was also a wrong kind of development, namely that which might raise the possibility of independence and endanger Western influence. It was for these reasons that, in 1965, the ostensibly inoffensive prospect of an Arab League economic development office being opened in the Gulf was regarded by the British as a political threat, given the League's Arab nationalist leanings and the inclination of the poorer Trucial States to welcome the League.

London immediately used its influence behind the scenes to have the more loyal emirates found a Trucial States Development Office, jointly funded by Britain and the wealthier Gulf states, in order to render the League office unnecessary. When the dissident emirates continued to support the Arab League's advances, Britain backed a palace coup that deposed the Sheikh of Sharjah, at which point the remaining dissidents fell quickly into line.[72] For all the strategic reversals it had suffered, Britain still retained the capacity to play the role of imperial power-broker in the Gulf.

Empire's sunset, imperialism's survival

Overall however, a drawdown from the Gulf was fast becoming an inevitability. In the mid-1960s, Britain was spending 7 per cent of GDP on its military (more than treble the present figure), which was now regarded as unsustainable. When originally mooted, a proposed reduction of the British presence east of Suez was met with strong American opposition and appeals from Saudi King Faisal to reconsider.[73] But the sterling crisis of June 1966 put the increasingly chaotic imperial retreat beyond further debate, and the devaluation of the pound in November 1967 (brought on partly by the effect on the cost of oil of the recent closure of the Suez Canal) merely reinforced the rationale. Britain was driven from its strategic stronghold Aden in 1967 by nationalist forces, and the following year London announced that it would withdraw from the Gulf by 1971.[74]

Britain's balance of payments problems had returned during the 1960s, culminating in the currency crisis of 1967. By this point, Treasury and Bank of England officials had begun to question whether propping up sterling and maintaining its international role was worth the cost (not least the military cost) to the UK. They concluded that it was not and that the City would not suffer unduly from a devaluation, which was duly effected. Britain then set about dismantling the sterling area.[75]

British hegemony in the Gulf had been highly important to both US power and the functioning of global capitalism, not just to Britain's own imperial needs and the survival of the Gulf monarchs. President Lyndon Johnson, upon hearing of Britain's intent to withdraw, wrote to Wilson to express his dismay, emphasising the impact the decision would have on both the Western powers' collective interests. Wilson replied that Britain's military commitments were extended unsustainably beyond its economic capacities and that the UK was being forced to reconcile itself to the reality of its diminished status in the world.[76]

King Faisal reportedly feared that the Saudi monarchy would now be exposed and that his kingdom and its neighbours on the Gulf could be the next of the West's regional allies to fall. Some Gulf rulers even suggested that they might cover the cost of British forces remaining in situ, but, as Whitehall quickly made clear to them, they vastly underestimated what that cost actually was.[77]

The immediate question raised by the coming withdrawal was how to secure the survival of the vulnerable Gulf elites which now had to contemplate life without their imperial patron. London's initial preference was for a loose confederation to emerge, encompassing Bahrain, Qatar and the seven Trucial States. However, as the British-led negotiations played out, Bahrain and Qatar took their own independent path, leaving a union of the Trucial States (today's United Arab Emirates) that would inevitably be dominated by its largest members, Dubai and Abu Dhabi.[78]

One piece of fortune London and its allies enjoyed during this period was the outcome of the June 1967 Arab–Israeli war, in which the forces of Arab nationalism had suffered a swift and humiliating defeat whose effects were felt region-wide. An internal Foreign Office minute on these events remarked that 'The June war was the turning point . . . we would never have had a chance of making an orderly withdrawal from the Gulf nor would the Sheikhs have had a chance of survival if the revolutionary Arabs had not been completely deflated by the results of the June war.'[79]

The Gulf monarchs immediately sought protection from the United States, but Washington was reluctant to extend itself further, given its existing Cold War commitments and the ongoing conflict in Vietnam, now at its height. The preference was to build up Iran, and Saudi Arabia to a lesser extent, to act as local policemen, in accordance with the wider 'Nixon doctrine' that local allies should take greater responsibility for managing their own regions. It would take the fall of the shah, the Iran–Iraq War and finally Saddam's invasion of Kuwait to bring the US to adopt the role Britain had performed in the Gulf for the 150 years up to 1971.[80]

Fortifying monarchical rule

Britain's priorities after the formal withdrawal were to ensure the stability of the regional order in the Gulf, allowing British exports to continue, oil supplies to be maintained, and British investments (especially through the oil companies) to be safeguarded.[81] For these reasons, the withdrawal is better described as a drawdown and was certainly not a complete relinquishment of British influence, which would become less visible but still remain. The militaries and internal security forces of the new states would receive British support, and London would remain committed to the continuation of monarchical rule. Through the 1950s and 1960s, Britain had been building up the Gulf states' internal security forces so as to reduce its need to intervene militarily if any of its clients were threatened. The British effort to ensure that the Gulf monarchies were well protected by police forces and intelligence services armed and trained by the UK continued after 1971.[82]

Military bases in Bahrain and Sharjah were evacuated but those in Oman were maintained until 1976. British officers outnumbered Omani officers in the Omani military until the early 1980s, and only in 1985 did Omanis begin to take positions of military command. In the UAE, British advisers retained influential roles in the armed forces and the judiciary. The military and civil services of Kuwait, Bahrain and Qatar each retained scores of British citizens, and even the defence secretary and chief economic adviser to the Sultan of Oman were British for a period after 'independence'.[83]

Meanwhile the Saudi National Guard continued to be trained by the British army on their duties protecting the king, while the Saudi oil minister was guarded by a team of former SAS troops. Additionally, Britain signed a £250 million deal with the Saudis in 1973 to train its air force pilots and service its aircraft.[84] A former senior British diplomat in the Gulf region, Anthony Parsons, noted in 1988 that there were 'perhaps over a thousand British officers on secondment or under contract to the armed and security forces of the Gulf states, and British military equipment, including aircraft, tanks and armoured cars, is in widespread use and makes a valuable contribution to British industry and the balance of payments.'[85]

From 1966 until 1998, a Briton by the name of Ian Henderson, who had previously served as a colonial official in Kenya, acted as director general of Bahrain's Public Security Directorate, Criminal Investigations Directorate (CID) and State Security Directorate (SSD) before serving a final two years as adviser to the Interior Ministry in Manama. Opposition groups accused him of playing the leading role in a severe campaign of repression against Bahraini dissidents. Human rights groups accused the CID and SSD of a series of severe human rights violations over many years, especially torture under interrogation, including such methods as pulling off fingernails, using dogs to attack prisoners, and sexual assault.[86]

With extensive British support behind the scenes, local rulers continued to suppress domestic challenges to their rule. Bahrain's national assembly, elected in 1973, contained an array of nationalists and other forces, but the ruling family dominated the leading cabinet positions, and the bureaucracy was stuffed with regime allies from the wealthy merchant class. The nationalist bloc made demands for women's votes, the expulsion of the US navy and full nationalisation of the oil industry, and before long the emir's patience ran out, leading to the dissolution of parliament in 1975. A similar scenario played out in Kuwait, where Arab nationalist challenges on matters of oil and foreign policy prompted the emir to dissolve parliament in 1976 and rule by decree.[87]

In Oman, the British had come to realise that one of the most important factors undermining monarchical stability was the unpopularity of the monarch himself. Sultan Said bin Taimur showed no interest in taking measures to address popular grievances and, despite his government's healthy fiscal position, made no attempts to invest in economic development, leaving the regime vulnerable to a nationalist overthrow supported by Britain's Cold War enemies. After some discussion between Whitehall officials and British diplomatic and military staff in Oman, the decision was taken on 16 July 1970 to support a coup against the sultan, who, on 23 July, was deposed by his son, the Sandhurst-educated Qaboos, who rules Oman to this day.[88]

The background to this action was the growing nationalist threat to the Omani monarchy. From the mid-1960s, the government had fought a counter-insurgency war against a rebellion which started in the western Dhofar province but in 1970 spread to the interior of Oman, a development that proved the trigger for the coup. The rebels received support from Iraq, China and the Soviet Union and operated out of sanctuaries in the neighbouring People's Democratic Republic of South Yemen, but they were fundamentally an indigenous force, arising as a result of the poverty in the country, and shared the familiar socialist, nationalist and anti-imperialist outlook that was confronting British clients across the region. The sultanate's armed forces were dominated by the British. As Fred Halliday put it in his seminal work *Arabia without Sultans*, '[t]he blunt fact was that the British directed and commanded the war and all orders came from them.'[89] British officers seconded to Oman, SAS troops, and former British soldiers acting as mercenaries organised Omani forces and fought alongside them, with British air power in support.[90]

Punitive tactics of collective punishment were used against the communities out of which the rebellion arose, including an economic blockade leading to widespread malnutrition, burning homes, bombing pastures, poisoning and blowing up wells, killing livestock, and burning crops at harvest time.[91] In December 1973, the Shah of Iran sent several thousand troops into Oman to come to the aid of a fellow Gulf monarch and assist in crushing the sort of forces that could also threaten his own rule. By 1975, this combined external support for the sultan had ensured the crushing of the rebellion. Qaboos's longer-term policy of investing in economic development (unlike his father) may ultimately have helped to deal with some of the underlying causes of the unrest, or at least served to consolidate his legitimacy in the country overall to the extent necessary to secure his position.[92]

Petrodollars: crisis and opportunity

When in late 1973 the Organization of the Petroleum Exporting Countries (OPEC) raised the price of oil and the Arab producer states embargoed the United States for supporting Israel in the Arab–Israeli war, the resulting crisis had dramatic consequences for London. The impact on the world economy and the sharp increase in revenues (petrodollars) to the producer states resulting from the oil shock represented a serious recalibration in the balance of power between the West and the Gulf monarchies and elevated the status of Saudi Arabia in particular, as well as that of the UAE and Kuwait. Overall, the crisis was a seminal moment in the creation of the modern relationship between the UK and the Gulf states.

In the 1950s and 1960s, the producer states had gradually managed to secure themselves better deals with the oil majors, from (typically) a concession sum plus a small royalty rate in the early twentieth century to a 50–50 split of the profits. The formation of OPEC in the mid-1960s – prompted in part by concerns about price cuts, which affected producer-state domestic budgets but were decided by the majors without consultation or consent – was the prelude to the producers securing yet better deals with the multinationals, including significant ownership stakes and, crucially, real control over prices. A second factor setting the scene for the crisis was a rise in global demand for oil, which afforded the producers markedly increased leverage.[93]

The OPEC price hike and the embargo by the Arab producer states happened to coincide. The former was about getting a better deal for producers while the latter came in response to the Arab–Israeli conflict. The combined effect was devastating. The price of oil quadrupled in just over two months. At that time, oil supplied more than half the world's energy needs, with the Gulf providing 30 per cent of total production; 70 per cent of British oil imports originated from the Gulf, and 30 per cent from Saudi Arabia itself. The disappearance of cheap oil was a transformative event, impacting harshly on consumer states everywhere, including the UK,[94] whose economic woes in the 1970s, particularly with regard to inflation, cannot be fully understood outside this wider international context.

Saudi policy during the oil crisis was far less hostile to the West than it might have appeared on the surface. The six-month price freeze and the lifting of the embargo in early 1974 were both Saudi diplomatic achievements, as the kingdom sought to contain the influence of the more militant oil producers, reassure its Western allies and improve its market position in the process. The Saudis, with British support, were instrumental in softening the position of OPEC. Along with Abu Dhabi, they provided Britain with additional oil supplies to ease the crisis in late 1974 to early 1975, and they also lobbied within OPEC for prices to be lowered. The historian Mark Curtis notes that British officials were full of praise for the Saudis' 'moderating' role.[95]

Meanwhile, oil revenues for the Gulf states shot up dramatically. Between 1972 and 1974, Saudi Arabia's annual revenues rose from US$2.7 billion to $22.6 billion and Kuwait's from $1.4 billion to $6.5 billion. After the crisis, the producer countries either took larger ownership shares of their oil industries from the Western majors or imposed full nationalisation. The boost in revenues transformed their economies, funding the development of power generation, port facilities, petrochemical industries and, at a more basic level, paved roads.[96] Those petrodollars not absorbed domestically flowed northwards into the global financial system. By attracting the surge in petrodollars into their financial industries, Washington and London were also able to use their Gulf alliances to turn the crisis to their advantage.

Britain and Saudi Arabia now sealed what Curtis describes as 'a profound economic alliance, the consequences of which are still evident'.[97] As well as direct investment in the British economy and investment opportunities for British industry in the Gulf, Whitehall sought a wider influx of surplus oil revenues into the financial system, whereby recycled petrodollars would play a similar stabilising function to the recently expired Bretton Woods system of managed exchange rates. By 1975, the Saudi kingdom held the equivalent in today's prices of around £20 billion worth of investment in the British economy, as well as supporting the pound by holding large proportions of their surplus funds in sterling. The petrodollar boom also turned the Gulf into a leading global south export market for the UK.[98]

Another significant benefit for the UK was that higher oil prices helped to make exploration for reserves in the North Sea economically viable. In the medium term, Britain's interests were if anything slightly closer to OPEC's than had first been apparent. After an initial few years of pain caused by the oil shock, Britain could envisage becoming a net oil exporter, providing a considerable boost to its balance of payments from the 1980s.[99]

Britain became the world's fifth-largest producer in the 1980s, which left OPEC with less leverage over British policy and Britain less exposed to events in the Middle East, although, given the relatively modest size of Britain's reserves, it was clear that this situation would not last. Gulf wealth continued to represent a major opportunity for capital accumulation for exporters and the financial industry.[100] Broader imperialist interests, moreover (in terms of maintaining Anglo-American dominance of the Gulf region), were unchanging.

As British influence in the Gulf gradually waned over the 1970s and 1980s, the US was moving to become the dominant power in the area. The initial policy to build up Iran and Saudi Arabia as 'twin pillars' of a conservative regional order was fatally undermined by the

Iranian revolution of 1979. In response to this, and the Soviet invasion of Afghanistan, President Jimmy Carter stated that the United States would not tolerate, and would use all means to prevent, the Gulf coming under the domination of any hostile power. The Rapid Deployment Force (later incorporated into the US military's 'Central Command', based in the Gulf region) was set up to enforce the 'Carter Doctrine'.[101]

Britain and the GCC: the current relationship emerges

This period therefore represents the hinge between a century and a half of British imperial hegemony over the Gulf and the subsequent half-century of asymmetric interdependence between the UK and the Gulf Arab monarchies. The contours of Britain's current relationship with the Gulf states had now taken shape. London saw the stability of oil flows, the investment of petrodollars in the UK economy, and continued access to Gulf markets for British exporters as matters of high importance, and the British government was committed to the defence of local political structures to ensure that this relationship continued. Saudi Arabia was regarded as Britain's most important ally in the Middle East in political, economic and military terms. By the 1980s, the kingdom was well established as the largest market for British exports outside Western Europe and North America. The Gulf states themselves saw the British relationship as economically beneficial but ultimately about their own defence.[102]

Prime Minister Margaret Thatcher made a concerted effort to maximise London's interests in the Gulf commercially and strategically, most notably in the field of arms exports, and tended to the relationship with a regular flow of royal and ministerial visits.[103] The giant Al Yamamah arms deal represented both the ultimate fruit of her efforts and a significant enhancing of Britain's strategic position in the Gulf after decades on a steady downward trajectory. The first memorandum of understanding between London and Riyadh under the Al Yamamah framework, signed on 26 September 1985, committed the UK to supply seventy-two Tornado military jets, thirty Hawk trainer jets (both made by BAE Systems, then British Aerospace) and thirty PC-9 basic training aircraft (made by the Swiss company Pilatus). Britain also agreed to provide ongoing support and maintenance services, components and ammunition and to make all future developments of the aircraft available to the Saudis as well.[104]

The memorandum was state to state, but BAE would act as the supplier, with the contract paid for by means of an oil-trading scheme handled by BP and Shell. They were to receive 500 barrels per day of Saudi crude which they sold onto the world market. The proceeds were then transferred to the British Ministry of Defence, which paid out to BAE and the other contractors.[105]

At an estimated £20 billion, the contract was thought to be the largest arms deal in British history. Luck, rather than just Thatcher's lobbying, had also played a decisive role. As Nonneman points out, the deal was only '[c]oncluded after five years of Saudi attempts to buy F-15 fighter-bombers were defeated by effective opposition from the pro-Israel lobby' in the United States.[106] The fact that Britain was able to step in when the US government was politically unable to provide these arms is an indication of the important role London is capable of playing from Washington's point of view.

To describe the Al Yamamah programme as a mere sale of jet fighters would be to downplay its significance to the point of distorting its true nature. The contract effectively provided for the creation of a modern air force and aerial defence system. As well as purchasing Tornado aircraft and Hawk trainer jets and ongoing support for both, the Saudis bought a number of improvements to their airbases. Al Yamamah II, signed in 1988, was an even larger deal and included, along with Tornados and Hawks, fifty helicopters, four minesweepers and the building of an airbase. Notwithstanding the primacy of the Washington–Riyadh relationship, the Royal Saudi Air Force was now also dependent on the UK to a highly significant extent.[107]

The significance of Al Yamamah was not, primarily, about jobs, much as this concern is stressed in public by politicians and BAE executives. Rather, it was the way in which Gulf petrodollars were available, through Britain's long-standing relationship with Saudi Arabia, to fund an enormous export order for the British arms industry, an industry whose health is vital to Britain maintaining its role as a global military power. In addition, through the negotiation and performance of the contract, close and enduring relationships were forged at several levels of the British military–industrial–political complex and its counterparts in the Saudi system. The contribution of this boost to visible exports to Britain's balance of trade should be noted as well.

In 1980, Saddam Hussein's Iraqi regime attacked Iran, aiming in the first instance to seize the same oil fields that the British had originally discovered seventy years previously. As the war ground on, the West increasingly tilted towards Baghdad. The US shared classified satellite imagery with Saddam to aid him in the war effort and also intervened to protect oil shipping out of Kuwait.[108]

During the war, the Gulf Arab monarchies saw Iraq as a bulwark against revolutionary Iran, and Saudi Arabia and Kuwait contributed billions of dollars to Iraq's war effort. In 1981 the five small Gulf states plus Saudi Arabia formed the Gulf Cooperation Council (GCC), mainly to collaborate more closely in the security sphere. In particular, Saudi Arabia, Bahrain and Kuwait were concerned by the potential effect of the Iranian revolution on their own Shia populations.[109] But in both the Iran–Iraq War and the subsequent Gulf War, despite the emergence of the GCC, it was others who would do the fighting to protect the Gulf Arab rulers.

For Britain, the prospect of an Iranian victory was regarded as a major threat to the Arab Gulf states, particularly Kuwait. In 1987, the US, Britain and other European states had sent naval forces into the Gulf to protect oil shipping. Britain also provided material support for Saddam's regime throughout the 1980s, including £3.5 billion in trade credits which effectively freed up resources for the Iraqi military. Despite Saddam's use of chemical weapons and his repeated targeting of civilians, Britain continued to sell dual-use (civilian and military) materials to Iraq. Some British arms also went to Iran during the war, but Iraq was the favoured destination.[110]

After the Iran–Iraq War, Kuwait flatly rejected debt forgiveness for Baghdad, while its production in excess of OPEC quotas helped depress oil prices, thus undermining Iraq's economic recovery. Baghdad also accused Kuwait of drawing more than it was entitled to from the oil field lying across the border between the two countries and demanded a renegotiation of the borders defined under British rule in the 1920s that had rendered Iraq almost landlocked. In the absence of the outcome that it wanted on these issues, Iraq invaded Kuwait on 2 August 1990. This proved a grave miscalculation.[111]

The Western powers were not prepared to tolerate Saddam's move, and Britain joined the major US-led coalition that expelled Iraqi forces from Kuwait. Thatcher had been a leading voice encouraging US President Bush to act militarily.[112] For the Saudis' part, US$50 billion was contributed to the war effort.[113] During the war, Iraq fired SCUD missiles at US troops in Saudi Arabia, and the ongoing threat from Saddam perceived by the Saudis, as well as their continued rivalry with

Iran, prompted them to invite the Americans to set up a permanent military presence in the kingdom.[114]

From London's point of view, its own involvement was consistent with commitments it had maintained to the Arab Gulf monarchs since the early nineteenth century. The oil of the Gulf region was a major source of strategic power, of vital importance to the health of the world economy, and the oil wealth of the GCC states provided the UK with a lucrative export market, particularly for its strategically crucial arms industry, and a leading source of inward investment. It was ultimately these interests that had led Britain to help expel Iraqi forces from Kuwait and in doing so demonstrate its commitment to the maintenance of the status quo in the Arab Gulf, and it was these interests that would continue to shape policy in the period after the end of the Cold War.

Conclusions

Three principal lessons can be taken from this brief survey of the history of Britain's relationship with the Gulf Arab monarchies. First, far from being a simple encounter between the liberal democratic West and the autocratic East, the Anglo-Arabian relationship was one of governing elites in Britain and the Gulf making common cause (albeit not as equal partners) to the benefit of both British power and monarchical rule in the region. The Gulf has been a site of complex, lively and continuing socio-political contestation in which London has worked consciously to bolster the rule of the Arab monarchs – and not, it must be stressed, because those monarchs were always the most progressive force involved in that contestation. Neat binaries based on broadbrush characterisations of 'culture' therefore obscure more than they reveal about the collusive relationship between the two sides.

Second, oil and the revenues generated from its sale have been of high and central significance to these relationships throughout the last hundred years. Control of the Gulf reserves constitutes a major advantage for any imperial power, and Gulf oil wealth has mattered enormously to British policy-makers, whether in terms of defending sterling in the 1950s or securing export orders for Britain's strategically vital military industry in the 1980s.

Third, Gulf wealth continues to play an important role for British capitalism and British power in the world because the deep ties formed during the British Empire's domination of the region have endured and continue to be available for Anglo-Arabian elites to take advantage of. It is these second and third lessons that best explain the relationship described in the first lesson.

By the end of the Cold War, Britain's status had been severely downgraded, from the global power that helped create the state system in the Middle East to lieutenant to the now undisputed broker of Gulf security, the United States. Britain's stake in the region was still highly significant, but it now operated in the shadow of Washington.

Nevertheless, as we turn our attention to our own historical moment, it is important not to overstate the extent to which the UK has become diminished as a global actor. It remains one of the five permanent members of the UN Security Council, one of a tiny minority of nuclear powers, a leading arms exporter, and home to what is currently the world's premier financial centre. The Gulf is no longer a 'British lake', but it remains a region where Britain wields a considerable degree of power and influence.

As we have seen, the British government has consistently regarded its interests in the Gulf region as a means of maintaining its global role, in defiance of the general trend of imperial decline. At the end of the Cold War, Britain used a combination of major strategic arms deals, the promise of decisive military protection in times of crisis, and extensive commercial relations in many sectors to secure its ties to the Gulf monarchs. The following chapters will detail the nature and scope of those interests and connections in the three main areas in which they manifest themselves today: oil and gas; trade and investment; and arms sales and military cooperation.

2

Oil and Gas: The Strategic and Commercial Prize

As discussed in the Introduction, the importance of Gulf oil and gas is best understood in the following terms: first, as a source of geostrategic power (for the United States, in the present era); second, as a source of energy crucial to the functioning of the global economy; third, as a site of capital accumulation for the world's energy firms and, fourth, as a generator of sizeable revenues for the producer states (petrodollars), which can often be recycled back into the global economy to the advantage of the major capitalist states. The last of these factors will be addressed in subsequent chapters, while the present chapter will address the first three. It will examine the extent to which the UK is directly or indirectly reliant on the Gulf states for energy imports; the wider geostrategic value of Gulf oil and gas to the United States (the UK's main strategic ally) and to the UK itself; and the value of Gulf energy to the British and Anglo-Dutch firms BP and Royal Dutch Shell – two of the world's leading multinationals whose commercial health is a key concern for the British government.

Gulf hydrocarbons have long been a major material prize, but the West's commercial grip on them has loosened considerably over the years. As noted in chapter 1, oil production in the Gulf was initially managed by the international oil companies (IOCs) associated with the leading imperial powers. The monarchies of the producer states received little more than an allowance from a process of extraction and commercial sale that was out of their hands. Over the course of the late twentieth century, British corporate interests in Gulf oil were increasingly limited, first by competing American firms and later by producer-state nationalisations. In the 1970s, a new relationship emerged between the GCC producers and the IOCs, as the former sought greater autonomy. Ownership and control would now reside with the state, while operations, shipment and sales would be the domain of the firms. However, the producers were also increasingly selling directly to the market themselves: the proportion of OPEC exports sold without the oil majors acting as middlemen rose from 8 per cent in 1973 to 42 per cent in 1979. Not only was the IOCs' involvement in upstream operations (discovery and extraction) severely curtailed, but their downstream role (shipping and sales) was also being encroached upon. The shift to national ownership was pushing the major British and American oil firms out of the global south.[1]

After the 1973–4 oil crisis, the Iranian revolution in 1978–9 helped to trigger a further oil price shock. The Iran–Iraq War, which commenced in 1980, might have been expected to push prices up even further, but a reduction in global demand, together with the Saudi policy of increasing supply in order to moderate the price, combined to have the opposite effect. Other factors at play included additional production from non-OPEC countries such as Norway and Britain (when North Sea oil came on-stream) as well as Alaska.[2] The price spikes of the 1970s had made 'unconventional' oil more economically viable, as was the case again in the late 2000s.[3] Lower prices in the late 1980s also prompted producer governments to seek ways to increase production to try and increase revenues. This offered a small reopening to the IOCs, as several national oil companies (NOCs) sought expert and technologically adept commercial partners for upstream development.[4]

The value of these vast energy reserves is far from purely commercial or economic. The geopolitical rationale for US hegemony over Gulf energy resources, to which the UK is substantively committed through its deep strategic alliance with the United States, was articulated in explicit terms by President Jimmy Carter in January 1980:

The region which is now threatened by Soviet troops in Afghanistan is of great strategic importance: It contains more than two-thirds of the world's exportable oil. The Soviet effort to dominate Afghanistan has brought Soviet military forces to within 300 miles of the Indian Ocean and close to the Straits of Hormuz, a waterway through which most of the world's oil must flow. The Soviet Union is now attempting to consolidate a strategic position, therefore, that poses a grave threat to the free movement of Middle East oil. . . .

Let our position be absolutely clear: An attempt by any outside force to gain control of the Persian Gulf region will be regarded as an assault on the vital interests of the United States of America, and such an assault will be repelled by any means necessary, including military force.[5]

Here, Carter was setting out a long-established imperialist logic which has shaped US foreign policy through major episodes, including the reflagging of Kuwaiti oil tankers during the Iran–Iraq War and the military operation to expel Iraqi forces from Kuwait in 1990–1. The UK House of Commons Foreign Affairs Committee cited several factors creating the 'imperative' to act militarily against the Iraqi invasion of Kuwait, including 'the threat of disrupted access to two-thirds of the world's oil reserves'.[6] In making the case for war, US President George H. W. Bush and his defence secretary, Dick Cheney, both pointed to the threat represented by Saddam Hussein's seizure of Kuwait's vast oil reserves and the proximity of his forces to the even greater Saudi fields just across the border.[7] Britain's own military support for the Gulf states (covered in chapters 5 and 6), together with its involvement in US-led military interventions, complement and support US imperial commitments in the region, which are fundamentally oil-centric.

While Western governments have tended to justify their domination of the Gulf in defensive terms, invoking threats posed variously by the Soviet Union, Saddam Hussein's Iraq, revolutionary Iran, and so on, this is a one-sided and somewhat self-serving view. Washington and London have been driven by broadly similar motives to those they attribute to others. Gulf energy is a major source of wealth and power, and it is predictable that it should be coveted by powerful states. In this and in much else, the US and the UK are scarcely more innocent than their rivals, whose ability to seriously challenge them has, in any case, been limited.

The strategic importance of Gulf energy to the UK

The strategic importance of Gulf energy has a narrower and a broader dimension. The first has to do with securing the UK's own energy needs, while the second has to do with the wider geostrategic importance of the GCC region's energy reserves to US global hegemony and British policy in this context. We will begin by looking at the narrower dimension of the UK's energy supply.

UK energy supply

The period after the Cold War was a turning point for Britain in terms of its own direct energy needs. North Sea oil production peaked in 1999 and declined gradually thereafter as reserves were run down and new discoveries failed to compensate. The UK became a net importer of gas in 2003 and of oil in 2005 (see figure 2.1). Twenty years earlier, oil had represented around 20 per cent of total exports, but these and the resulting revenues subsequently fell sharply. Nonetheless, the UK remains one of the largest petroleum producers and exporters world-wide, with 86 per cent of its exports in 2016 going to EU countries.[8]

Oil and gas currently represent 69 per cent of Britain's energy consumption mix, with petroleum accounting for 36 per cent, gas for 33 per cent, coal for 16 per cent and renewables for 15 per cent. The vast majority of petroleum demand is for transport (72 per cent) and industrial use (22 per cent). Major sources of demand for natural gas are

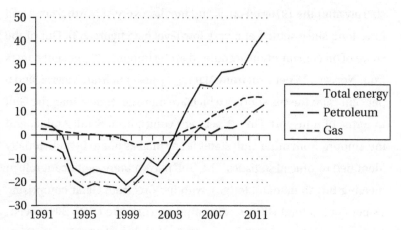

Figure 2.1 UK petroleum and gas imports as a percentage of primary supply
Source: P. Bolton, Energy Imports and Exports.[9]

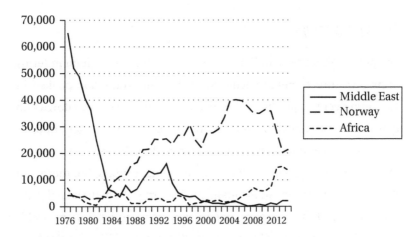

Figure 2.2 UK crude oil imports by country/region of origin (thousand tonnes)

Source: Department of Energy and Climate Change.[10]

residential (36 per cent), for electricity (25 per cent), industrial (22 per cent) and commercial (11 per cent).[11]

Britain is not heavily reliant on the GCC states for direct supplies of oil and gas. UK crude oil imports from the Middle East declined sharply after the 1970s oil crisis and the discovery of North Sea oil and have long since settled at a very low level (see figure 2.2). Out of the share of oil consumption accounted for by imports, 47 per cent comes from Norway, 15 per cent from Algeria, 11 per cent from Nigeria, and 6 per cent from Russia, sources which are more accessible than the Gulf in terms of transport. Only 3 per cent comes from Saudi Arabia, and the amount from other Gulf states is so small as not to be individually identified by official statistics. The Gulf plays a more significant role in meeting British demand for gas, with imports from Qatar comprising 13 per cent of total UK gas consumption, compared with 30 per cent from Norway, 8 per cent from the Netherlands, and 47 per cent that is produced domestically.[12]

Since Gulf producers meet an insignificant amount of Britain's oil demand and a larger but still relatively modest proportion of its gas demand, the UK's close relationship with the states of the GCC cannot be narrowly attributed to its direct energy supply needs. However, as will be discussed in more detail below, the weight of Gulf oil and gas reserves, as opposed to current production, combined with the decline of Britain's own energy industry, means that this picture could change in the future. In particular, Qatari gas is likely to become a larger part of the UK's energy mix. In addition, the growing capacity of Gulf energy supplies to affect the global price, and then impact on the world economy, is inescapable, wherever Britain's direct supplies for its own needs are sourced from. Supply and price disruptions can affect the UK directly, and also indirectly via the global investments and interests of British capital.

Gulf energy in global context

The value of Gulf oil and gas to the UK therefore needs to be understood in a global context, by looking at the significance of Gulf production and reserves to the world economy and to key emerging powers.

The GCC's considerable share of global oil production has grown steadily since the end of the Cold War, from 19.6 per cent in 1991 to 23.4 per cent in 2015. Its more modest but still significant share of world gas production has grown appreciably over the same period, from 3.7 per cent to 11.5 per cent. Adding the shares of Iraq and Iran provides a fuller picture of the significance of the Gulf as a geographical region. In 2015 the area produced 32.1 per cent of the world's oil and 16.9 per cent of its gas.[13]

However, it is by looking at proven reserves that we can assess the true importance of the region for meeting rising global demand in the long term. Together the GCC states account for 29.3 per cent of proven

Table 2.1 Share of global proven oil reserves, 2016

Producer	% of proven reserves	Producer	% of proven reserves
Saudi Arabia	15.7	Kuwait	6.0
UAE	5.8	Qatar	1.5
Oman	0.3	Iran	9.3
Iraq	8.4	Venezuela	17.7
Canada	10.1	Russia	6.0
All GCC	**29.3**	**All Gulf region**	**47.0**

Source: BP Statistical Review of World Energy, 2016.

reserves, and, adding Iran and Iraq, the entire Gulf region accounts for 47 per cent of the total (see table 2.1). It should also be noted that the cost of recovering oil in Saudi Arabia is considerably lower than it is in Venezuela, the country with the largest proven reserves.[14] (One should be slightly wary of the claims producer states make about the size of their reserves, but, notwithstanding this, the data provided in the *BP Statistical Review of World Energy*, used here, is widely recognised to be among the most reliable.

According to the US Energy Information Administration, 'Saudi Arabia has usually kept more than 1.5–2 million barrels per day of spare capacity on hand for market management', thus, if necessary, allowing it to increase production quickly to stabilise prices.[15] The size and nature of Saudi reserves, and its resulting ability to affect the global price, is what grants it the status of 'swing producer'.[16] This also allows it to put pressure on rival producers of oil that is more expensive to recover, such as US shale, as it did by sharply increasing production in 2014, causing the global price to plunge.[17] Equally, cutbacks can have a clear effect on the price in an upward direction.

The states of the GCC are able to affect the global price of oil not only through their own output but also through their influence within the producers' cartel OPEC. OPEC accounts for 41.4 per cent of current global production, and the GCC states account for 53.5 per cent of OPEC production. Saudi Arabia alone is responsible for 31.4 per cent of OPEC production (adding Iraq and Iran, the Gulf region accounts for 74.4 per cent). Again, however, it is by looking at proven reserves that a true sense of OPEC's significance, and GCC influence, can be established. OPEC holds 71.4 per cent of the world's proven oil reserves and the GCC states account for 40.5 per cent of OPEC reserves, with Saudi Arabia alone holding 21.9 per cent (adding Iraq and Iran, the Gulf region accounts for 65.2 per cent).[18]

Subject to internal cohesion, the OPEC cartel is therefore likely to have serious and increased influence over the global price of oil, and the GCC states will have serious and increased power as a result. British policy-makers are cognisant of these prospects, just as they are of the projected future importance of natural gas and the capacity of GCC gas reserves – 22.4 per cent of the world's total – to meet this growing demand.[19]

The size and significance of Gulf energy reserves lend geostrategic importance to the supply routes connecting the region to world markets. There are two major 'transit chokepoints' around the Arabian peninsula – narrow shipping lanes which are critical to the world's energy security because of the high volume of oil and other liquids that are transported through them. The Strait of Hormuz, at the mouth of the Gulf, is most important of these chokepoints worldwide. In 2013, 17 million barrels of oil per day flowed through the strait, representing 19 per cent of total world supply. In addition, more than 30 per cent of the trade in global liquid natural gas passes through the strait. There are some land-based pipelines which can be used as alternative outlets in an emergency, but these are no adequate substitute. In addition, the Bab el-Mandeb Strait, located between Yemen, Djibouti and Eritrea, saw the passage in 2013 of 6 per cent of world maritime oil trade and 4 per cent of total world supply. Closure of this strait would keep tankers from the Persian Gulf from making their way north towards the Mediterranean. This represents one aspect of Yemen's strategic value to Western states and their GCC allies.[20]

Supply and demand: the shift eastwards

The importance of GCC oil and gas is further underlined by dramatic and long-term increases in global energy demand, principally from the growing Asian economies, putting upward pressure on prices. This accounts for the post-2000 oil boom that boosted the revenues of the GCC states, with major implications for British capitalism (we will consider these more closely in chapters 3 and 4).

China is set to become the world's largest oil importer by 2020 and India the second largest around 2035.[21] Non-OECD (global south) energy consumption is expected to rise by 71 per cent between 2012 and 2040, compared with 18 per cent in the OECD (broadly, the global north) countries, with non-OECD consumption reaching almost two-thirds of the world total. Over the same time-frame, global oil consumption is projected to rise from 90 million to 121 million barrels per day, while natural gas consumption is projected to rise from 120 to 203 trillion cubic feet.[22] One attraction of gas is that, while not strictly green, it produces lower carbon emissions than oil. Another is that advances in technology, such as the process of liquefaction, have made it easier to transport long distance via tankers rather than only through pipelines.[23]

Andreas Goldthau argues that, as a result of these trends, oil prices have lost a structural source of stability, by virtue of the fact that consumption by global north states, backed by their strategic reserves, is declining whereas non-OECD consumption, which does not have the similarly robust safety mechanisms, is increasing.[24] The issue of price stability is therefore becoming even more important, underlining the significance of GCC producers (particularly the Saudi kingdom).

Trends on the supply side have also enhanced the strategic importance of Gulf energy. By the start of the 1990s, there were no significant new non-OPEC discoveries – like the North Sea or Alaska – waiting to come on-stream, as there had been ten to fifteen years earlier, partly because the low price undermined the economic case for exploration and development. Going into the first decade of the twenty-first century, the fear grew that short supply was a structural rather than a cyclical problem, a combination of the failure to find new, economically viable reserves and the relentless growth of China and India.[25] Global energy supply is commonly understood to be tight, relative to demand, and analysts disagree only on the extent of the problem. This underlines the strategic importance of proven, economically viable, and comparatively large reserves, such as those found in the Gulf.[26]

The GCC states currently provide 33 per cent of China's oil imports, and the Gulf region as a whole accounts for 51 per cent. Qatar provides a third of Chinese gas imports.[27] Energy imports from the Gulf region are therefore vital to China, the major long-term rival to Washington as a global power, and this dependence can be expected to grow in the future. This underlines the strategic value of control over Gulf energy reserves to the United States, and by extension to the UK, given the latter's commitment to US global supremacy.

Just as GCC energy imports have become vital to developing markets in Asia, those markets have now become highly significant to the GCC producers: 68 per cent of Saudi oil exports go to Asia compared with 19 per cent to the Americas and 10 per cent to Europe, and 75 per cent of Kuwaiti oil exports go to the Asia-Pacific region, along with 72 per cent of Qatari liquefied natural gas exports. As of 2014, the UAE exported 96 per cent of its crude oil to Asia.[28] From the point of view of the Gulf monarchies, therefore, the importance of their Western allies is not as customers of their oil and gas industries.

Strategic importance of Gulf energy – the 'dual logic'

In *Global Energy Security and American Hegemony,* Doug Stokes and Sam Raphael describe US policy as guided by a 'dual logic': first of energy security and second of geopolitical leverage.[29] Their concept of the 'dual logic', adapted to the British case as appropriate, will provide a framing for the remainder of this section, which examines Anglo-American policy responses to the growing strategic importance of Gulf energy.

From the points of view of both Washington and London, energy security is not only a question of ensuring supplies for their own national needs – including those of their large militaries.[30] The globalised economy as a whole requires a reliable supply of oil and gas at a broadly stable price, and, given the extent to which US and British capital is invested in and interdependent with the rest of the world economy, national energy security cannot be easily disaggregated from global energy security. This is particularly true in an era of global energy markets, where consumer nations are affected by the price changes that may be dictated by events in the Gulf, irrespective of where their own supplies come from.[31] Ensuring the secure flow of Gulf energy to world markets is therefore the first element of the 'dual logic'.

Second, by securing the stable flow of Gulf energy, which serves as a broad common good for international capitalist interests, Washington places itself in a position of 'immense *structural* power. By acting as the ultimate guarantor of global energy security, US hegemony over the international system is consolidated, with potential rivals to its position forced to be (and in some instances content to be) reliant upon American power.'[32] The US role in the Gulf therefore represents 'a significant political lever to be operated (or threatened) should the current conditions of intracore peace break down.'[33]

This second element of the 'dual logic' is a concern primarily for Washington rather than for London. Only the United States has the capacity to play this, not just imperial, but hegemonic role in the global system. However, since Britain's relegation to the second tier of global powers in the latter half of the twentieth century, London has perceived its own interests as best served by the continuation of US hegemony. In this sense, therefore, the second element of the 'dual logic' is of high strategic relevance to British power.

Given the importance of Washington's strategy to that of the UK, let us then first briefly examine some articulations of the 'dual logic' from key US figures, before turning to articulations of the 'dual logic' coming from British policy-makers themselves.

US articulations of the security logic

In 1998, Anthony Zinni, commander in chief of the United States Central Command (CENTCOM – the military command structure responsible for the Middle East and Central Asia), noted: 'our strategy is basically energy driven, or it's at least one of the prime considerations in determining our interests.'[34] Kenneth Pollack, who under the Clinton administration served as the US National Security Council's director of Persian Gulf affairs, wrote in 2003 that 'America's primary interest in the Persian Gulf lies in ensuring the free and stable flow of oil from the region to the world at large.' This interest was not an altruistic one but, rather, due to the fact that, 'if Saudi oil production were to vanish, the price of oil in general would shoot through the ceiling, destroying the American economy along with everyone else's.'[35]

Pollack cited three principal threats to 'Persian Gulf security': the geopolitical positioning of Iraq, the alleged Iranian nuclear weapons programme, and 'potential internal unrest in the countries of the Gulf Cooperation Council', where, if 'reforms do not succeed and revolution or civil war ensues, the United States might face some very difficult security challenges.'[36] The survival of the Gulf monarchies was therefore crucial to US imperial interests.

In addition, the April 2008 summit declaration by the North Atlantic Treaty Organization made explicit mention of the importance of energy security, committing the alliance to 'projecting stability' and 'supporting the protection of critical energy infrastructure'.[37] In a February 2010 speech, then US Secretary of State Hillary Clinton suggested that NATO's 'spirit of collective self-defence must also include non-traditional threats' such as 'energy disruptions',[38] an approach that, if it were ever formalised, would effectively commit the entire alliance to upholding the Carter Doctrine.

US articulations of the geopolitical logic

Although the 'security logic' is easier to express within a predominantly liberal political discourse (with the US cast as securing the common good of liberal energy markets), US policy-makers have often been quite open about the importance of Gulf energy in geopolitical competition and power considerations. Henry Kissinger, a former US secretary of state and long-time *éminence grise* of Washington's foreign policy community, remarked in 2005 that competition between the major powers over energy resources risked forming the basis of a new 'Great Game', echoing the strategic conflict over Central Asia between Britain and Russia in the nineteenth century.[39] Similarly, the US National Intelligence Council argued in 2004 that the rise of China and India was set to 'transform the geopolitical landscape', given that their 'lack [of] adequate domestic energy resources' and resulting dependence on imports would likely 'be a major factor in shaping their foreign and defense policies'.[40]

The sense in which control over Gulf oil represented a form of critical leverage over key geopolitical rivals has been openly acknowledged on both sides of the political divide in Washington. In 1995, Zalmay Khalilzad, a key figure in the future Bush administration, noted with specific reference to China that '[t]he US position in the Gulf . . . helps the United States to prevent the rise of another global rival. And should one arise, Washington's position in the Gulf would be a great advantage.'[41] Pollack, of the Clinton administration, noted with reference to the 2003 invasion of Iraq that the US 'has an interest in preventing any potentially hostile state from gaining control over the region and its resources and using such control to amass vast power or blackmail the world. If the United States were denied access to the Persian Gulf, its ability to influence events in many other key regions of the world would be greatly diminished.'[42]

One does not have to accept Pollack's defensive framing of the policy imperatives here. Given the enormous discrepancy in military power between the US and its nearest rivals, the prospect of a 'hostile state . . . gaining control over the region' appears remote, as does that of the 'United States [being] denied access to the Persian Gulf'. What these statements demonstrate is that Gulf oil is understood by US policy-makers – Republican and Democrat – as a source of geostrategic power. The real issue is Washington's possession of that power, not any threat that it might be taken by a rival.

UK articulations of the security logic

Elements of the 'dual logic' have also been frequently articulated by British policy-makers during the post-Cold War period. In 2003, the Labour foreign secretary Jack Straw identified the aim 'to bolster the security of British and global energy supplies' as one of the UK's seven foreign policy priorities.[43] A Department for Trade and Industry white paper that same year argued that 'we need to give greater prominence to strategic energy issues in foreign policy.' This would be achieved through 'maintain[ing] strong relations with exporting countries ... [and] work[ing] to minimise the risk of disruption to supplies from regional disputes.'[44] Of course, 'strong relations with exporting countries' means supportive relations with governments such as those of the GCC.

In December 2001, in a letter subsequently declassified by the Iraq Inquiry headed by Sir John Chilcot, the private secretary to the head of the UK Secret Intelligence Service wrote to the prime minister's chief foreign policy adviser on the possibility of a coming US–UK invasion of Iraq. In the section headed 'Why Move?', the first point made is that 'the removal of Saddam remains a prize because it could give new security to oil supplies.'[45]

In their foreword to the UK's *National Security Strategy* in 2010, Prime Minister David Cameron and Deputy Prime Minister Nick Clegg stated that '[t]he security of our energy supplies increasingly depends on fossil fuels located in some of the most unstable parts of the planet.' In the document itself, '[d]isruption to oil or gas supplies to the UK, or price instability, as a result of war, accident, major political upheaval of deliberate manipulation of prices' was identified as a '"tier three" 'priority risk', where 'tier one' risks include direct terrorist attacks on the UK and 'tier two' risks include a civil war overseas which terrorists are able to exploit to their advantage. 'All [tiers] are significant areas of concern and all of them require government action to prevent or mitigate the risk.'[46]

In 2013, Alistair Burt, parliamentary under-secretary of state for foreign affairs and the lead minister on the Middle East region, described the Gulf as 'critical ... for the UK's national security and prosperity ... We depend on the region for the security and stability of the global energy market.'[47] In written evidence to the House of Commons Foreign Affairs Committee, the Foreign and Commonwealth Office (FCO) stated that

> Around one third of global oil supply originates in the Gulf. Although the UK imports very little directly from the region, the Gulf is still of vital importance to the stability of global supply and the market price at which our energy is consumed. UK gas imports from the Gulf have increased dramatically over recent years, with around 20% of domestic consumption coming from the region last year. The strategic importance of the Gulf's energy producers is only likely to grow as global demand increases over the coming decades. This will put further pressure on export routes, particularly the Strait of Hormuz, through which around 35% of seaborne traded oil passes.[48]

In written evidence to the same committee's inquiry into the Arab uprisings of 2011, the FCO listed a number of reasons why this series of events 'matters to the UK's national security and prosperity interests'. 'Energy security' is second on the list, after 'conflict prevention'.[49] In a report the following year on the UK's relationships with Saudi Arabia and Bahrain, the committee concurred with this analysis, noting that 'the Gulf is critical to global energy security and market stability.'[50] In evidence to that second inquiry, the FCO spelled out the importance of Saudi Arabia in this regard.

Saudi Arabia has a vital role in securing the reliable and affordable energy supply that is needed to underpin global economic recovery. It is the world's largest oil exporter and is the only country where capacity to extract and export oil exceeds to a meaningful degree the level at which it chooses to do so. This spare capacity gives it the unique ability to provide additional market supply to mitigate disruption elsewhere. This was graphically illustrated in 2011 when Saudi Arabia was able to pump an additional million barrels per day to compensate for the reduction in global supply caused by the conflict in Libya, thereby helping to ensure that the market remained relatively stable during a period of reduced supply and heightened tension in a key oil producing region.[51]

The FCO also noted that 'Bahrain is critical to the protection of Gulf shipping lanes ... and global energy supplies', providing onshore bases for the UK Maritime Component Command, which allows the UK Royal Navy to operate in the Gulf, and out into the Red Sea, the Gulf of Aden and the north-west Indian Ocean. Bahrain also provides bases for four UK mine-hunters, which are stationed in the Gulf to keep the Strait of Hormuz clear.[52] The committee concurred that Bahrain is 'of great strategic significance in terms of energy security as it is critical to the protection of Gulf shipping lanes ... and global energy supplies.'[53]

UK articulations of the geopolitical logic

Leading British politicians also alluded to the aspect of the 'dual logic' relating to geopolitical competition. Prime Minister Gordon Brown, in a speech in 2007 in which he made a point of praising the UK's alliance with the United States in strong terms, noted that 'as energy supplies are under pressure there is a new global competition for energy resources.'[54] The Brown administration's *National Security Strategy* said that

> the premium attached to energy security and the rising risk of energy shortages will increase the potential for disputes and conflict. Countries including China and Russia are already making control of energy supply a foreign policy priority . . . competition for energy is a global challenge . . . with potentially serious security implications . . . .. [I]t is one of the biggest potential drivers of the breakdown of the rules-based international system and the re-emergence of major inter-state conflict, as well as increasing regional tensions and instability.

Later on, the document affirmed that Britain must 'guard against the re-emergence of a state-led threat through maintaining strong national capabilities' so as to protect its 'vital interests'.[55]

The *National Security Strategy* produced by Brown's successors also identified the fact that '[g]reater demand for scarce natural resources is attracting interest in countries which control those resources . . . . Competition for resources may also increase the prospect of global conflicts over access to them.'[56] As noted previously, this familiar defensive framing should not obscure the power that the US – Britain's key strategic ally – gains over its rivals from its domination of the Gulf.

Britain's own military power projection into the region, and its arms sales and diplomatic support to the local monarchies, serve to complement and reinforce Washington's hegemonic role.

Anglo-American power and the geopolitics of Gulf energy

Throughout the post-Cold War period, British policy-makers and their American allies expressed a specific, consistent, and broadly shared understanding of the strategic importance of Gulf energy resources. The principal way in which this manifested itself in terms of concrete policy was through security commitments to the GCC states (to be discussed in chapter 5), as well as military interventions in the region. The US has taken the lead on the deployment of military force, including arms sales, and the provision of training to key security forces.[57] CENTCOM has its forward headquarters and principal base in Qatar, while the 5th fleet of the US Navy is based in Bahrain.[58]

This is not the place for an in-depth discussion of the invasion of Iraq, a topic that has been amply discussed elsewhere. However, it is worth briefly noting, for the present purposes, the extent to which the Anglo-American intervention was related to their common geostrategy for oil.

With long-term energy supply tightening, the fate of Iraq became an even more important issue for the West. British and American policy-makers were faced with the need to bring Iraq's oil huge reserves back online, but the danger was that it was Russia, China and France that, thanks to their relations with Baghdad, were best placed to capitalise on the end of the post-Gulf War sanctions regime, in terms of their geopolitical advantage and the commercial advantage to their firms. Invasion and occupation negated those dangers. Philip Carroll, formerly CEO of the US branch of Royal Dutch Shell, was put in charge of the restructuring of the Iraqi oil industry, with the aim of massively increasing output over a short space of time.[59] The British government sought to help establish a pro-Western regime in Baghdad, serving to weaken OPEC from within.[60] Britain's approach to the commercial exploitation of Iraqi oil, and its hopes for how this might impact upon the energy industry in the GCC states, will be discussed further below.

To summarise, the strategic importance of Gulf oil for the UK is not a matter of direct supply but, rather, follows a 'dual logic', first in terms of security of supply for the world economy on account of the indirect importance this has for British state and capitalist interests and, second, in terms of a geostrategic imperative to ensure that it is Washington, London's close ally, that dominates the crucial energy reserves of the Gulf region, given their large and growing importance to the rivals, and allies, of the Atlantic powers.

British commercial interests in Gulf energy

Setting geopolitics aside, the Gulf is also a crucial site of capital accumulation for Britain's leading IOCs, BP and Royal Dutch Shell.

Rather than being solely British, Shell is an Anglo-Dutch firm. From 1907 to 2005, the Royal Dutch Petroleum Company and the UK's Shell Transport and Trading Company acted as joint public parent companies of a group of firms known collectively as the Royal Dutch/ Shell Group. In 2005, Royal Dutch Shell plc became the single parent company of the Shell group, registered in England and Wales and headquartered in the Netherlands at The Hague.[61] Any reference here to Shell as a 'British IOC' should be read with this qualifier in mind. BP plc (originally the Anglo-Persian Oil Company) is a more straightforwardly British firm, in so far as it is both headquartered and registered in London.[62] Both corporations are listed on the FTSE 100 index of leading shares on the London Stock Exchange.

In the remainder of this chapter we will examine how the GCC region has become more important to the UK's two IOCs in recent years, look at the close relationship between those firms and the British state, and evaluate their involvement in Gulf oil and gas production in the modern era.

Changes in the international oil business

The rise of global south national oil companies (NOCs) has pushed global north IOCs such as BP and Shell out of key areas such as the Gulf since the 1970s, making them increasingly reliant on less profitable and harder-to-access reserves. During the twenty-first century, the IOCs have failed to grow their reserves substantively or continually.[63] They are largely shut out from the largest conventional reserves with the lowest associated production costs, making it hard to replace their own reserves as they are run down. Simultaneously, with changes in the global consumption patterns, the centre of gravity of the downstream industry is now shifting to Asia, where the IOCs are not well placed. In addition, global south NOCs are increasingly moving into downstream operations, thus putting a further squeeze on the global north IOCs.[64]

Additionally, since the 2007–8 financial crisis, investors have been less willing to support large long-term, high-risk projects such as those required to replace upstream reserves.[65] Since the IOCs' future prospects depend on this sort of work being carried out, the need to find a way back into areas like the Gulf, in some shape or form, is only accentuated.

Partly as a result of the challenges noted above, the post-Cold War period has been one of merger and consolidation, with forty-five IOCs in 1998 becoming sixteen by 2004.[66] BP sealed a US$48 billion merger with Amoco in 1998 and bought the US firm ARCO for $26.8 billion the following year.[67] The Amoco merger was part of a BP strategy to get into the growing gas business, and it saw gas rising from 12 per cent of the company's hydrocarbon production to 47 per cent.[68] By 2013, the new cast of international 'supermajors' comprised ExxonMobil, BP, Shell, Chevron, ConocoPhillips, Total and ENI.[69] At the end of this period of upheaval, the two British firms had survived as independent major players among the IOCs, albeit in transformed and challenging circumstances.

The IOCs have not been shut out of GCC production entirely, and, to the extent that limited opportunities in the region still exist, these corporations may retain some hope of strengthening their long-term position. Those Gulf producer states who had nationalised their oil industries in the 1970s have more recently begun to permit a limited reopening to foreign firms, for example in complex offshore projects or enhanced oil-recovery operations requiring the use of particularly advanced technologies and specialist skills.[70] In these cases, IOCs work as service providers, through technical service contracts, and generally on a fee-for-service basis which excludes them from revenue sharing.[71] This opening is limited however, given that Gulf states with ballooning current account surpluses are not necessarily in need of IOC capital for investment and that the service companies to whom IOCs outsource much of the relevant work and technology are increasingly willing to supply these direct to the NOCs.[72]

As noted above, a large proportion of global proven oil reserves is concentrated in a handful of countries. Among these, Saudi Arabia is closed to IOC upstream investment in oil, Iraq after Saddam Hussein is not open on the attractive terms previously hoped for (as will be discussed below), Iran remained internationally isolated until 2016, with sanctions having forced the IOCs out of agreements that had not in any case been made under particularly attractive terms, and Venezuela was regarded as hostile to IOC involvement and highly unreliable politically. This lack of access has seriously undermined the whole basis of the IOCs' previous success in the twentieth century.[73]

In these constrained circumstances, any opportunity for involvement in GCC hydrocarbon production on comparatively decent terms is to be welcomed by the British IOCs, and indeed by their competitor firms based in other leading capitalist nations, primarily the US and France. British IOC commercial interest in the hydrocarbon sector of the GCC economies has only increased over the period under review.

Current health of the UK IOCs

According to a composite index including reserves, production, refining capacity and sales, *Petroleum Intelligence Weekly* ranks Shell and BP second and third among their fellow IOCs.[74] As regards non-sector-specific comparisons, BP and Shell are two of Britain's leading corporations and among the largest companies worldwide as measured by market capitalisation. According to PricewaterhouseCoopers, at the end of the financial year 2015–16, Shell and BP were the first and sixth largest UK firms, the twenty-fourth and seventy-fifth largest global firms, and the third and sixth largest oil and gas firms respectively. The UK had a total of seven firms in the global top one hundred, which serves to underline the significance of these two IOCs for British capitalism.[75]

Both British IOCs suffered a precipitous decline in these rankings from the end of financial year 2008–9, when they had respectively ranked ninth and sixteenth at a global level. Four of the five companies that suffered the sharpest falls were in the oil and gas sector. BP was one of those four – its market capitalisation plunging by US$32 billion between 2009 and 2016. This can be attributed in part to the longer-term problems facing the IOCs described above, but also to more recent issues such as sluggish demand and the sharp drop in oil prices that commenced in 2014.[76]

UK IOC relations with the British government

Given their historic and continuing importance to the UK economy relative to other firms, BP and Shell have predictably enjoyed close relations with the British state. These can be illustrated by the frequent movement of leading personnel between the higher echelons of both sides. The former BP chairman Sir David Simon was ennobled and appointed minister for trade and competitiveness in Europe by the Blair government in 1997, and Blair's director of government relations Anji Hunter left Downing Street in 2002 to become director of communications at BP.[77] A former head of MI6, Sir John Sawers, joined the BP board in May 2015, following the former MI6 deputy head Mark Allen, who took up an advisory role with the firm in 2004.[78] Sir Nigel Sheinwald, a former foreign policy and defence adviser to Prime Minister Tony Blair, and then British ambassador to Washington from 2007 to 2012, now serves as a non-executive director on the board of Shell.[79]

These latter appointments are particularly noteworthy because they demonstrate the high value that the IOCs place on experience in intelligence and diplomacy. In their endeavours in the Gulf, the British IOCs have long benefited from the support of Whitehall and UK diplomats on the ground. Referring to the period immediately before the withdrawal from 'East of Suez', Rosemary Hollis says that 'a former British ambassador to the Gulf [had told her] that BP would never tell him what they were up to, or forewarn him of the potential political repercussions, until something went awry or they needed his intercession to help clinch a deal. Then they would show up at his residence expecting him to do as they asked.'[80] Returning to the present day, an investigation in 2000 by *The Observer* newspaper into multinationals' staff working inside government departments revealed that 'BP has paid for employees to work in the British embassy in Washington and on the Foreign Office's Middle East desk in London . . . Both BP and Shell have had staff working inside the DTI [Department for Trade and Industry].'[81] Other forms of support will be described further below.

These close and broadly supportive relationships should not be taken to mean that the government is subordinate to the IOCs. According to Anthony Sampson, BP and Shell were not sufficiently powerful or connected to wield decisive influence over British foreign policy in the case of the invasion of Iraq, which was opposed by the chairmen of both companies, because of concerns about the potential destabilisation of the region.[82] However, while the US–UK invasion itself was opposed, BP and Shell were certainly not against Britain being involved if the invasion were to go ahead, given the likely benefits to them. Indeed, once it was clear that the invasion would be taking place, and after the country had been occupied, the UK government worked with the British IOCs to create the new commercial foothold they needed in the Gulf region.

Iraqi oil needed to be brought back onto the global market, investment and expertise was required to achieve that, and the UK IOCs were looking for just such an opportunity. Furthermore, it was hoped that a successful and productive return to Iraq for the IOCs would serve as an exemplar to the GCC states and encourage them to open up their industries to BP and Shell.[83]

For London, the point was not purely or specifically to seize Iraqi oil for BP and Shell but, rather, 'to expand Iraqi oil production, through foreign investment' for the reasons highlighted earlier. Nevertheless, the potential involvement of BP and Shell was a significant additional benefit. The British government was determined that its leading role in the invasion and occupation should be matched by a leading role for the British firms in the new Iraqi oil industry.[84]

However, Iraqi domestic political opposition prevented the privatisation of the Iraqi NOCs, and even the entering into of production-sharing agreements that would have been more favourable commercially for IOCs than the terms usually available in the neighbouring GCC region. Instead, the IOCs had to settle for the standard service contracts on offer elsewhere in the Gulf. BP and Shell took significant joint stakes in those contracts, and the return to Iraq was undoubtedly welcome from their point of view, given the wider commercial environment. But the Anglo-American occupation had not been the bonanza originally envisaged, and nor had it provided the desired effect on the political economy of oil production in the GCC states further south.[85]

To summarise, Shell and BP are two of the UK's biggest and most important corporations, not just compared with other leading British firms but also on a worldwide basis. They are also among a small, dominant elite of international energy companies. The British state has a close and supportive relationship with the UK IOCs and works to advance their interests to the extent that they are consistent with its own. This is particularly true in the Gulf, a region of major and increasing importance to BP and Shell. With that context established, we can now evaluate the commercial fortunes of those firms in the GCC region itself.

BP and Shell in the Gulf

BP and Shell's scope for commercial opportunity differs from one GCC state to another. In Saudi Arabia, Kuwait and Bahrain, upstream oil production is controlled by the NOCs: Saudi Aramco, the Kuwait Oil Company (KOC) and the Bahrain Petroleum Company. The industry is a little more open in the UAE, where each emirate has its own NOC, and there is considerable foreign investment through their subsidiaries. The Abu Dhabi Company for Onshore Oil Operations (ADCO) is 40 per cent owned by foreign IOCs and 60 per cent by the state NOC, the Abu Dhabi National Oil Company (ADNOC). Foreign companies accounted for one-third of Qatar's oil production capacity in 2007. Petroleum Development Oman – responsible for over 90 per cent of the sultanate's exploration and production – is a joint venture between the government (with a 60 per cent share), Shell (34 per cent), Total (4 per cent) and Partex (2 per cent).[86] These are the commercial parameters within which Britain's two IOCs must operate.

Given the growing importance of Gulf energy reserves to the IOCs, competition for opportunities between those firms is robust, with the relevant states of the major capitalist powers (the UK, the US or France) providing diplomatic support for their own IOCs. Unlike the geostrategic sphere, the UK and the US are rivals in this context. Any success in the GCC enjoyed by BP and Shell represents both a commercial victory for the company over its IOC rivals and, as such, a victory for the British state over its leading capitalist competitors.

Saudi Arabia

The UK government helps British firms seize what opportunities may become available in the Gulf region. From 2003 until its absorption into the new Department for International Trade in 2016, UK Trade and Investment (UKTI) was the non-ministerial government department dedicated to supporting UK corporations overseas, with personnel working in London and British embassies around the world. The government's High Value Opportunity Programme, led by UKTI, identified a number of promising projects in the Saudi energy sector for British firms and formed dedicated campaign teams, supported by industry specialists, to promote the capabilities of those firms, complemented by ministerial lobbying. One such project is 'Red Sea Oil and Gas', which is expected to add considerably to Saudi oil reserves and will require the sort of high-technology inputs and new infrastructure development that the international energy industry often provides to Gulf NOCs.[87]

Generally, however, opportunities have been few and far between. The late 1990s and early 2000s saw a long stand-off between several major IOCs and the Saudi government over the terms under which the firms might be involved in the development of gas production, which the IOCs saw as a potential step on the road to wider readmittance to the Saudi hydrocarbons sector.[88] In June 2001, the 'Saudi Gas Initiative' was even the subject of an elaborate signing ceremony attended by King Fahd and the chairmen and presidents of eight IOCs, including Shell and BP, who would between them invest between US$20 and 30 billion exploring for natural gas in the kingdom.

However, the Saudi oil minister Ali Naimi drove a hard bargain, insisting that the IOCs would buy any gas they found from Saudi Aramco, which would dictate the price, whereas the IOCs insisted that only direct access would provide an acceptable rate of return.[89] In the end, the deal was never finalised, and instead a series of smaller contracts were signed, including one in 2003 worth $5billion for gas exploration in which Shell took a 40 per cent stake. It was the IOC's first upstream involvement in the Saudi hydrocarbon sector since the 1970s, but also an illustration of the obstacles they still faced there.[90]

Other opportunities presented themselves downstream, where Shell entered into the 'Motiva' 50–50 joint venture with an Aramco subsidiary covering three refineries in Louisiana and Texas. A $7billion project was announced in 2007 to upgrade the Port Arthur refinery in Texas, making it the biggest such facility in the US.[91] However, the joint venture was unwound in 2016, with the Saudis buying Shell out so that Shell could offset the cost of its £35 billion acquisition of the BG Group.[92]

Kuwait

Kuwait's economy is heavily dependent on petroleum exports, and the country has a constitutional ban on foreign ownership of natural resources. IOCs are allowed involvement through enhanced technical services agreements and contracts for enhanced oil recovery, which tend to be performance related.[93] Shell signed one such agreement in February 2010 to develop the Jurassic natural gas field, but the project did not produce the anticipated yields.[94] Kuwait also holds medium-term contracts with Shell and BP for its own gas imports.[95]

A major deal that was subject to negotiations during the modern era was known as Project Kuwait. This envisaged a twenty-year contract under which a consortium would help develop known reserves, while Kuwait would retain ownership of all assets and revenues and the firms would employ and train Kuwaitis to eventually take over operations. Originally mooted in 1991, by 2001 a shortlist of nine major IOCs, including BP and Shell, had been settled upon to take the project forward, with rival consortiums being led by BP, ExxonMobil and Chevron.[96] However, this faced the same political obstacles as the 'Saudi

Gas Initiative', with the plan repeatedly stalled in the Kuwaiti parliament. Again, the large project was never finalised.[97] Downstream, both BP and Shell worked jointly with the Kuwait Petroleum Corporation in 2005 to explore investment opportunities in China, hoping that this might smooth their path to involvement in Project Kuwait, but these efforts too have been fruitless.[98]

Oman

The situation is somewhat different in Oman, where Shell has a 34 per cent shareholding in Petroleum Development Oman and a 30 per cent share in Oman Liquefied Natural Gas.[99] However, the firm suffered an unexpected defeat in 2005 when the concession to develop the Mukhaizna gas field was awarded to the American firm Occidental, which was promising more investment. This was a blow to Shell given its long-standing interests in the sultanate, which date back to the 1930s and are facilitated by the UK's close relationship with the Omani monarchy. In terms of the ongoing competition between Western capitalist interests, this was a clear defeat for the British.[100] Meanwhile, BP has interests in Omani oil exploration and also signed a US$700 million deal in 2007 to exploit hard-to-extract gas in the country.[101]

Qatar

Qatar is heavily reliant on energy exports to support its economy. Earnings from its hydrocarbon sector accounted for 49 per cent of total government revenue in 2014. Qatar was the world's fourth largest dry natural gas producer and the largest liquefied natural gas (LNG) producer in 2013.[102] The state-owned Qatar Petroleum controls all aspects of the oil and gas industry, with the latter sector run by Ras Gas

Company Ltd and Qatargas Operating Company Ltd. Qatargas operates the major LNG ventures with a consortium of IOCs that includes Shell.[103]

Shell has recently developed two highly significant energy infrastructure projects in Qatar: 'Pearl' and 'Qatargas 4'. Qatargas 4 is an LNG project, while the Pearl plant is for gas-to-liquids, a process whereby natural gas is converted to liquid fuels such as gasoline, jet fuel and diesel. Both projects represented huge capital investments for Shell, made with the view that there were significant long-term returns to be had in gas. In 2009, Shell began to suffer financial difficulties, had its credit rating downgraded and was forced to cut thousands of jobs. This increased the importance of the Qatari projects to the company's corporate health, given that they were expected to generate up to a fifth of its cash flow once fully operational.[104] The value to the GCC states of this sort of foreign direct investment from the global north is considerable (and will be discussed in more detail in the next two chapters).

The Pearl facility began operations in June 2011, having cost US$19 billion to develop, Shell's largest single investment. The *Financial Times* reported that the plant 'is the size of Hyde Park and Kensington Gardens; the amount of concrete used [in its construction] could build eight Wembley stadiums; and the steelworkers erected the equivalent of 40 Eiffel Towers.'[105] Pearl's managing director Andy Brown hailed it as 'the most valuable asset Shell has anywhere in the world'.[106]

The slump in oil prices in later years, however, caused Shell to scrap plans for one of the world's largest petrochemical plants with Qatar Petroleum. The plant had been planned to serve largely Asian markets with 2 million tonnes of petrochemical products a year, with Shell taking a 20 per cent stake in the US$6.5 billion joint venture. The high capital costs required for such a venture became prohibitive once the energy industry was hit by the sharp fall in oil prices from 2014 onwards.[107]

Qatar is also an increasingly important supplier of LNG to the UK, and the British gas industry has worked hard in recent years to secure supplies to meet that demand. In February 2011, Centrica, the parent company of British Gas and Scottish Gas, signed a £2 billion deal for 2.4 million tonnes of Qatari LNG to be delivered over a three-year period.[108]

The following year it emerged that Centrica had been prepared to offer Qatar a stake in its business, including a seat on the board, in return for a twenty-year gas supply deal worth up to £30 billion delivering 4 million tonnes of LNG per year. The revelations came in a government briefing paper leaked to the *Financial Times*. The briefing recommended that energy minister Charles Hendry ask the Centrica chief executive whether it would be possible to announce the deal in advance of a forthcoming prime ministerial visit to Qatar. In the end, however, only the aforementioned three-year deal was secured.[109] This was followed in 2013 by a new £4.4 billion four-and-a-half-year deal with Qatar for a further 3 million tonnes per year.[110] All this commercial activity underlines the growing importance of Qatari gas to British energy firms.

UAE

Hydrocarbons remain very important to the economy of the United Arab Emirates. Abu Dhabi is the emirate central to UAE oil production with policy set by the Supreme Petroleum Council.[111] Contract structures are based on long-term production sharing agreements between the Abu Dhabi National Oil Company and various IOCs. BP and Shell are among those involved in the oil and gas sectors.[112] In 2008,

Shell lost out to the American IOC ConocoPhillips on a US$10 billion deal to develop the Shah sour gas field; it then lost out again when ConocoPhillips pulled out of the deal and another US firm, Occidental Petroleum, won the second competition.[113]

The most prominent recent episode where the fortunes of the British IOCs in the Gulf were affected by the British state's relationship with the regional monarchies occurred in the second half of 2012, when BP's long-standing and lucrative 9.5 per cent stake in Abu Dhabi's huge onshore oil concession appeared to come under threat as a result of differences between the UAE and UK governments. BP was excluded from a list of IOCs invited to bid for a renewed concession deal, which would potentially have represented a loss of 3.5 per cent of its global production.[114] In the context of the uprisings around the region and the perceived threat those forces posed to monarchical rule, an unnamed UAE official expressed concern to the *Financial Times* that the British were taking an insufficiently hard line on the Muslim Brotherhood and its affiliates. In the same report, an oil industry source said that other UAE officials had confirmed that political rather than commercial considerations were behind the exclusion of BP.[115]

These events complicated efforts being made by David Cameron's government to deepen the UK's ties with the Gulf monarchies, and London spent several months trying to repair relations with Abu Dhabi, including a prime ministerial visit in November 2012.[116] It later emerged that the threat to BP had been part of a far wider range of threats made by the UAE, to arms deals, investment and intelligence cooperation, on account of concerns that the Brotherhood was making use of London as a base despite representing an 'existential threat' to the Middle East, quoting UAE government papers seen by *The Guardian*.[117]

Nonetheless, in December 2012 BP re-emerged as a candidate to have its concession renewed, indicating either that British diplomacy had had some degree of success or that the UAE had not been willing to follow through on its apparent threats.[118] There was little appreciable shift in British Middle East policy after the episode, save for an official Whitehall investigation into the Brotherhood, run by the UK ambassador to Saudi Arabia and reporting back in 2016, which was strongly critical of the group and its various political positions but stopped short of recommending a ban.[119]

This episode indicates that, while the importance of Gulf energy reserves to British capitalist interests may provide GCC states with a degree of bargaining power, ultimately that power is relatively modest and, in this case at least, insufficient to shift British policy in a substantive way.

When the oil concessions from which BP had been temporarily excluded came up for renewal in January 2014, Abu Dhabi National Oil Company was forced to take over full control of operations for the first time as it had been unable to agree new terms with the IOCs. Although a deal was signed with Total in January 2015, BP and Shell continued to hold out in resistance to Abu Dhabi's attempts to levy a multibillion dollar signing-on fee. The low oil price had encouraged the IOCs to bargain harder in order to ensure an acceptable rate of return on any investment. Other IOCs were reported to be offering significant signing-on fees, but Shell and BP's extensive knowledge of the Abu Dhabi fields placed them at an advantage. BP's chief executive expressed the view that he was content to 'wait and see' given that any deal 'has to be economic for us'.[120]

Conclusions

The fact that the immense oil and gas reserves of the GCC region are a central factor in Britain's relationship with the Gulf states is, in a broad sense, clearly not a new analytical finding. What this chapter attempts to contribute is a systematic and detailed evaluation of the specific ways in which Gulf hydrocarbons are important to the UK. A number of key points emerge.

Britain does not rely on Gulf oil for its own supplies to any significant extent. Qatari gas, however, does have a growing part to play in Britain's domestic energy consumption mix, and securing these supplies is a commercial priority.

However, the price of oil and gas is determined largely through a global market and is highly vulnerable both to any supply disruptions from the Gulf and (in the case of oil) to decisions made by OPEC within which the GCC states are highly influential. Given the relative size of its energy reserves, the importance of the Gulf in terms of price stability is likely to increase. Price volatility can negatively affect the UK economy directly, as well as indirectly through British capital's global investments and trading relationships. Security of Gulf oil and gas exports are therefore of considerable, if indirect, importance.

In addition, it should be noted that, as an oil producer, Britain (like the US, another producer) gains from higher oil prices in a way that its rival powers in the global north such as France and Germany, as non-producers, do not. High oil prices have an inflationary effect on all the global north economies, but only in the case of the oil producers such as the UK is this offset through oil revenues. Therefore the optimum price for the UK and the US is different from that of their rivals. For this reason, a close relationship with the swing producer Saudi Arabia, with its unique ability to influence the global price of oil, represents an additional benefit of the alliance.

There is also a strong geopolitical element shaping Britain's interest in Gulf energy. Although the UK is not a superpower on the scale of the US or a potential emerging superpower such as China, it does have a clear preference for and active commitment to the continuation of US hegemony, both worldwide and in the Middle East specifically, with its own state and capitalist interests seen as best pursued within that over-all framework. A key aspect of maintaining US hegemony, as American policy-makers have openly articulated, is dominance over the Gulf, especially given the burgeoning demand for Gulf oil and gas coming from China and India. Washington's position in the Gulf constitutes a major strategic advantage over its primary long-term rival, Beijing, and British security commitments to the GCC monarchies should be understood as complementing and reinforcing US efforts to entrench a conservative regional order oriented towards Western power, which is to London's own geopolitical benefit.

The UK also has an important commercial interest in Gulf energy by virtue of the fact that two of Britain's leading corporations are major IOCs, and London works actively to ensure that British firms are best placed to seize opportunities in this sector as they arise. The UK IOCs have met with considerable challenges in attempting to gain a stronger foothold in the Gulf oil and gas industry on commercially acceptable terms and in the face of competition from their rivals. In one high-profile incident, the UAE used this vulnerability as a pressure point on London, albeit to limited discernible effect. We have also seen that, while such commercial interests are important, both the British government and the UK IOCs nevertheless remain in a fairly strong position relative to the Gulf states.

Finally, a further crucial aspect of the importance of Gulf energy is the considerable revenue it generates for the Gulf states and the scope for those petrodollars to be drawn into the UK economy or to form the basis for significant arms deals. This adds to the complex and multi-layered ways in which Gulf wealth matters to Britain, as the next three chapters will explore.

3

British Neoliberalism and Gulf Capitalism: A Perfect Fit

British capitalism did not develop in isolation within the UK's national borders but, rather, as part of a complex, dynamic process of interaction with the outside world during the age of the British Empire. Within the imperial dimensions of this process, the contributions that came from the Atlantic slave trade and the plunder of India were only the more egregious examples of the role of power and violence in what was fundamentally a system of coercion and exploitation.[1] As we saw in chapter 1, and as we will see in chapters 5 and 6, state violence has long played, and continues to play, an important role in enforcing the relations of power under which the GCC region has been integrated into the global economy on terms that primarily serve local elites and Western state and capitalist interests. It is important to bear these background realities in mind as we examine the precise ways in which relations between Gulf capitalism and British capitalism have developed over the years.

In the post-Cold War epoch, British capitalism runs along neoliberal lines. The neoliberal model, introduced by the Thatcher government in the 1980s and retained in modified forms by her various Conservative and Labour successors, is characterised by an increased role for the private sector in the economy, a laissez-faire approach to business regulation, and the growing size and importance of the financial industry. At the same time, capitalism in the Gulf Arab monarchies has developed in such a way as to complement British capitalism, where the opportunities offered by one meet the needs of the other in a number of respects. For Britain as a capitalist power, the GCC area represents a unique combination of significant petrodollar wealth and deep military and security ties emerging from a long imperial history. This chapter will detail the ways in which these two capitalisms have come to fit together in the modern era, which is a key part of the reason why Gulf wealth matters to Britain.

The chapter will start with some focused background on the development, first, of the UK's relationship with the rest of the world economy and, second, of Anglo-Arabian trade and investment in the decades between the Second World War and the end of the Cold War. There will then follow an overview of Britain's relationship with the global economy in the post-Cold War era, covering the status and power of the UK financial sector and the health of Britain's export industry, as well as a discussion of the modern economy of the GCC area and the opportunities it provides to British capitalism, focusing on the effects of the post-2000 oil boom, the significance of GCC sovereign wealth, and the key areas of growth and development in the region.

As noted in the Introduction, state and capitalist interests are interlinked and complementary. This does not mean that governments are narrowly at the service of individual corporations or concentrations of capital. Rather, the state performs a management role in the wider system in which capital operates, and the most powerful states do so on an international basis. Within those parameters, states will work to advance the interests of those corporations and capitalists headquartered in their countries in so far as this is consistent with the broader managerial role.

As one of a handful of leading states within the global system, the UK

has long had (and retains to a reduced but still important degree) a privileged capacity to create, maintain and promote global opportunities
for capital accumulation for UK-based capitalist interests. This, rather
than the acquisition of control over territory, is the essence of imperialism when understood as a global structure of political-economic
relations. The large capital surpluses generated by the GCC states from
oil and gas sales represent a unique opportunity for British capitalism
in terms, first, of those states' capacity to purchase UK exports and provide returns on UK investments and, second, of capital flows that can
be attracted into the UK economy. Within this picture, Britain's world-
leading financial industry has come to play a crucial role.

In the mid-twentieth century, the UK was a major industrial power
with a large trade surplus in manufactured goods.[2] However, its share
of world trade fell steadily over subsequent decades, while the focus
of that trade moved from the Empire and Commonwealth to Europe.[3]
The defining trend was a relative shift in status of the key economic
sectors, away from visible exports and towards financial and other services. In addition, Britain experienced recurring balance of payments
problems, where income from exports and investments was increasingly insufficient to offset expenditure on imports, which deficits in
turn put downward pressure on sterling.[4]

London's growing status as a financial centre during the later Cold
War period helped to offset the UK's troubles on the current account
(that is to say, the growing overall deficit in the balance of trade,
returns on investment and other income). After the 1973–4 oil crisis,
petrodollars recycled to the City from the newly enriched oil producers
helped to stabilise the currency at a time when the price of oil and the
government's own expansionary economic policies might otherwise
have caused sterling to depreciate.[5] So, while the UK's current account
deficit was putting downward pressure on sterling, capital inflows,

including those from the Gulf, financed that deficit and kept sterling stable. This is a central dynamic in UK–Gulf economic relations and one which retains high significance to this day.

This in turn had implications for manufacturing industry. The effect of the oil shock on sterling could have given a boost to British manufacturing by raising the cost of imports and cutting the price of exports. It might also have prompted government to take strategic measures to strengthen exporting industries in order to help balance the current account in the face of higher energy prices. But the influx of petrodollars that helped finance the current account deficit and prop up the pound thereby also reduced the incentive to take this alternative path.[6] This provides some of the context for Britain's shift to the more financialised form of neoliberal capitalism in the following years.

The oil shock was a win for the City in other ways. International commercial banks, mostly in London and New York, were recipients of US$154 billion in short-term petrodollar deposits over the rest of the 1970s. Countries incurring balance of payments deficits caused or exacerbated by the crisis sought to borrow from those same international banks, which were thus able to turn petrodollar deposits into loans. The bulk of this activity was arranged in London and, given the size and risk of the lending, often advanced by syndicates of banks.[7]

As Cain and Hopkins note, the City survived the loss of formal empire by becoming an 'offshore island' servicing capital from parts of the global north where industry and commerce remained more dynamic.[8] Major regulatory reforms undertaken by the Thatcher government in 1979 and 1986 allowed the British financial sector to take full advantage of the accelerating internationalisation of global finance.[9] These reforms were undertaken with the expectation that many established British financial firms would end up in foreign hands, suggesting that policy was driven not by the influence of City institutions over the government but, rather, by the government's own sense of the right direction for the UK financial industry and British capitalism more broadly. Finance was simply seen, rightly or wrongly, as a better strategic bet than manufacturing.[10]

This shift in orientation had a marked effect on the balance of payments. After the end of the Bretton Woods system and the relaxation of capital controls in the 1970s, Britain's current account began to fluctuate between larger surpluses and deficits than had hitherto been experienced since the end of the Second World War. From the 'Big Bang' reforms in financial regulation onwards, the trend was for large and sustained deficits, despite the exports of North Sea oil.[11] Capital inflows from overseas – not least the Gulf – had become vital to financing the UK's current account deficit and propping up the pound.

The development of UK–GCC trade and investment: 1945–1991

Gulf capital started flowing to the UK after the Second World War, with investment from Kuwait and Abu Dhabi combined with returns on UK investments in the Gulf offsetting oil imports on the balance of payments. In the 1970s, the sharp rise in the cost of oil imports (by 80 per cent in 1974 alone) was accompanied by a considerable increase in the value of exports to the region (by 40 per cent in 1975) as a result of the producers' new spending power. The development of Gulf infrastructure and hydrocarbon-related industries from the 1970s onwards provided opportunities for British firms in a number of sectors, including exports of machinery and services such as civil engineering.[12]

While the Thatcher government's policies had a deleterious effect on manufacturing during the 1980s, Britain still developed a substantial trade surplus with the Gulf states over that period. This was of course largely attributable to North Sea oil negating the need for oil imports from the region, but the value of UK exports to the Gulf also rose as the GCC economies continued to grow. Besides the Al Yamamah arms contract (to be covered in chapter 6), the UK aeronautics sector benefited from the Saudi purchase of ten Boeing 747 airliners in 1984, powered as they were by Rolls-Royce RB-211 engines.[13]

Britain was able to benefit financially from the 1970s petrodollar boom in no small part because of the relationships that had developed between the Gulf elites and London throughout the imperial era. The British Bank of the Middle East (BBME) was the first bank in Kuwait, Dubai, Sharjah, Abu Dhabi and Oman and played a key role in handling oil revenues up until the 1970s. It was taken over by the Hong Kong and Shanghai Bank (now known as HSBC and still one of Britain's largest banks) in 1960, after which a strengthened BBME continued to operate under its own name.[14]

The Kuwait Investment Board (KIB), a precursor of today's sovereign wealth fund, was established in 1953 to help offset the state's reliance on oil, with the Kuwait Investment Office (KIO) set up in London to pursue those objectives. It was the British government that had initiated the establishment of the KIB, and the board originally consisted of five British bankers and was chaired by the director of the Bank of England's Middle East Department. The Abu Dhabi Investment Board was established in 1967, again with its headquarters in London, and the Abu Dhabi Investment Administration, set up after independence in 1971, later took sole control of the emirate's sovereign wealth.[15]

After the British withdrawal of 1971 and the subsequent petrodollar boom, the Gulf elites began to develop their own financial sectors. In London, the Saudi International Bank, the Qatar National Bank, and the National Bank of Abu Dhabi set up offices, the purpose of which was to channel funds profitably from their home countries into the UK, while the purpose of British banks in the Gulf region was to attract capital to the City (while also reinvesting some in the region where possible and repatriating any profits).[16]

As Gulf oil wealth grew, the Kuwaiti approach was to spread their portfolio investments thinly across a range of reliable leading firms, with a low enough stake so as not to invite attention or public concerns over foreign ownership. In addition, in the 1970s the KIO became one of the biggest operators in the UK property market.[17] The policy of spreading investments widely enough to avoid vulnerability to the fortunes of individual investments, and thinly enough to maintain confidentiality, have been broadly maintained since then.[18]

The academic Rosemary Hollis, who has researched the changes in the UK's commercial relationships with the Gulf region during the 1970s and 1980s, described to this author the response to the petrodollar boom of the 1970s:

> The [British] bankers told me that, as soon as the nationalisation [of oil] took place and the Gulf Arabs became rich overnight, the big scramble was to get them to put that money into . . . their [British] banks . . . the alternative the British were afraid of, or the British bankers were afraid of, [was] an alternative Islamic banking system . . . [which would mean that the oil revenues would not] come into the international banking system where the London based banks are at the top . . . Unless an Islamic banking sector was created there really were only two places [the oil revenues] could go [i.e. Wall Street and the City of London].[19]

Overall, British financiers were highly successful in attracting petrodollar investment and winning the spoils of the 1970s oil shocks.

Furthermore, the continuation of these capital flows over subsequent decades has proven to be highly significant, given the state of Britain's foreign economic relations today.

Britain in the global economy: 1991–2017

The balance of payments

Britain's consistent and established balance of payments situation since the end of the Cold War has been one of a current account deficit financed by significant capital inflows (see figure 3.1).[20]

Looking at the component parts of the current account (the side of the balance of payments concerned with trade in goods and services, investment income and other cash transfers) the size and persistence of the deficit is largely a result of the deficit on trade in goods, which is offset to some extent by income from the export of financial and

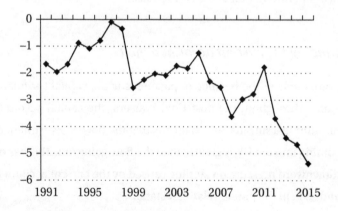

Figure 3.1 UK current account deficit since the end of the Cold War, as a percentage of GDP

Source: World Bank.[21]

insurance services. The deficit on investment income is smaller and not persistent; in fact, the UK was in surplus on investment income during the boom years between 2000 and the financial crisis of 2007–8.[22] Overall, the current account deficit has been higher than 3 per cent for most of the period since the financial crash of 2007–8 and higher than 4 per cent since 2012. As Coutts and Rowthorn note, some studies regard current account deficits as unsustainable when they reach 4 to 5 per cent of GDP.[23] This of course depends on individual circumstances.

This illustrates the extent of the importance of financial services to the UK economy. On the current account, it is financial and insurance services and investment income that either consistently offset or are capable of offsetting the downward pressure exerted by the large and persistent deficit in visible trade. Even then, the UK is increasingly running current account deficits close to or at a level at which they may become a cause for concern. These must be financed by capital inflows that the City of London, with state support, must take the lead in attracting, including from the Gulf region, with its large capital surpluses generated by oil and gas revenues.

Financing the current account deficit

The other side of the balance of payments is the capital (or financial) account. Throughout the post-Cold War era, the capital account has been running a surplus, which means that the flow of investment capital coming into the UK is greater than the flow going out. This has offset the downward pressure on sterling caused by the current account deficit and so kept the pound relatively stable.

Looking at the component parts of the capital account surplus, a major contributing factor since the turn of the millennium has been inward portfolio equity investment, which is favoured, for example, by the Kuwait sovereign wealth fund (as noted above) and which is also very difficult to trace. Since the crisis of 2008, net outflows of direct investment have been replaced by net inflows, bolstering the surplus further. This in part reflects the UK's increased reliance on foreign capital to fund domestic investment.[24] It also coincides with a period where the UK has been making strenuous efforts to attract GCC capital investment, and where GCC investments in the UK have started to become larger and more visible (as will be discussed in the next chapter).

Attracting foreign capital into the UK, as well as financing the current account deficit, also provides the funds for subsequent outward investment and may lead to a deficit on Britain's international investment position (IIP), where liabilities to external parties exceed external assets. However, it is possible to run an IIP deficit while still maintaining an account surplus on investment income, or at least while running a smaller deficit than one might expect. This is on account of the specific forms and locations of the investments in question. UK direct investment in the global south, including the Middle East, for example, earns a significantly higher rate of return than, to take another example, portfolio equity investment and bank deposits in the UK.[25]

The capacity of the UK to take advantage of such opportunities in the global south is directly related to its status as a powerful and developed capitalist economy. Global south capital deposited in UK-based banks can be recycled into productive investment in global south countries whose own financial industries do not have the expertise or capacity (even where they do have the available capital) to mobilise and put into effect such forms of investment. Because foreign direct investment (FDI) in the global south provides higher returns than global south deposits in global north banks, this process of recycling constitutes a good deal for global north financial centres such as the City of London.

The importance of the financial industry

The UK financial industry therefore performs a crucial function for British capitalism. It attracts the necessary capital inflows to finance a large current account deficit, exports professional services and receives investment income that somewhat reduce that deficit, and facilitates the status, power and reach of British capitalism. The City of London should be seen not as separate from or shorthand for British capitalism as a whole but, rather, as a facilitator of it, as well, of course, as a major revenue earner for the British state.

The City has benefited from the emergence of English as the global business language, the development of an ecosystem of complementary businesses and services in London, and a location that allows it to conduct business 'with Asia in the morning, North and South America in the afternoon, and Europe all day'.[26] It has thus emerged as the world's leading financial centre: by the turn of the millennium it held 20.1 per cent of outstanding global assets and liabilities, compared with 10 per cent held in the US.[27]

This being the case, the UK government has consistently protected the City and treated its overall (if not necessarily sectional) interests as crucial to the wider interests of British capitalism and British power. Even after the financial crisis of 2007–8 (when the total state bailout of financial institutions, including undrawn guarantees and contingent liabilities, reached £1,200 billion) the UK Treasury under Gordon Brown's Labour government rejected any move fundamentally to restructure the industry or to break up the large banking conglomerates, preferring instead to return to something as close to the status quo ante as quickly as possible.[28]

The enduring importance of manufacturing

While a shift from manufacturing to services is common to developed economies, the UK's shift from a manufacturing trade surplus of 6.3 per cent of GDP in 1962 to a deficit of 4.4 per cent in 2010 far exceeds that experienced by any other advanced economy. Coutts and Rowthorn describe 'a widespread feeling' among analysts and policy-makers 'that ... the [UK] economy had become dangerously unbalanced.'[29] However, they also note that manufacturing remains significant, with the country still exporting 'over 50 per cent more than the whole of the City of London and all knowledge-intensive services put together'. Furthermore, '[t]he balance of trade in manufactures is the difference between two very large magnitudes and a modest percentage difference to either exports or imports can have a large effect [on the balance of payments].'[30] This being the case, any surplus in visible trade with the GCC, and any successful attempt to win a major contract for such exports, is of high importance to British capitalism and the UK economy. Major arms export deals fall into this category, aside from their military and geostrategic value.

The GCC economies: opportunities for British capitalism

Bearing in mind the preceding account of the UK's foreign economic relations, let us now turn to the GCC economies and the opportunities they offer to British capitalism.

The political economy of states such as those in the GCC are often analysed with reference to the 'rentier state' paradigm. While most states support themselves by extracting taxation from society, what distinguishes a rentier state is that it supports itself, and society, principally through rents collected from the outside world – in the specific case of the GCC, from hydrocarbon sales.[31] Adam Hanieh, an academic expert on Gulf capitalism, notes that, in the case of the GCC, the state is an expression of the class and familial relations of the ruling monarchies, who owe their privileged position in part to their interaction with the wider global capitalist system and its leading powers.[32]

The Gulf's specific place in that global system has shaped the nature of its own forms of capitalism and class. First, hydrocarbon production has dominated the Gulf economies, and Gulf capitalism and capitalist classes have also developed around related activities such as petrochemicals and construction. Second, many domestic sectors of production have remained comparatively less developed, which, combined with the growing wealth of the GCC states, has made the region a significant market for foreign imports, providing lucrative opportunities for local elites to act as import agents. Third, the Gulf financial sector has been able to develop by benefiting from the channelling of capital surpluses, both outwards to the wider global economy and into domestic and intra-regional investment. In each area, it is elites and the ruling families that have been the primary beneficiaries.[33]

Gilbert Achcar, a specialist on the political economy of the Middle East, notes some other characteristics of Gulf capitalism, connected to the character of the ruling monarchies. Speculation and short-term profit-making is prioritised ahead of long-term economic development. This is exemplified by the prominence of major construction projects in the Gulf, including tower blocks of increasingly extravagant height, which, as Achcar points out, stand 'at the intersection of land speculation, encouraged by the pursuit of safe-haven investments in real estate, and a commercial and tourist-oriented service economy heavily fuelled by the regional oil rent.'[34]

Gulf petrodollars played a key role in the financialisation and neo-liberalisation of global capitalism from early 1970s onwards. Recycled petrodollars formed a significant proportion of the loans made to states hit by the oil shock, and, when the US interest rate rise of 1979 pushed those states into repayment crises, the Bretton Woods institutions made bail-outs conditional on the enactment of 'free market' economic reform.[35]

Meanwhile, Saudi Arabia agreed to invest heavily in US assets and for its oil to be traded in US dollars, thus helping to ensure the dollar's role as the global reserve currency, insulating the US from the effects of running large balance of payments deficits and giving the Gulf states a stake in US financial power.[36] These points, taken together with the geopolitics of energy, provide a fuller account of why, in Hanieh's words, 'the Gulf region has become increasingly central to the functioning of the overall [capitalist] system.'[37]

Hanieh identifies three major developments accompanying the post-2000 oil boom. First, GCC oil exports shifted eastwards as South and East Asian development took off. Second, 'GCC petrodollars helped to sustain the precarious global imbalances that maintained US dollar hegemony and the US economy's central role in world consumption.' Third, the rapid development of the GCC states expanded the region's import market. These three trends further enhanced the GCC's importance in the global economy.[38]

Oil boom and current account balances

In the 1980s and 1990s, Gulf states became net capital importers, and they accumulated deficits as a result of the low oil price.[39] However, the sharp price rise from 2000 to 2008 resulted in major current account surpluses, which in turn had a dramatic effect on their economies and on their significance as a source of potential accumulation for British capitalism.

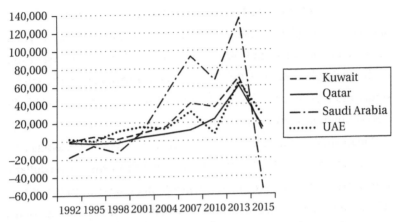

Figure 3.2 GCC major hydrocarbon producer-state current account balances, in current prices (US$m)
Source: UNCTAD.[40]

As the authors of a report on the GCC economies for the European Central Bank (ECB) observe, '[t]aking cumulative current account surpluses as a rough benchmark for measuring the pool of petrodollars available for (financial market) recycling is common practice.'[41] Figure 3.2 shows the annual current account balances of the major GCC oil and gas producers during the post-Cold War period, which closely correspond to the price of hydrocarbons. To give a sense of scale, figure 3.3 compares total current account surpluses for the whole of the GCC with those of two major world economies also running significant surpluses over the same period. Total GCC surpluses are broadly comparable in scale to those of China and Germany, but the Gulf states of course have far less capacity to absorb those surpluses domestically.

The ECB report's authors describe the post-2000 price rise as 'in many respects comparable to the oil price shocks of the 1970s, even if it is taking much longer to unfold.' The effect was that '[t]he nominal GDP of GCC economies has more than doubled since 2001, adding an

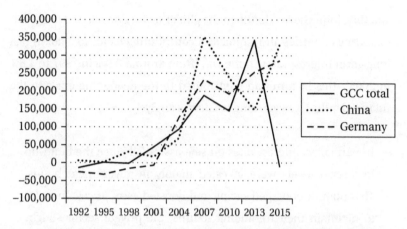

Figure 3.3 GCC total current account surpluses in global context, in current prices (US$m)
Source: UNCTAD.[42]

economy the size of Sweden to the GCC in terms of aggregate output.'[43] The decision in 2014 to increase oil production, thereby cutting the global price and undermining rival US shale producers, was clearly taken with the comfortable position built up over the preceding decade and a half very much in mind. Without that cushion of accumulated surpluses, an aggressive move such as this would have been much more difficult to take. As Hanieh puts it,

> [f]rom 1998, petrodollar flows essentially switched places with Western Europe as the second major origin of global savings, complementing those from East Asia. In early 2007, oil exporting countries were the biggest source of global savings, having surpassed East Asia in 2005 and adding half a trillion dollars in assets in 2006, close to 40 per cent of the total from the world's surplus countries.[44]

In a speech delivered in March 2008, during the early stages of the financial crisis, the Bank of England's deputy governor for financial stability, John Gieve, identified the glut of savings developed in the oil-exporting countries and China as a contributing factor to a fall in real long-term interest rates in the UK, 'from around 3.9% in 1997 to 1.6% in 2005'. This in turn had contributed to the deepening crisis in the financial industry, according to Gieve's analysis.

In particular, interest rates on safe assets fell since the build-up in foreign assets were invested mainly in government bonds. That both discouraged saving and boosted asset prices. In order to maintain their traditional returns, the private sector sought higher yielding strategies and were too ready to believe that these could be attained through new products without running bigger risks. We are now dealing with the consequences of that mistake.[45]

This analysis can be debated, but the fundamental point is that petrodollar flows into the global economy, and the financial system in particular, were significant enough during the 2000s oil boom to be regarded by policy-makers as having a major macroeconomic, even systemic effect.

This 'recycling' of petrodollars, through a relationship established in and inherited from the days of formal empire, is central to UK–GCC relations today. In a paper for the International Monetary Fund, Saleh Nsouli defines petrodollar recycling broadly as 'the reflows to the rest of the world that result from the use oil-exporting countries make of their oil receipts. A portion may be spent to purchase foreign goods and services, and another saved in foreign assets held abroad. Such foreign assets may range from deposits held in foreign banks to bonds and private equity.'[46] Nsouli identifies two channels of petrodollar recycling: the 'absorption channel', where petrodollars finance domestic consumption and thus increase demand for goods and services, and the 'capital account channel', where they are saved in foreign assets abroad, resulting in a capital outflow.[47] Gulf wealth matters to British capitalism in both these contexts (and matters more specifically to the British state in helping it to sustain a domestic military industry through major arms sales, as discussed in chapter 5).

An additional dimension, relevant to the post-2000 oil boom, is that (as discussed in chapter 2) Gulf hydrocarbons are increasingly sold to Asia rather than the West. Therefore, in contrast to the 1970s, the petrodollars coming to the British economy from the Gulf are not literally 'recycled' from British oil purchases. Rather, for the most part, the money is flowing first to the Gulf producer states from their Asian customers and thenceforth to Britain as investments and income from UK exports. We can still speak of petrodollars being broadly recycled back into the world economy, but the direction of flow has shifted substantively.

GCC sovereign wealth

The key vehicles of petrodollar recycling on the 'capital account channel' identified by Nsouli are the producer-state sovereign wealth funds (SWFs). Sara Bazoobandi, an expert on sovereign wealth management, defines these as 'a state-owned investment fund composed of financial assets including properties, stocks and bonds'.[48] Common SWF characteristics include the fact that they are usually established through balance of payments surpluses such as those arising from high commodity prices; that they tend to place their assets abroad to avoid appreciation of the domestic currency; and that they are often used to protect against commodity price swings[49] (including deliberately engineered swings such as that effected in 2014).

The bulk of GCC petrodollar investments is made by SWFs, which absorbed most of the current account surpluses from the 2000s oil boom.[50] The leading Gulf SWFs are the Abu Dhabi Investment Authority (ADIA), the Saudi Arabian Monetary Authority (SAMA – the central bank, which acts as the Saudi SWF), the Kuwait Investment Authority (KIA) and the Qatar Investment Authority (QIA). There are also several smaller funds.[51]

Gulf SWFs are well known for their secrecy and reluctance to set out the nature and location of their investments in a systematic and transparent way. Many of them do not publish information on their assets and allocation of investment.[52] The ECB report authors remark that, '[a]s only about half of these financial resources can be tracked with the help of international statistics, a large part of investment activities by the GCC countries remains opaque to international financial market participants.'[53]

The Sovereign Wealth Fund Institute (SWFI), an organisation that studies sovereign wealth funds and other long-term public investors, draws up rankings of SWFs by estimating the size of their assets. While this is extremely difficult to do with accuracy, these best estimates, set out in table 3.1, give us some indication of the significance of Gulf capital as a proportion of the global sovereign wealth.

Fourteen of the seventy-eight SWFs in operation around the world are from the GCC, and their combined assets are estimated to comprise 40 per cent of the world total of sovereign wealth managed by such funds. Within the almost US$3 trillion of assets under management by Gulf state funds, 35 per cent ($1,034.6 billion) is held by Abu Dhabi vehicles, 25 per cent ($758.4 billion) by Saudi Arabia, 20 per cent ($592 billion) by Kuwait and 11 per cent ($335 billion) by Qatar.[54]

The growth of the Gulf SWFs in the 2000s represents another shift in the extent to which capital in the world economy flows from south to north, rather than from north to south. The Gulf states have therefore become significant players in global financial markets.[55] This should

Table 3.1 Leading sovereign wealth funds, including all from GCC, June 2016

Ranking	Country	Name	Assets (US$bn)
1	Norway	Government Pension Fund – Global	850
2	China	China Investment Corporation	813.8
3	Abu Dhabi (UAE)	Abu Dhabi Investment Authority	792
4	Saudi Arabia	SAMA Foreign Holdings	598.4
5	Kuwait	Kuwait Investment Authority	592
6	China	SAFE Investment Company	474
7	Hong Kong (China)	Hong Kong Monetary Authority Investment Portfolio	442.4
8	Singapore	Government of Singapore Investment Corporation	350
9	Qatar	Qatar Investment Authority	335
10	China	National Social Security Fund	236
11	Dubai (UAE)	Investment Corporation of Dubai	196
Other GCC			
13	Saudi Arabia	Public Investment Fund	160
14	Abu Dhabi (UAE)	Abu Dhabi Investment Council	110
20	Abu Dhabi (UAE)	International Petroleum Investment Company	66.3
21	Abu Dhabi (UAE)	Mubadala Development Company	66.3
31	Oman	State General Reserve Fund	34
39	UAE (Federal)	Emirates Investment Authority	15
41	Bahrain	Mumtalakat Holding Company	10.6
45	Oman	Oman Investment Fund	6
60	Ras Al Kaimah (UAE)	RAK Investment Authority	1.2
		Total SWF assets worldwide	**7,369.5**
		Total GCC SWF assets	**2,982.8 (40% of world total)**

Source: Sovereign Wealth Fund Institute.[56]

not be overstated. Bazoobandi compares the $4.2 trillion managed by SWFs in 2011 with the $21.6 trillion held by insurance funds at that time, the $24.7 trillion held by mutual funds and the $31.1 trillion by pension funds. That being said, the SWFs also outstrip other significant classes of investor, for example the $1.8 trillion held by hedge funds and the $2.6 trillion held by private equity funds.[57]

Given that there was a limit to the capacity of their own domestic economies to absorb the new petrodollar wealth, Gulf SWFs invested a large and growing proportion of it in equities, bonds, real estate and other investments in the global north.[58] Other sectors in which they invest include aerospace, healthcare and transport. However, they disproportionately favour financial firms, in particular large banks, which are seen as having significant potential for growth and profitability.[59] This matches the preference for speculative investment over more productive investment requiring a more active managerial role, as described by Achcar (noted above). In addition, it should be recognised that, by investing in the global north, particularly states such as the UK and the US with their commitment to protect the Gulf monarchies, GCC SWFs are making partly political rather than purely economic decisions.

The Gulf SWF preference and reputation for passive, low-profile investment changed to some extent during the mid-2000s as some (but not all) of the Gulf SWFs decided to become more visible.[60] Bazoobandi characterises the differing strategies of the various Gulf SWFs. SAMA finances US government debt partly in exchange for the political and military security that Washington can provide. The KIA invests the country's surpluses outside Kuwait as an insurance policy in the case of a potential crisis. The Abu Dhabi SWFs work to support government ambitions to turn the emirate into an energy, technology and education hub. ADIA often invests in high-profile assets to gain reputation in the global financial system and establish itself as the Gulf's largest SWF.

It holds between 25 and 35 per cent of its investments in Europe and between 35 and 50 per cent in North America. Mubadala pursues joint projects that can bring technology to Abu Dhabi.[61] The approach of Qatar's QIA perhaps most closely resembles that of the ADIA, particularly in terms of its high-profile investments in Britain, a topic which the next chapter will discuss in detail.

Compared with the 1970s boom, GCC capital since the mid-2000s has been more likely to flow into financial securities than into bank deposits.[62] The 2007–8 financial crisis saw a series of Gulf SWFs acquire or increase shareholdings in major Western banks. In addition to the Qatari stake in Barclays discussed in the next chapter, the Abu Dhabi SWF bought a 4.9 per cent share in Citigroup, while Kuwait's bought a 5.7 per cent share in Merrill Lynch. Despite the economic turmoil of the period, Western financial corporations were still seen as fundamentally good long-term investments, and the availability of shares at comparatively low prices made them an attractive proposition to Gulf SWFs. In addition, there was a perceived strategic advantage in establishing closer links between these major international banks and the domestic banking and industrial sectors of the Gulf states. Finally, there was the potential for reputational benefit in being seen to help rescue failing banks during the crisis and to be exerting their economic power in benign rather than a threatening way.[63]

Questions often arise over the extent to which Gulf SWFs may act as foreign policy instruments of their governments, particularly given the centralised, patrimonial and opaque nature of the GCC states and a lack of transparency from the SWFs themselves.[64]

Bazoobandi argues that foreign policy informs the location of SWF investments to a significant degree, with SAMA's holding of the large majority of its portfolio in US treasury bonds reflecting the long-term

Washington–Riyadh alliance and mirroring the KIA's historic emphasis on investing in the UK.[65] In her view,

> it is unlikely that the governments of Kuwait or Saudi Arabia will find it easy to diversify their financial strategies from their political alliance with the former colonial powers that assisted them in creating their sovereignty. After all, there would have been no SWF if there was not a sovereign. However, the political alliance would direct these funds towards strategies in support of the West, if at all, rather than to impose national security threats on Western host countries.[66]

Key areas of domestic growth

The post-2000 oil boom also increased opportunities for British capitalism on the 'absorption channel' as the GCC states used their windfall to expand their domestic economies. As member states embarked on a range of large infrastructure and industrial development projects, the GCC became the world's largest project finance market, with the value of projects reaching US$1.9 trillion, or 170 per cent of GCC GDP, by November 2008.[67] In addition, the GCC was developing as a regional trade hub, investing heavily in roads, ports, airports and other physical infrastructure, and in 2003 formed a customs union and a common market with free movement of labour (for GCC citizens) and capital.[68] As will be discussed in the next chapter, this boom presented a range of opportunities to UK firms, from project financiers to exporters of goods and services.

The 2007–8 financial crisis prompted a temporary fall in oil prices, which recovered by 2011. In that period, the GCC states intervened to boost their economies and announced a range of new infrastructure and industrial projects, providing a further opportunity for UK firms.[69] For Bahrain and Oman, which were not benefiting from the hydrocarbon bonanza in the same way as the larger producers, a US$20 billion 'Marshall-type plan' was announced by the GCC to develop infrastructure and create jobs.[70] The region had become the world's largest market of construction megaprojects, including highways, skyscrapers and shopping malls, much of which were built using heavily exploited migrant labour.[71]

Some attempts were also made to diversify away from hydrocarbons production, both to reduce vulnerability to changes in global prices and to generate greater employment opportunities for the GCC populations. Initial efforts were concentrated on heavy export industry such as petrochemicals, fertiliser, metals and plastics production, where energy producers hold a comparative advantage. This in turn required complex technical and design work, necessitating the extensive involvement of international engineering and construction firms, and there is a good deal of competition between US, European and East Asian corporations for these lucrative contracts.[72]

The infrastructure and wider construction boom of the 2000s was not only financed by domestic and regional capital but provided rich investment opportunities for international capital as well. Dubai in particular borrowed heavily to support its construction boom. While the GCC has an abundance of capital, there remains a need to attract foreign direct investment from elsewhere, often for the specific associated transfers of technology. So, while East Asian investors are able to compete for some investment opportunities in the Gulf, firms from states such as the UK often have the competitive edge.[73]

Consumer goods in the GCC are largely imported, representing a lucrative opportunity for UK brands and retail firms. Import businesses have concentrated on Saudi Arabia and the UAE in particular, with the Saudi kingdom the most populous of the GCC markets and the UAE acting as an entrepôt for the other four. Hence UK exports to the GCC are disproportionately weighted towards the UAE in particular.[74]

Conclusions

The modern economic relationship between the UK and the Gulf Arab monarchies is the product of a number of interrelated processes coming out of the age of empire and into the present day. These have culminated in a situation whereby the British and GCC economies complement each other in several ways. This is not to imply that the nature of the relationship is necessarily a desirable one – merely that it fits together in a certain fashion.

On the one hand, the relative decline of British manufacturing industry and the rise of the City of London to the position of the world's leading financial centre have resulted in the UK having a chronic and growing current account deficit financed by large capital inflows and an ailing but economically important export industry in need of foreign markets. On the other hand, the Gulf economies benefited from significant windfalls during the oil shocks of the 1970s and the post-2000 oil boom, resulting in the dramatic growth of their domestic economies and large surpluses of capital becoming available for foreign investment.

Twenty-first-century capitalism retains some important aspects of the age of empire in which it was born, to the extent that major capitalist states are able to use their advantages, power and status to benefit from opportunities for capital accumulation available in the global south. In the UK–GCC context, this includes not only the drawing of Gulf capital into the UK financial industry but also the ability of other

British firms to benefit from the economic boom that took place in the Gulf region from the turn of the millennium, in terms of FDI, joint ventures and the export of goods and services. UK–GCC trade and investment cannot be explained purely as a set of market transactions. Britain played a key role in the creation of the Gulf states and their economies, and the modern relationship between British and Gulf capitalisms was originally forged in the days of empire. Furthermore, Gulf foreign investment is state-directed, and on a foreign-policy as well as a commercial basis. The Gulf monarchs are well aware of the importance of the diplomatic and military support they receive from the UK, particularly in the wake of the Arab uprisings that began in 2011. The UK–GCC relationship therefore constitutes a unique combination of economic and strategic ties.

Having established *why* Gulf wealth matters to British capitalism, we can now attempt to evaluate just *how* important it is. This is the question that will be addressed in the next chapter.

4

How Important is Gulf Wealth to British Capitalism?

This chapter will evaluate the importance of Gulf wealth to British capitalism in both relative and absolute terms. It will detail the precise forms that UK–GCC trade and investment take and the role of governments in promoting and facilitating these movements of goods, services and capital. The analysis will be focused on the Gulf's relevance to some specific dimensions of the UK's status as a leading capitalist power: the size of its economy, its ownership of foreign assets, the international prominence of its banking sector, and the status of its currency. The role of Gulf capital in addressing two of the main strategic challenges facing the British economy – the current account deficit and the weakness of manufacturing industry – will also be discussed. Gulf wealth is important to British capitalism in myriad different ways, and this chapter will attempt to provide as rich and detailed a judgement as possible on just how important it is.

What we will find is that, in a number of crucial respects, the GCC area is at least as important to British capitalism as the leading global south economies of China and India, and sometimes considerably more so. To make a judgement like this we need to do two things: first, identify the key economic components of Britain's status and strength as a capitalist power (the military aspect will be discussed in chapter 5) and, second, evaluate the specific relevance of GCC wealth to these key components. Existing scholarship can help us with the first of these tasks.

Tony Norfield's recent book *The City: London and the Global Power of Finance*[1] explains how an understanding of structural power within global capitalism can help us to make sense of Britain's place in the world economy. Norfield is a former financial dealer with twenty years' experience in the City, and his book is based on his recent doctoral thesis. While it focuses on the financial industry, Norfield repeatedly stresses that the City must be seen as an integral part of the rest of the UK economy and of Britain's enduring status and power within global capitalism. His account of what that power consists of also suggests ways in which we can assess the importance of Gulf wealth to British capitalism.

To illustrate the economic dominance of the major capitalist powers, Norfield notes that, in 2012, ten banks, including four from the US and three from the UK, accounted for nearly 80 per cent of the global foreign exchange market. Of the world's top 100 non-financial firms, three-quarters were based in just six countries: the US, the UK, France, Germany, Japan and Switzerland.[2] These major corporations, in turn, own many other firms, an additional dimension of their power and influence. The support they receive from their associated states, such as the US and the UK, and the economic benefits those states derive from the success of those corporations, is a crucial power dynamic within modern capitalism.[3]

Global north states with major financial centres are able to draw in the world's capital and enjoy the revenues thus generated, while corporations based in those rich countries then enjoy greater access to investment funds, empowering them to extend their global reach and influence. UK–GCC economic relations are an example of Britain using its economic status in this way. The provision of financial services is bound up with questions of power and capacity, because countries in the global south have less well-developed financial systems to channel capital efficiently or profitably. The power relations are even more stark for those global south nations that, unlike the GCC states, lack capital as well as financial capacity.[4]

The key components of British capitalist power

Norfield argues that four factors can be used to evaluate the economic power and status of leading capitalist nations such as the UK, the US, France, Germany and China: the size of their economy, their owner-ship of foreign assets, the international prominence of their banking sector, and the international status of their currency.[5] Under those criteria (as well as military expenditure), Norfield ranks the UK as one of a handful of countries in the world with real global power.

Britain's GDP (which as Norfield notes is partly 'boosted by value appropriated from elsewhere') places it fifth in the world, behind the US, China, Japan and Germany. On ownership of foreign assets it ranks second, some distance behind the US but ahead of Germany and France.[6] On the international prominence of its banking sector, Britain comes out top – ahead of the US – measured by the size of international assets and liabilities of banks operating in the UK (with the qualifier that many UK-based banks are not UK-owned or controlled). This is the one measure where the UK comes first internationally; even when restricted to UK-owned banks, Britain is a close second behind the US. On the fourth criterion, the UK is judged to have the third-ranked national currency, a long way, of course, behind the US dollar and a shorter distance behind the Japanese yen. Norfield does not include the euro as it is not a national currency, although this approach is debatable given the power and influence of certain states within the eurozone, particularly France and Germany.

Bringing his calculations together as an index of global power (including military spending), Norfield concludes, predictably, that the US is by far the leading capitalist power in the world, followed a long way behind by a second tier including the UK, China, Japan, Germany and France. Britain ranks marginally ahead of the others in this small group as a result of the prominence of its banking sector and the extent of its foreign investment, but it is of course due to be overtaken in the near future by fast-growing China.[7]

Therefore, notwithstanding Britain's dramatic decline in status since the early twentieth century, the UK remains one of a very small number of genuine global powers, when power is understood as residing not merely in the state but, rather, in a nexus of state and capitalist interests. A major aspect of the UK's continued status as a major power – perhaps more important than its military strength or its diplomatic influence, which are also exceptional compared to those of most states – is its position in global capitalism. The City of London is central in this regard.

Questions can of course be raised with Norfield's approach. One is to do with how the relationship between capital and the state varies from country to country. Accepting that these two centres of power tend to be closely linked together, having overlapping and complementary (though not identical) interests and objectives, variations in the precise nature of those links, from country to country, remain of relevance. For example, the power to direct investment lies with or very close to the state in the GCC (e.g. through sovereign wealth funds), whereas in the UK this power lies overwhelmingly with the private sector. This has a bearing on the extent to which this dimension of a country's power can be exerted in a deliberate and focused way (for example, by making or withdrawing investments as a foreign policy decision).

Nevertheless, if we accept Norfield's four criteria as broadly indicative of the economic dimensions of Britain's economic power, it follows that we can use his schema to identify which aspects of UK–GCC relations are important and derive from this some methods and tools for evaluating the relationship. This chapter will therefore evaluate the importance of UK–GCC trade and investment to the size of the UK economy, UK ownership of foreign assets, the international prominence of the British banking sector, and the status of the pound sterling. Given the strategic challenges facing British capitalism identified in the previous chapter, we will also examine the GCC's relevance to the UK's balance of payments problems and its ailing manufacturing industry.

It should be emphasised that there are no exact or comprehensive ways to evaluate UK–GCC economic relations in respect of each of these criteria. One measure applied to a certain criterion will not tell us the whole story, relevant data may be only partially available, comparisons or proxies that are used may be inexact, and so on. That being said, enough information exists – either covering the entire post-Cold War period or giving detailed snapshots in time – to piece together a reasonable, indicative picture of the relationship. Taken together, the facts and figures here can provide a reliable overall sense of how much GCC capital matters to British capitalism.

Before we begin, it is worth pausing to make a brief point regarding the statistical information being used. Economic data covering the period after the vote to leave the European Union have not been included as it is too early to tell how factors such as the subsequent sharp fall in the value of the pound have affected the overall picture. To ensure a more reliable understanding of UK–GCC economic relations in the current historical epoch, pre-referendum data will generally be preferred. The post-Brexit situation would need to develop more fully before it can be analysed in a productive and helpful way.

UK–GCC trade and investment: 1991–2017

British politicians recognise the GCC region's importance as an export market and source of inward investment. As commercial secretary to the Treasury in 2010, Lord Sassoon described the Gulf as an 'extremely significant region to be working with . . .. the UK's 7th largest export market . . . a growing consumer market. And the Gulf states are critical to the inward investment that the UK vitally needs.'[8] The same year, the minister of state for the Middle East, Alistair Burt, told the Abu Dhabi Investment Forum, 'we export around £14 billion in goods and services to the [Gulf] region each year. That's on a par with our exports to China and India combined; three times more than we export to Russia; and five times more than we export to Brazil. British companies are also major investors across the region.'[9] In its 2013 assessment of the UK's relations with Saudi Arabia and Bahrain, the House of Commons Foreign Affairs Committee classed trade and investment, energy security, counter-terrorism and defence as the four areas in which the Gulf States are particularly important to the UK.[10]

Ministers are particularly conscious of the opportunities offered by the post-2000 petrodollar boom. In 2012, the Foreign Office minister Lord Howell remarked that 'governments across the [Gulf] region are embarking on ambitious investment programmes. They are seeking to diversify their economies, and to meet the growing aspirations of their people. In infrastructure alone there are plans to invest an estimated US$2 trillion over the next decade. Here in Britain we are striving to be the Gulf's commercial partner of choice.'[11]

Size of economy: how GCC trade and investment contributes to UK GDP

As per the key factors highlighted above, we begin by examining how the GCC contributes to the size of Britain's economy. This will involve looking at the value of goods and services exported to the Gulf states; the income derived from British investments in the Gulf; some specific examples of the sorts of goods and services Britain exports; the economic opportunities in the region that the UK government identifies as particularly important; and the ways in which the government works to help firms take advantage of those opportunities. What we learn is that the GCC region is highly important to British capitalism by the standards of the rest of the global south, if less so by those of the global north.

British exports to the GCC area rose in value considerably during the oil boom period, particularly in respect of the smaller Gulf monarchies (see figure 4.1), and the economic crisis of 2007–8 interrupted this trend only briefly. It should be noted that the UK Office of National

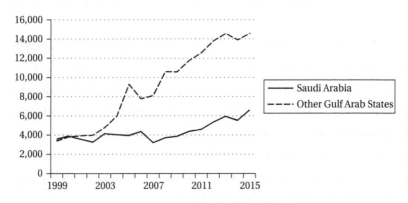

Figure 4.1 UK exports of goods and services, in current prices (£m)
Note: The ONS category 'Other Gulf Arabian Countries' includes the rest of the GCC plus Iraq and Yemen.
Source: Office of National Statistics.[12]

Statistics categorises all GCC states other than Saudi Arabia together with Iraq and Yemen as one group, 'Other Gulf Arabian Countries', making no separate breakdown of statistics for individual states available. Given the size and state of development of the Yemeni economy and the conditions there during the period in question, it is unlikely that exports there were of more than marginal value. Iraq's economy is considerably larger, however, notwithstanding the conflict there since 2003, so data on 'Other Gulf Arabian Countries', here and in the following sections, must be read with this point in mind.

Table 4.1 places the value of the Gulf region to the UK as an export market in a global context. Developed markets are by far the most

Table 4.1 UK exports of goods and services worldwide, 2015, in current prices (£m)

Export destination	Goods	% of total goods	All exports (goods and services)	% of total goods and services
Saudi Arabia	4,679	1.6	6,587	1.3
Other Gulf Arabian Countries	10,058	3.5	14,561	2.8
All Gulf	14,737	5.2	21,148	4.1
Germany	30,480	10.7	44,755	8.7
France	17,920	6.3	32,073	6.3
All EU	133,524	46.9	222,433	43.5
United States	47,229	16.6	100,273	19.6
Japan	4,552	1.6	10,450	2
China	12,721	4.5	16,313	3.2
India	4,250	1.5	6,545	1.3
All BRICS	24,346	8.5	36,346	7.1
Total	**284,855**		**510,340**	

Note: The ONS category 'Other Gulf Arabian Countries' includes the rest of the GCC plus Iraq and Yemen.
Source: Office of National Statistics.[13]

significant to British exporters, but the combined GCC is significant compared to other export markets in the global south. The value of all UK exports to the entire Gulf area in 2015 was less than half the value of British exports to Germany alone. However, combined exports to the Gulf Arab region were worth 58 per cent of combined exports to the BRICS countries (the leading global south economies, comprising Brazil, Russia, India, China and South Africa). The Gulf area purchased more British exports than China, and Saudi Arabia alone purchased more than India, Russia, South Africa or Brazil. While this is a snapshot in time and does not account for the potential of, say, China and India to grow much further, it is clear that the Gulf is a highly significant market for UK exporters in the developing world.

Given the need to strengthen the UK's manufacturing exports in order to better balance the economy, table 4.1 isolates the export of goods to assess the significance of the Gulf area as an export market in this regard. Again, developed markets account for the clear majority of goods exports, but the Gulf is significant compared to the rest of the developing world. The combined Arab Gulf area purchases more British goods than China, and goods exports to the region were worth 60 per cent of those to the combined BRICS market. Again, the Gulf stands as a significant global south market for British manufacturers.

At this point it is worth stressing the significance of military items within the category of goods exports to the GCC. According to data collated by Campaign Against Arms Trade, the UK government licensed £3.3 billion of military equipment for export to Saudi Arabia during 2015, the year covered by table 4.2. The total value of goods exported to Saudi Arabia that year was £4.68 billion, though it should be noted that military goods licensed for export in a given year may not necessarily be exported that same year. The £3.3 billion figure for 2015 was unusual (the 2014 figure was £107 million) and comes in the context of the war in Yemen. What this demonstrates is the relative significance of arms as a proportion of total goods exports and the dramatic effect those particular exports can have on a given year's export figures.[14] The value of UK arms exports to the GCC states will be discussed in more detail in chapter 5.

Another way the Gulf region contributes to the size of the British economy is through income earned by UK-based parties on investments made in the Gulf area. Table 4.2 shows the data for 'primary income' from the Gulf compared with the rest of the world. The Office for National Statistics includes investment income under the heading 'primary income', together with employee remuneration and some other forms of income such as rent. The earnings here are much

Table 4.2 UK primary income, 2015, in current prices (£m)

	Primary income, 2015	% of total
Saudi Arabia	733	0.5
Other Gulf Arabian Countries	1,275	0.9
All Gulf	2,008	1.4
Germany	7,936	5.7
France	8,564	6.1
All EU	50,662	36.3
United States	35,686	25.5
China	1,902	1.4
India	2,103	1.5
South Africa	3,072	2.2
All BRICS	9,427	6.7
Total	139,656	

Note: The ONS category 'Other Gulf Arabian Countries' includes the rest of the GCC plus Iraq and Yemen.
Source: Office of National Statistics.[15]

smaller than those for the export of goods and services. Again, the Gulf area is eclipsed by the developed world but comparable with individual BRICS states.

To obtain a more detailed picture of the role of the state in these foreign economic relations, we can look at the specific areas in individual GCC economies identified by the UK government as offering opportunities to British firms and examine the various ways in which the state provides support to those firms seeking to take such opportunities.

Of the six GCC states, perhaps the two most important to Britain in economic terms are the UAE and Saudi Arabia. Foreign Minister Burt described the UAE in 2010 as

> our 13th largest [export market] globally. We exported more to the UAE last year than to many other 'big names' around the world – among them Japan, India, Australia, Russia and Brazil. Just as the UK is a gateway to Europe, the UAE is not only a market in its own right, but an important bridge to emerging economies in the wider Middle East, South Asia and East Africa.[16]

The Foreign Affairs Committee noted that Britain is 'the second largest cumulative investor in Saudi Arabia after the US . . . and there are approximately 200 UK/Saudi joint ventures with a total investment of more than £11 billion. Thousands of British expatriates work in Saudi Arabia and British companies involved in the country include Shell, GlaxoSmithKline, BAE Systems, Rolls Royce and Marks & Spencer.'[17]

Guidance for British investors and exporters provided by the Department for International Trade offers an overview of where the government believes the major opportunities lie in the GCC. The UAE is identified as an import entry point for other GCC countries and Dubai, in particular, as a regional hub and major commercial capital in West Asia and North Africa. Education, energy, financial services, healthcare, construction and aerospace are the key areas of opportunity. Several British schools are exporting their services and ten UK universities are represented in the country. Emirati infrastructure plans are 'huge' and very promising for UK construction firms.[18]

In Saudi Arabia, 'massive government investment in transport, infrastructure, healthcare, education and energy' and attempts to grow the private sector and open up more areas to foreign investment offer a range of opportunities for British business. The Department for International Trade also identifies specific 'High Value Opportunities' arising from an estimated US$1,000 billion of public investment over the next twenty years, including £14 billion on railways, £60 billion on healthcare, £30 billion on water, and £37 billion on education. An expected US$100 billion investment in sixteen new nuclear reactors promises opportunities for firms specialising in project management, engineering and technical consultancy.[19]

Qatar is described as the UK's third-largest export market in the Middle East and North Africa (MENA) region, and the UK as the fourth-largest exporter to Qatar, the leading visible exports areas being aeronautics and motor cars. Qatar plans to invest up to US$220 billion in infrastructure in time for the 2022 World Cup – 'one of the most ambitious infrastructure programmes in the world'. Other promising areas identified by Whitehall include rail, where Doha is planning to invest $36.5 billion and where UK engineering firms are winning contracts; education, where Doha wants to draw on the UK's expertise, including the establishment of a campus of University College London; and also healthcare and financial and professional services.[20]

Kuwait is identified as 'one of the UK's largest and most important trading partners', since bilateral trade doubled from £2 billion to £4 billion in the two years to February 2015. Again, infrastructure development is the area of major opportunity here, with a projected government spend of £71 billion. Likewise in Oman, British firms are pointed to 'large [infrastructure] developmental projects worth about £50 billion'.[21]

The coalition government that came to office in 2010 placed a lot of emphasis on UK–GCC trade and investment, for example in targeting a doubling of trade with Kuwait and Qatar by 2015.[22] It was, however, nothing new for a British government both to value and vigorously to promote bilateral trade and investment with the Gulf region. Under the previous Labour government, for example, Prime Minister Gordon Brown had been accompanied on a state visit to the region by leading executives from a range of top UK companies, including Shell and BP; the major financial firms HSBC, Standard Chartered and Royal and Sun Alliance; the construction sector companies Serco, Carillion, Balfour Beatty, and Foster and Partners; and high-tech manufacturers such as Rolls-Royce and BAE Systems; as well as senior figures from educational and cultural institutions such as Sheffield University, University College London and the British Museum. Similar delegations have accompanied prime ministerial visits to the Gulf before and after the Brown government.[23]

In talking up and promoting British goods and services exports to the Gulf, ministers provide several specific examples of instances where those exporters have enjoyed success in the region. In 2013, Prime Minister David Cameron welcomed orders for a total of 100 passenger aircraft placed by two UAE airlines – Etihad and Emirates – with the European aircraft manufacturer Airbus, which has production facilities in the UK. Cameron said that the Emirates deal alone would be worth £15 billion to the British economy, where the planes' wings are designed and assembled, and the Etihad deal (involving Rolls-Royce engines) a further £3 billion.[24]

The commercial secretary to the Treasury, Lord Sassoon, hailed the success of 'Ultra Electronic [in] winning a £200 million contract to upgrade Oman's airports' and 'Carillion's involvement in the re-development of Doha to the tune of £300 million'.[25] The minister of state for energy and climate change, Charles Hendry, noted that Rolls-Royce had won a memorandum of understanding with the Emirates Nuclear Energy Corporation to assess Abu Dhabi's civil nuclear industry potential.[26] Lord Sassoon pointed to the fact that, in a fast-growing market, the UK's insurance firms are the leading insurers in the Gulf.[27]

Not all the promotion of UK firms' involvement in the Gulf was being carried out by the British government. The *Financial Times* reported in October 2011 that Saudi Arabia was making 'an aggressive push to increase trade with the UK', with the Saudi finance minister highlighting 'more than US$400bn of infrastructure opportunities in the kingdom'. A few weeks earlier, trade experts from the UAE, Saudi Arabia and Qatar had visited the north-east of England to encourage local firms to pursue more business opportunities in the Gulf.[28] This push came at the height of the Arab uprisings, so the rationale for seeking to deepen economic ties with the UK may well have had at least some political dimension.

Beneath the ministerial level, government departments and agencies provide ongoing practical support to British exporters to the Gulf. UK Trade and Investment (UKTI) was a non-ministerial government department formed in 1999 to assist British exporters and attract inward investment. In July 2016 its functions were absorbed into the new Department for International Trade.[29] UK Export Finance (UKEF), a ministerial department separate from the Department for International Trade but under the responsibility of the latter's secretary of state, supports UK exporters by arranging finance for buyers and providing insurance against buyer default.

As the then Middle East minister Alistair Burt told the Foreign Affairs Committee in 2013:

each Gulf Embassy works to a performance agreement with UKTI headquarters based on targets relating to two things; how much help it can give to how many companies, and how much value it can derive for British business from campaigns focussed on high-value opportunities within the market. . . . Our posts also work hard to encourage investment into the UK from the Gulf, and we are now looking to put more people into the region to do this.[30]

UKTI lobbied Emirati officials in support of the British firm Serco, which was bidding for various infrastructure projects in the UAE. Serco operates the Dubai Metro (and won a £350 million seven-year contract renewal in October 2013), as well as other public transport systems in the Emirates. Chris Rayner, managing director of Serco Dubai Metro, commented that, 'To be taken seriously by a public body in the UAE, a British company must be seen to have a strong relationship with the British government . . . our association with UKTI and the British Consul General strengthens our credibility.'[31]

In 2015, UKEF helped Carillion win a US$110 million contract for the Dubai World Trade Centre conference facility by financing the procurement of its services through a buyer credit loan arranged by Deutsche Bank, which also provided 50 per cent of the required lending.[32] UKEF support has also included nearly £2 billion of credit guarantees for Typhoon aircraft and spare parts exported to Oman.[33] In 2013, UKEF announced that it would guarantee $700 million of finance to British companies bidding for contracts on a new £12 billion petro-chemical facility in Saudi Arabia.[34]

To summarise, the export of goods and services to the Gulf is an important area of capital accumulation for British firms in the global south, promoted and facilitated by the government, and making a positive contribution to the size of the UK economy. This includes exports in high-tech manufacturing, a sector whose health is particularly important given the imbalances in the British economy. Investment income from the Gulf also makes a positive contribution to the size of the UK economy. This is an outcome of asset ownership in the GCC, the second important dimension of British economic power that we will examine.

UK asset ownership in the GCC

Ownership of foreign assets is one indicator of how a nation's capitalist class exerts its power and influence overseas.[35] The official data indicate that UK asset ownership grew modestly in the late oil-boom years in Saudi Arabia but grew significantly from the early boom years in the rest of the Gulf, and then very dramatically just before the global economic crisis of 2007–8, whereupon the figure broadly stabilised (see figure 4.2).

Again, the UK's Office of National Statistics places all GCC states other than Saudi Arabia in a single category, together with Iraq and Yemen. It

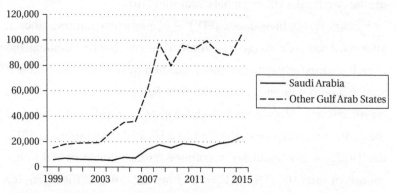

Figure 4.2 UK asset ownership in the Gulf region over time, current prices (£m)

Note: The ONS category 'Other Gulf Arabian Countries' includes the rest of the GCC plus Iraq and Yemen.

Source: Office of National Statistics.[36]

is theoretically possible that British investment in Iraq had some effect on the overall picture, but this is doubtful. In 2011, the director of UK Trade and Investment said that British investment in the country post-invasion had been very modest.[37] BP had won the rights to develop Iraq's largest oil field, but this was not until 2009, after the increase in UK asset ownership in the Gulf had peaked. It therefore appears that Iraq can be discounted, and that this was another instance in which British capitalists have been able to take advantage of the opportunities represented by the post-2000 boom in the GCC economies.

We must place these figures in a global context to understand their relative importance. The Gulf region accounted for 1 per cent of UK asset ownership worldwide, compared with 28.6 per cent for the US and 40.2 per cent for the EU. Again, the closer comparison is with the BRICS economies. British investors held more assets in the GCC area than in Brazil or China and twice as much as in India. The combined Gulf-located total of UK-owned assets was equivalent to 38 per cent of the combined BRICS-located total. So the Gulf is a leading investment destination for the UK by global south standards.[38]

Foreign direct investment (FDI) is of particular interest since it affords a degree of managerial control to the asset holder. Although the overall balance of payments data published by the Office of National Statistics do not provide comprehensive figures for FDI in the Gulf, a recent article published on its website gives a snapshot indication of the relative importance of the Gulf as a UK FDI destination. In 2014, the 'Gulf Arabian Countries' accounted for £6.8 billion of FDI in the context of total UK FDI worldwide of over £1 trillion. The figure for Saudi Arabia was evidently too small to be displayed. Brazil accounted for £14.7 billion, Russia for £13.7 billion, South Africa for £12.7 billion and China for £7.4 billion. The Gulf states are therefore not a significant destination for British FDI.[39]

However, it appears that UK FDI is important to the Gulf economies (notwithstanding the fact that the data provided by the United Nations Conference on Trade and Development – UNCTAD – is fairly patchy). In the latest years for which figures are available, Britain was the sixth-largest holder of FDI stock in Saudi Arabia (2010), the second largest in Qatar (2009) and the largest in Oman (2011). In terms of FDI flows, the UK was the largest source for the UAE in 2011.[40] While this is not a comprehensive or definitive picture, it does at least indicate that the UK is an important source of FDI to the Gulf states. This is significant for two reasons: first, because it indicates that UK investors have a notable degree of influence and control within the GCC economies in comparison with investors from the rest of the world, and, second, because the GCC states need FDI to gain the managerial skills and technology transfers required to diversify their economies. The character of UK investment in the GCC states therefore is very different from the more passive, low-profile and speculative investment coming in the other direction.

The British government claimed in 2016 that the UK was Saudi Arabia's 'second largest cumulative investor with approximately 200 joint ventures, estimated to be worth around £11.5 billion'.[41] It also described the UK as 'Oman's biggest foreign investor . . . with over £3 billion of investment, mainly in the hydrocarbons sector'.[42]

One avenue for UK investment in Saudi Arabia is through the Saudi British Offset Programme, set up following the Al Yamamah arms deal discussed in chapter 1. The programme is run by two committees, one Saudi and one British, each staffed by representatives from the respective governments, with the UK side including staff from the Ministry of Defence and UKTI, as well as representatives from BAE Systems and Rolls-Royce. The purpose is to offset some of the Saudi expenditure on the Al Yamamah deal by facilitating FDI into the kingdom. Examples include a major sugar refinery in Jeddah set up with investment from Tate & Lyle and Synthomer Middle East, a joint venture between Dhahran Chemical Industries and the UK chemicals firm Synthomer Ltd.[43] Another leading sector for British FDI in the Gulf region is of course oil and gas (as discussed in chapter 2).

The importance of Gulf capital to the UK banking sector

The next factor to examine in terms of Britain's enduring status as a major capitalist state is the strength of the UK's financial industry. Gulf capital surpluses represent a major opportunity for British financial firms, as is explicitly recognised by state officials. The former Bank of England deputy governor John Gieve described '[t]he rapid growth in SWFs' in 2008 as 'a fillip for London as a leading international financial centre'. Given the historic preference for portfolio equity investment among the Gulf states, it is also worth noting his observation that 'the prospective increase in the demand for equities relative to bonds [from SWFs] could have a positive impact on London and sterling. Whereas the value of the UK market for public debt securities is only 3.3% of the global market, UK equities account for 7.5% of the value of global equities.'[44]

Here, Gieve is explicitly identifying Gulf capital as a key opportunity for British capitalism, an assessment that is widely shared. As the Foreign Affairs Committee notes, the Lord Mayor of London (a major part of whose role is the promotion of the City's interests) takes a trade delegation from the City of London to Saudi Arabia on an annual basis.[45]

One example of how Whitehall seeks to attract Gulf capital to the City is the area of 'Islamic finance', banking arrangements compliant with the stipulations of sharia law (for example, in respect of the charging of interest). Prime ministers Gordon Brown and David

Cameron both spoke of their ambitions to make London a global centre of Islamic banking.[46] Cameron's foreign secretary William Hague noted in a speech to business leaders in 2010 that the UK was the leading Western centre for Islamic finance, with six fully sharia-compliant firms and twenty banks supplying Islamic financial services.[47] In 2013, the Treasury announced the creation of the Global Islamic Finance and Investment Group, chaired by the minister for faith and communities Syeeda Warsi, which would include chief executives of financial firms and central bank governors from Kuwait, Bahrain, Qatar, the UAE, the UK and Malaysia and help the UK government to understand the key trends and developments in Islamic finance globally.[48]

Gulf capital also has the potential to play an important stabilising role in times of crisis. As the authors of a report for the European Central Bank noted, the amount of capital available is vast, the favoured investments are long term, there is a reluctance to engage in highly leveraged positions, and the SWFs' portfolios are highly diversified.[49] As Gieve observed in 2008, 'SWFs have long investment horizons and generally have no commercial liabilities.' They are therefore 'well placed to play a contrarian role and help to stabilise markets by investing in times of stress . . . [A] number of SWFs have played an important and welcome stabilising role during the current turmoil by providing . . . new capital to some of the world's biggest commercial and investment banks.'[50]

Oil-producer funds played an important role in bailing out major international financial institutions after the 2008 crash, potentially saving the world from a longer and deeper recession.[51] The 2008 emergency recapitalisation of the US firm Citigroup included injections of capital from Kuwaiti, Saudi and Emirati investors,[52] although this was not sufficient to save the bank from government intervention later in the year. The then prime minister, Gordon Brown, led a ministerial delegation on a trip to the Gulf at the height of the financial crisis, in November 2008, to appeal for capital investment to stabilise the British and international financial systems.[53] For the City of London, the key case was that of Barclays, which will be discussed later on in this chapter.

Both British finance and Gulf capital perceive advantages in the relationship. The *Financial Times* noted in 2006 that 'the UK is popular with Middle Eastern investors because of the stability of sterling and the attractive banking environment.' Foreign policy considerations may also be at work. 'Sensitive to security concerns in a turbulent region, the smaller Gulf states use investments partly as a strategic tool to buy in interest from other countries outside the region', such as the United Kingdom. The report quoted Youssef bin Kamal, then Qatari finance minister and head of the Qatar Investment Authority, saying that '[w]e are a small country but with our investments we can be bigger than our size.'[54]

Gulf SWFs favour London and New York because of the wider range of investment opportunities available and a high level of liquidity which allows the absorption of large volumes of capital.[55] As Hanieh points out, even when the money goes to New York, London may still benefit, since, on account of 'a desire to keep purchases anonymous', Gulf buyers of US financial assets often use UK brokers to make third-party purchases.[56]

Given the poor transparency of the Gulf economies, there is no exact measure of the extent to which Gulf petrodollars flow into the UK financial system. The best information available is from the Gulf economies counterparties, including banks reporting to the Bank of International Settlements (BIS). This gives only part of the picture, since petrodollars are now more likely to be channelled directly into asset markets than they were in the 1970s, when banks tended to act as the intermediary.[57] Nevertheless, data from BIS, and from the Bank of England, can give us some indication of the extent to which Gulf

Table 4.3 Liabilities to counterparties resident in GCC, by location of bank (US$m)

	UK	US	Leading other	Total cross-border liabilities of international banks to each state
Saudi Arabia	90,487	14,177	26,171 (France)	221,562
UAE	30,458	14,664	14,218 (Switzerland)	160,922
Kuwait	23,189	15,951	2,653 (Hong Kong)	102,286
Qatar	11,370	2,127	3,946 (Guernsey)	34,013
Bahrain	3,590	1,578	4,140 (Belgium)	28,041
Oman	2,625	1,708	2,149 (Switzerland)	13,630

Source: Bank of International Settlements.[58]

capital favours UK-based financial institutions and the extent to which those financial institutions receive capital from the Gulf compared with other sources. UK-based financial institutions are not always UK-owned, but financial business done in the City of London is still of benefit (through fees, taxes, and so on) to British concentrations of capital, British capitalism and the British economy.

Table 4.3 shows the cross-border positions of banking offices located in the UK, the US and one leading other location in respect of liabilities to counterparties in the GCC states. In each case (except Bahrain), and often by some distance, the UK (not including offshore crown dependencies such as Guernsey and Jersey) is the leading location for liabilities to counterparties from the Gulf. UK-located banking offices hold 41 per cent of global cross-border liabilities to Saudi counterparties, 19 per cent of those to Emirati counterparties, 23 per cent of those to Kuwait counterparties, and 29 per cent of those to counterparties in the GCC region overall. By this measure, the City of London is highly significant to Gulf capital.

An indication of how significant Gulf capital inflows are to the City of London can be gained from Bank of England data on the external liabilities of monetary financial institutions operating in the UK (table 4.4). These figures allow us to compare Gulf capital flows into UK-based financial institutions with capital flows from elsewhere in the world.

Liabilities to counterparties based in the global north constitute the clear majority, 56.7 per cent, of all external liabilities of UK-based finan-

Table 4.4 External liabilities of monetary financial institutions operating in the UK (US$m)

Location of counterparty	Liabilities	Percentage of total
Saudi Arabia	97,249	2.1
UAE	35,939	0.9
Kuwait	17,806	0.4
Qatar	14,697	0.3
Bahrain	3,546	–
Oman	2,060	–
All GCC	*171,719*	*3.7*
United States	799,273	17.4
Germany	280,689	6.1
France	233,776	5.0
Ireland	218,297	4.7
All developed countries	*2,603,073*	*56.7*
China	78,695	1.7
Russia	20,810	0.4
India	16,793	0.4
South Africa	16,644	0.4
Brazil	19,581	0.4
All developing countries	*467,574*	*10.2*
Cayman Islands	177,610	3.9
Jersey	157,084	3.4
All offshore centres	*642,473*	*14.0*
Total	**4,586,277**	

Source: Bank of England.[59]

cial institutions. Liabilities to US-based counterparties by themselves constitute 17.4 per cent of the global total. By contrast, total liabilities to counterparties in the entire GCC region, at 3.7 per cent, come to between a half and two-thirds of those to counterparties in Germany alone (6.1 per cent) and a little less than those for the offshore centre of the Cayman Islands.

However, the GCC states are highly significant by global south standards. Total liabilities to GCC counterparties constitute 36 per cent of the total to the entire developing world. Comparing the GCC states to the BRICS, liabilities to counterparties in Saudi Arabia are greater than those to China and India combined, with the UAE broadly equivalent to Russia and South Africa combined and Kuwait above both India and South Africa. Total liabilities to counterparties in all GCC states, at US$172 billion, exceed the total to those in the BRICS group of emerging economies (US$152 billion).

Another way to gauge the importance of the GCC to the UK financial industry is to examine the relative size of assets held by UK-based financial institutions in the Gulf states compared with those in the rest of the world (table 4.5). This is distinct from the figures discussed earlier in this chapter, which were for assets owned by all UK-based parties, including non-financial corporations and other investors. The focus in the present section of the chapter is specifically on the importance of the GCC to the UK banking sector.

Here, the global north's significance is overwhelming, with 74.9 per cent of the external assets of UK-based financial institutions to be found there, 24.1 per cent in the US alone. By contrast, the GCC economies combined account for just 2.8 per cent of the external assets of UK-based financial institutions. Again, however, this is significant when placed in the context of the rest of the global south. Assets in the GCC area comprise 30 per cent of those in the entire developing

Table 4.5 External assets of monetary financial institutions operating in the UK (US$m)

Location of counterparty	Assets	Percentage of total
UAE	63,603	1.5
Qatar	29,740	0.7
Saudi Arabia	18,852	0.4
Bahrain	6,714	0.1
Kuwait	3,393	–
Oman	1,815	–
All GCC	124,117	2.8
United States	1,047,093	24.1
France	391,593	9.0
Germany	332,078	7.6
All developed countries	3,252,024	74.9
China	36,650	0.8
Brazil	28,747	0.7
India	27,124	0.6
Russia	19,427	0.4
South Africa	18,375	0.4
All developing countries	407,305	9.4
All offshore centres	540,149	12.4
Total	**4,340,280**	

Source: Bank of England.[60]

world. The US$124 billion of assets held by UK-based financial institutions in the GCC area falls not far short of the £130 billion held in the BRICS states. So the GCC area is a highly significant investment destination for the UK financial industry compared with the rest of the global south, and here it is worth reiterating that investments in the developing economies can yield a higher rate of return than those in the global north.

Barclays, Qatar and the 2008 financial crisis

The role played by Gulf investors in rescuing Barclays plc during the 2008 financial crisis illustrates the important stabilising role that Gulf capital is capable of performing for the UK financial industry. This is another benefit British capitalism derives from its long relationship with the Gulf monarchies.

As the early stages of the financial crisis unfolded, Barclays was facing persistent questions over the valuations of complex debt securities on its balance sheet. In an attempt to shore up its capital ratios, Barclays approached investors in the Middle East and secured £1.8 billion from the Qatar Investment Authority, plus £530 million from its chief executive, Sheikh Hamad bin Jassim bin Jaber Al Thani.[61] When the crisis turned into a full-blown crash, Barclays went back to the Gulf and raised a further £2.3 billion from Sheikh Al Thani (taking his shareholding to around 15.5 per cent) and around £3.5 billion from International Petroleum Investment Corp, chaired by Sheikh Mansour bin Zayed Al Nahyan, a member of Abu Dhabi's ruling family (which took his shareholding to over 16 per cent). This allowed the bank to meet its pledge to regulators to raise its capital reserves, thus avoiding a state bailout and the conditions that would have come with it.[62]

In a memorandum leaked to the *Financial Times*, Barclays' chief executive John Varley explained the reasons for seeking Gulf capital instead of a state bailout: '[The board] felt that our ability to do what our shareholders would expect of us [in terms of dividends and lending policy] would be compromised if Barclays was nationalised.' He denied suggestions that an additional concern had been the wish to escape restrictions on executive bonuses.[63]

In his autobiography, the then chancellor of the exchequer, Alistair Darling, wrote that 'Barclays . . . was determined not to take anything from the taxpayer. The board could see all too clearly that the political spotlight would turn on their arrangements for pay . . . and on their lending.' In 2013, people involved in the situation within Barclays during the crisis told the *Financial Times* that there was a desperation to stay out of government control and avoid imposed restrictions on bank strategy and executive remuneration.[64] There was some disquiet among other, longer-term shareholders concerned that Barclays had been too hasty in rejecting government support, but Chancellor Darling warned them that any terms they got from the government might well be tougher than those their board had agreed with Gulf investors. After this, and some minor commercial concessions from the board, the brewing shareholder rebellion fizzled out.[65] Once the worst of the crisis had passed, the Gulf investors began to pull out or reduce their stakes.[66]

Regulatory authorities later began to take an increasing interest in how Barclays had raised the capital. In June 2017, the Serious Fraud Office charged Barclays plc and four former senior executives – including the bank's former chief executive officer – with conspiracy to commit fraud and the provision of unlawful financial assistance, contrary to the Companies Act 1985, in relation to the fundraising from the Gulf during the 2008 crisis. Subsequently, the Crown Court dismissed the charges against the bank itself, but not those against the executives. At the time of writing, the trial is due to be held in January 2019, and all the accused deny the charges. (Separate to the SFO case, the Financial Conduct Authority levied a £72 million fine on Barclays for going 'to unacceptable lengths to accommodate' wealthy individuals, reportedly from Qatar, involved in a £1.9 billion deal in 2011 and 2012.)[67]

A number of conclusions can be drawn from this episode. First, in Norfield's words, it illustrates '[t]he value of the economic, political and social connections between the UK and foreign financiers', specifically those in the Gulf.[68] Second, it is possible, in light of Chancellor

Darling's almost explicit message to long-term Barclays shareholders not to challenge the Gulf rescue packages, that the UK government was glad to be able to avoid the responsibility and cost of taking over another major troubled financial institution. Third, it appears that, for some of the Gulf investors involved, the aim had been, in part, to demonstrate their worth and value to the UK. If this is correct, the controversy around the capital injection may have been a factor leading them to reduce or dissolve their stakes in 2009. As Qatari Sheikh Hamad bin Jassim bin Jaber Al Thani told the *Financial Times* in 2016, 'I regret the noise. We thought we had helped the British economy at a bad time and that someone would thank us for it.'[69] To the extent that the 2008 Gulf bailout of Barclays was motivated by the desire of Gulf elites to strengthen their ties with the UK – a state which had long supported and protected them – this is an example of the wider benefits to British capitalism of UK–Gulf relations.

UK banking and GCC capital: some other examples

Aside from investment opportunities in the UK, British banks offer important services to Gulf monarchies and associated elites in terms of public investment policy and private banking. HSBC and Barclays Capital were able to take advantage of the demand for project finance during the boom of the 2000s, and before the 2008 crisis the Royal Bank of Scotland was briefly the second-largest project financier in the Middle East and North Africa.[70] These UK firms had few international rivals in terms of the knowledge, experience and connections required to manage major funding projects.

British banks also play a role in facilitating Gulf investment into the UK. HSBC acted as an adviser to Dubai International Capital in its £700 million acquisition of the British engineering group Doncasters in

2006, while Barclays participated in the £675 million leveraged buyout of Travelodge Hotels by Dubai International Capital in October 2006.[71]

British financial corporations also help Gulf elites place their wealth offshore. In 2015, the International Consortium of Investigative Journalists reported the leak of documents detailing clients and accounts with HSBC Private Bank, a Swiss-based subsidiary of HSBC. Among these were 3,636 clients from the GCC states with deposits totalling approximately US$11.2 billion, including 475 clients in Kuwait with deposits totalling $1.1 billion, 1,504 clients in Saudi Arabia with deposits totalling $5.8 billion, and 1,126 clients from the UAE with deposits totalling $3.5 billion. Mentioned by name were Crown Prince Salman bin Hamad Al Khalifa of Bahrain, Sultan Qaboos of Oman and Saudi Prince Bandar.[72]

To summarise, Gulf capital is evidently significant to the UK financial industry compared to other sources of capital from the global south. The absorption, processing and reinvestment of Gulf capital represents an important capital accumulation opportunity for British banks. The Barclays episode demonstrates the important stabilising role that concentrations of Gulf capital are capable of playing for major British financial institutions in times of crisis, providing an alternative option to state bailout whose significance should not be underestimated. As an investment destination for UK banks the Gulf is not significant in absolute terms, although it compares favourably with other leading global south destinations.

From the Gulf elites' point of view, the UK financial industry is clearly of some consequence, offering as it does an almost unrivalled capacity to absorb, process and reinvest the GCC states' considerable capital surpluses, to facilitate project finance for infrastructure development, and to safeguard the fortunes of Gulf elites. It also represents an opportunity to deepen their ties to the UK, an alliance which is of high importance in securing their continued rule and privileges.

The importance of the GCC to the strength of the pound and the UK's balance of payments

A fourth economic factor that can be used to ascertain the power and status of British capitalism is the status of the pound sterling, evaluated in terms of how widespread its use is internationally. It is difficult to assess directly how the GCC economies contribute to this, since data on the size of any sterling reserves held by those states is unavailable.

However, the status of the pound is related to its strength in value, which is in turn affected by the UK's balance of payments; and, as discussed earlier in this chapter, the large and persistent deficit on the current account is a potential source of vulnerability in this regard. Therefore, to the extent that Britain is able to run a current account surplus with the GCC states, and to the extent that Britain is a net capital importer from the GCC states, these two factors will play a role in offsetting the pound's vulnerability, either by lessening the current account deficit or by financing it through the capital account. The role played by economies of the GCC region in preserving the strength of the pound can therefore be taken at least as an indirect indicator of how trade and investment between the UK and the Gulf states contribute to the status of Britain's currency. Furthermore, the state of the balance of payments is an important consideration in its own right in terms of the health of the British economy and of British capitalism.

British officials are keenly aware of the importance of Gulf sovereign wealth in financing the UK's chronic current account deficit. In his speech during the financial crisis, the Bank of England's John Gieve noted that, at least in comparison with the days of empire, when capital overwhelmingly flowed from north to south, in the twenty-first century capital was more likely to be flowing 'uphill' to the global north, directed by the central banks and SWFs of emerging market economies, many of which had switched from debtor to creditor status in the preceding decade. These 'uphill' capital flows were helping to finance the growing current account deficits of many developed countries (the UK, the US and others).

There was a danger here, Gieve went on to say, because,

[w]hile there are many examples of countries which have run deficits for many years . . ., history also shows how painful the eventual adjustment can be. There are many examples in which capital flight has resulted in a huge fall in GDP growth and broader financial crises . . . which, in turn, weakened global GDP growth or global financial institutions. . . . Countries with large deficits are vulnerable to a rapid reversal of capital flows. If investors are no longer willing to finance the deficit, domestic spending will need to be cut relative to output through a combination of reducing spending and switching production to the tradable sector.[73]

Since the GCC economies are one of the major sources of capital surplus worldwide, this gives a sense of the importance of Gulf capital inflows to the UK economy.

The next section will therefore examine what official statistics can tell us about any positive contribution that Gulf capital, and trade in goods and services with the Gulf, may have on the UK balance of payments. We will then look at UK state support for these capital inflows and some specific examples of Gulf investment into the British economy.

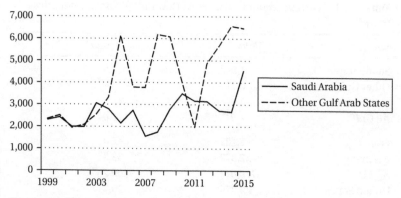

Figure 4.3 UK current account balances with the Gulf region, in current prices (£m)

Note: The ONS category 'Other Gulf Arabian Countries' includes the rest of the GCC plus Iraq and Yemen.

Source: Office of National Statistics.[74]

Positive contribution to the current account

The UK runs a consistent current account surplus with the Gulf region (see figure 4.3). The surplus with Saudi Arabia was fairly consistent during the pre-2008 oil boom, though it has increased subsequently. This is likely attributable to the 2007 Al Salam deal for the sale of Eurofighter Typhoons, with the specific spike from 2014 to 2015 probably due to the sharp increase in arms transfers coming in the context of the Saudi-led intervention in the Yemeni civil war. (Both issues are discussed in detail in chapter 5.) The surplus with the other Gulf Arab states increases significantly from the start of the oil boom in the early 2000s, with no major arms deals explaining this overall rise. It is likely therefore to be attributable to the overall economic growth in the region since the 1990s and the consequent rise in demand for goods and services, as well as increased returns on investments.

Table 4.6 UK current account balances worldwide, 2015, in current prices (£m)

State(s)	Value	% of total
Saudi Arabia	4,542	4.5
Other Gulf Arabian Countries	6,471	6.4
All Gulf	*11,013*	*11.0*
France	−7,781	−7.8
Germany	−32,372	−32.2
All EU	*−110,011*	*−109.7*
United States	29,375	29.3
Japan	−2,289	−2.3
China	−22,038	−22.0
India	−3,476	−3.5
All BRICS	*−20,024*	*−20.0*
Selected other positive contributors		
Australia	7,052	7.0
Switzerland	5,107	5.1
Singapore	3,665	3.6
Hong Kong	2,287	2.3
Total	**−100,261**	

Note: the ONS category 'Other Gulf Arabian Countries' includes the rest of the GCC plus Iraq and Yemen.
Source: Office of National Statistics.[75]

This is important because the Gulf area is one of a very small number of major markets with which the UK runs a significant current account surplus (see table 4.6). The combined Gulf area surplus in 2015 was equivalent to 11 per cent of Britain's worldwide current account deficit. The biggest positive contributor to the UK's current account balance was the United States, with which the UK ran a surplus equivalent to 29.3 per cent of its worldwide deficit. Aside from the US, the only state with which the UK ran a surplus comparable with that with the Gulf area was Australia. Otherwise, it ran a deficit with the majority of nations in the world and almost every state in the EU. Its overall deficit with the EU exceeded its (very large) overall deficit with the entire world, the deficit with China was 22 per cent of the total, and the combined deficit with the BRICS economies was one-fifth of the total.

So, on this measure, the GCC area is highly significant to the UK. Its combined positive contribution to Britain's current account balance in 2015, to give one example, matched and therefore negated the combined deficit with France and Japan. Aside from the US, only Australia and Switzerland made a greater positive contribution to Britain's worldwide current account balance than Saudi Arabia alone. Maintaining these surpluses is highly important to British capitalism and to maintaining the strength of the pound.

Breaking down the UK–Gulf current account balance into its major component parts helps us to see the precise areas in which the Gulf area makes its contribution (see table 4.7). Again, recall that Britain's major problem is its deficit on trade in goods. Here the Gulf area is very significant indeed, since it is one of a tiny number of major markets

Table 4.7 Gulf region contributions to total UK current account balance by sector, 2015, in current prices (£m)

State(s)	Goods	% of total	Services	% of total	Primary income	% of total
Saudi Arabia	2,772	2.2	1,558	1.8	−225	0.6
Other Gulf Arabian Countries	4,232	3.3	2,192	2.5	372	1
All Gulf	7,004	5.5	3,750	4.3	−147	0.4
Total	**−126,331**		**87,763**		**−37,106**	

Note: The ONS category 'Other Gulf Arabian Countries' includes the rest of the GCC plus Iraq and Yemen.
Source: Office of National Statistics.[76]

where the UK runs any surplus on trade in goods, let alone a significant one (the others being the United States, Ireland and Australia). The surplus with the Gulf area in 2015 was over half that with the United States, the world's largest economy. By providing that rare and valuable thing, a significant surplus on trade in goods, the Gulf economies play a vital role from the point of view of British capitalism.

Financing the current account deficit

While it is not possible to obtain a precise picture of the capital inflows that finance Britain's chronic current account deficit, the data provided by the Office of National Statistics on the UK's international investment position – its worldwide assets set against its worldwide liabilities – can act as an imperfect proxy measure.

Figure 4.4 shows the UK's net international investment position with

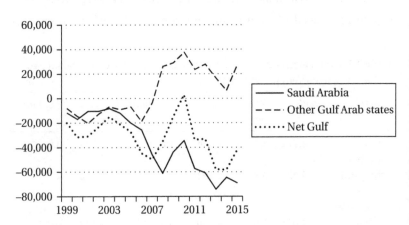

Figure 4.4 UK net international investment position with Saudi Arabia and other Gulf Arabian countries, in current prices (£m)

Note: The ONS category 'Other Gulf Arabian Countries' includes the rest of the GCC plus Iraq and Yemen.

Source: Office of National Statistics.[77]

respect to Saudi Arabia and the Gulf Arab countries. The figures represent the value of Gulf-owned investments held in the UK economy, minus the value of UK-owned assets held in the Gulf. They therefore show the extent to which the UK is a net importer or exporter of capital from or to the Gulf region. A minus value indicates net liability (a good thing in terms of the UK's balance of payments).

Overall, the UK is a net importer of capital from the Gulf area. However, this is entirely due to net capital imports from Saudi Arabia. Britain is a net capital exporter to the rest of the Gulf. The oil boom affected the flow of capital between the UK and the Gulf area in different ways. In the case of Saudi Arabia, the sharp rise in current account balances created a large surplus of capital, which in turn fuelled a growth in the stock of investments held in the UK. In respect of the rest of the Gulf, the growth of the economies there created opportunities which were taken up by British investors.

We can see the full significance of this by placing the contribution of the Gulf (specifically, Saudi Arabia) to financing the UK's current account deficit into its global context (see table 4.8). There are very few

Table 4.8 The UK's net international investment position and selected sources of capital imports, 2015, in current prices (£m)

States(s)	UK's net liability	Equivalent % of total
Saudi Arabia	−64,567	20.0
Ireland	−192,197	59.9
Luxembourg	−134,810	41.9
Germany	−73,300	22.8
All EU	*−293,704*	*91.4*
Norway	−58,673	18.2
Switzerland	−98,372	30.6
United States	−114,266	35.5
World Total	**−321,334**	

Source: Office of National Statistics.[78]

countries to which Britain's liabilities outweigh its assets to a similar degree similar. The UK's net liabilities to Saudi Arabia in 2015 represented one-fifth of its total net liabilities to the world, comparable to its position with Germany, Europe's largest economy, and Norway, another oil producer, like Saudi Arabia, enjoying large current account balances. Capital inflows from the United States, and from (or, rather, through) Ireland, Luxembourg and Switzerland, were more significant. Nevertheless, the data appear to show that Saudi Arabia plays a highly significant role in financing the UK's chronic current account deficit, and that its capacity to do so increased sharply as a result of higher oil prices after the turn of the millennium. This is perhaps one of the most important and fundamental senses in which Gulf wealth matters to Britain and to British capitalism.

Examples of Gulf investment in the UK and state encouragement

All capital inflows from the Gulf help to finance the UK's current account deficit to some degree, and British officials have shown a commitment to attracting Gulf capital into the UK. In 2010, the Treasury minister Lord Sassoon noted a number of recent successes, including the Qatar Investment Authority's £1.5 billion purchase of the prestigious Harrods department store; investment by the Abu Dhabi National Exhibitions Company to expand the ExCel conference centre in London, which it was claimed would bring '£1.6 billion of economic benefit to London in 2011 and will support tens of thousands of jobs'; and the plans of Dubai Holdings to expand its UK hospitality firm Travelodge from 390 to around 1,000 hotels by 2020.[79]

In 2012, the Foreign Office minister Lord Howell described the Qatari-owned 'Shard' skyscraper in London as 'the tip . . . of a very large iceberg', given that, behind these visible and high-profile investments, '[a] significant proportion' of GCC capital inflows was 'being channelled into financial assets'. The British government was 'reaching out to the Sovereign Wealth Funds across the Gulf to forge stronger, more strategic relationships. At a time of global financial turmoil, the world clearly sees Britain as a relative safe haven . . . So we are . . . helping [SWFs] to identify opportunities for investment here.'[80]

One such opportunity was infrastructure, where the government had outlined plans for £250 billion worth of investment across sectors such as energy, transport, utilities and communications. Given the Cameron administration's oft-repeated commitment to close the fiscal deficit, and an unwillingness to raise taxes, Howell argued that '[t]he GCC states are in a unique position globally to make these investments.'[81] The business secretary Vince Cable headed to the UAE in 2014 to launch a new UKTI Gulf Investment taskforce, headed by accountancy firm PricewaterhouseCoopers and charged with securing fifteen concrete investment projects from the Gulf states.[82]

A 2015 UKTI brochure attempted to persuade SWF managers to invest in the UK and domicile their funds in the City of London. London was 'the leading global centre for cross-border financial services' and in particular a 'gateway to Europe', where 'passporting benefits' allow fund managers to 'register funds in one Member State and then freely market them across the whole of the EU' (a major advantage which Brexit subsequently put into question).[83] Reasons to invest in the City of London, aside from its world-leading capacity as a financial capital, included its expertise in Islamic finance, the lowest corporation tax in the G20, and a particular facility called 'The Investment Management Exemption . . . [which] allows non-UK investment funds to appoint a UK based investment manager without creating a risk of UK taxation for the fund', permitting funds to benefit from the 'deep and diverse talent pool' of the UK financial services industry without incurring further tax exposure.[84]

The brochure pointed to leading SWFs with representative offices in London, such as the Kuwait Investment Authority and the Abu Dhabi Investment Authority, claiming that the UK had absorbed around one-sixth of global SWFs' direct investment in the preceding decade, including Abu Dhabi Investment Authority's investments in Kemble Water, the owner of Thames Water. UKTI itself claimed to have had a hand in more than 80 per cent of inward investment projects in the UK.[85]

In one striking example of the British state working to bring Gulf capital into the country, it emerged that the government had set up a secret Whitehall unit to encourage and facilitate investment from the UAE into the UK. The ten-person unit was headed by a Treasury minister and a director general in the civil service, codenamed Project Falcon, and focused on non-military investments. In a secret meeting with the UAE's Mubadala SWF in July 2013, and with the former prime minister Tony Blair in attendance as a lobbyist, Project Falcon officials presented a 'beauty parade' of potential investments for the Emiratis to consider. The fruits of these efforts appear to include a £1 billion deal with Manchester City Council for investment in the city, the first phase of which involves a £150 million property development project, as well as a £60 million gift to Great Ormond Street Hospital from the Crown Prince's mother. The project's remit was subsequently widened to include attracting investment from Qatar.[86]

In terms of visible Gulf investments (recalling again that these are far from the whole picture) the UAE and Qatar have been the leading players. Dubai's Emirates airline bought fifteen-year naming rights for Arsenal Football Club's new stadium (now known as 'The Emirates') for US$150 million, while Abu Dhabi United Group for Development and Investment purchased Manchester City Football Club in 2008 for $360 million, when their stadium was renamed 'The Etihad'. Abu Dhabi also reportedly entered into a $1.5 billion agreement in 2011 with Manchester City Council and the regeneration body New East Manchester.[87]

Leading Qatari officials have been reasonably explicit that these visible investments are strategic both in respect of long-term economic diversification and in terms of deepening ties with the UK. In a *Guardian* report on the opening of the Qatari owned 'Shard', the tallest skyscraper in Europe, Doha's ambassador to London commented:

> [t]he UK is a dear country to us. We have been investing in this country before and after the [2008 financial] crash. Our investment is a long-term investment. We don't need cash money now. This comes from a strategy of diversifying our economy over 10, 20, 30 years. We think the UK is the right place to put our investment. The UK is a strategic partner with our country.

The governor of Qatar's central bank said he was confident the Shard would become 'a symbol of the close ties between Qatar and the UK'.[88]

According to the UK Department of Trade, Qatar has around £30 billion in UK investments, including stakes in Heathrow Airport Holdings, Sainsbury's and the London Stock Exchange.[89] The QIA bought a 17.6 per cent share in Sainsbury's in 2007,[90] although research conducted for this book has found no evidence of this translating into any form of managerial control. Among other high-profile investments are the QIA purchase in 2014 of HSBC's headquarters – the second tallest skyscraper in the Canary Wharf financial district – for a reported £1.1 billion, making it London's most expensive office building at the time, and the South Hook LNG terminal, which supplies up to a fifth of the UK's total gas needs, which was built with £1.2 billion of Qatari investment.[91]

Qatar's investment strategy, however, can be distracting. Other more significant Gulf investors have chosen to adopt a lower profile. The UK Department of Trade describes Kuwait as 'one of the single largest investors in the UK with around £100 billion of official funds invested through the City of London', more than three times the figure it gives for Qatari investments.[92] It appears that the majority of this is comprised of portfolio equity investments. Saudi Arabia has a total of around £93.5 billion of assets in the UK, treble the figure cited by the UK government for Qatar, and again apparently mostly quite low profile.

Indirectly, then, in terms of the status of its currency, and directly in terms of its balance of payments, Gulf capital is very significant to British capitalism. It contributes positively on the current account, including on trade in goods, which is very rare, and it also appears to play a major role in financing the overall current account deficit.

Conclusions

A major theme of the analysis in this chapter has been the large capital surpluses built up by the GCC states over the post-2000 oil boom, which lasted around a decade and a half and came to an end with the fall in oil prices in 2014. Whether this is a cyclical or structural downturn will become clear only in the years to come, although it should be noted that the price fall was largely a result of conscious decisions taken by the OPEC producers themselves, with the aim of hurting rival producers in the United States who rely on a higher price to stay economically viable. The measure was intended to be temporary, and in 2016 the cartel moved to cut production, which pushed prices back up from $30 to $50 per barrel.[93] The underlying fundamentals, not least the relative size of Gulf hydrocarbon reserves and the projected growth in global demand, suggest that Gulf wealth will continue to be significant to the global economy, and to British capitalism, for some considerable time to come.

That being said, it is clear that Gulf elites know they cannot bank on their petrodollar riches indefinitely, and diversification and modernisation plans (ambitious, if not necessarily realistic) have been drawn up in an attempt to meet the challenge.[94] These plans, like those for infrastructure development during the 2000s oil boom, will also present a range of opportunities for British capitalism.

At the time of writing, plans are being mooted to float part of Saudi Aramco on the stock exchange in either New York or London, in what the *New York Times* described as potentially 'the biggest deal in capital-markets history'.[95] *The Guardian* reported that '[t]he company could be valued at $2tn (£1.5tn) [and its listing] would generate hundreds of millions of dollars in fees for investment bankers, lawyers and other advisers.' However, a proposal by the Financial Conduct Authority to allow state-backed firms such as Aramco to qualify for a premium listing on the London Stock Exchange (it would not qualify under existing rules) was strongly criticised by the Institute of Directors on the grounds that this might harm the UK's reputation for strong corporate governance. The question again arises as to how far British officials are prepared to go to attract Gulf petrodollars into the UK economy.[96]

Meanwhile, the importance of the GCC area as an export market and a source of investment has only been accentuated by the prospect of Brexit. In a speech to the leaders of the GCC states in December 2016, Prime Minister Theresa May expressed the desire to establish 'an ambitious trade arrangement for when the UK has left the EU . . . [encompassing] the whole of the Gulf area'.[97] The joint communiqué issued by the GCC monarchs and the prime minister after the summit stated that the parties would 'make it a priority, when the UK leaves the European Union, to build the closest possible commercial and economic relationship . . . [working to] remove barriers to trade and investment.'[98] A down payment on these aspirations came in March 2017, two days before the British government triggered the official process to leave the EU (the timing is unlikely to have been accidental), when Qatar announced a commitment to invest £5 billion in transport, property and digital technology projects in the UK.[99]

These, however, are matters for the future. For now, what we have learned from the analysis in this chapter is that UK–GCC trade and investment are highly valuable to British capitalism and particularly significant in some specific and important areas.

With assistance from the state, UK exporters were able to meet increased Gulf demand in key areas such as infrastructure development, industrial diversification and education, as the GCC became a leading global south market for Britain, contributing significantly to UK GDP. The City of London is more successful in attracting Gulf capital than any other world financial centre, and Gulf capital inflows are significant in value compared with those from elsewhere in the global south. Gulf investors played a vital stabilising role when Barclays turned to them for the capital it needed to avoid a state bailout in 2008 (an outcome which was also beneficial to the British government).

On the status of the pound sterling, it is clear that Gulf capital inflows make an important indirect contribution by helping to maintain the strength of the pound, and thus its attractiveness as an international currency. This is because, on the balance of payments, the GCC region plays a very significant role indeed. It is one of the few markets in the world with which Britain has a current account surplus, including on manufactured goods, and Gulf capital inflows, particularly from Saudi Arabia, appear to play a crucial part in financing the overall current account deficit. On these key measures, the Gulf region is not merely important to the UK compared to other leading economies in the global south (such as the BRICS) but important even compared to major economies in the global north.

Britain is also of high economic importance to the Gulf Arab monarchies. The UK is one of the GCC's leading sources of FDI, which is significant in terms of the Gulf's economic development and diversification. Additionally, the City of London remains the leading financial centre from the Gulf elites' point of view. In terms of its ability to marshal FDI in economic sectors where it is needed, but above all in terms of its ability to absorb, process and reinvest Gulf capital, the UK is of great economic significance to the Gulf monarchies.

Furthermore, it appears that Gulf investment in the UK is not made with purely economic considerations in mind but is also seen by Gulf elites in part as a way of maintaining close relations with Britain. This is important when we consider the role that London plays in arming and protecting the Gulf monarchies.

5

Arming Authoritarianism

Arms sales are perhaps the most high-profile and controversial aspect of UK–GCC relations. This has been the case particularly in recent years, given the authoritarian backlash against the Arab uprisings and the disastrous Saudi-led intervention in the war in Yemen. From London's standpoint, these arms sales have a value that is far from purely economic. They play a vital role in sustaining the UK's arms industry, which in turn is indispensable to maintaining Britain's status as a global military power – a core strategic aim for London through the period of imperial decline and beyond.

This is another reason, on top of those mentioned in previous chapters, why Gulf wealth matters to Britain, and why the British government works to shore up and defend the Gulf elites though military cooperation and power projection into the region. From the Gulf monarchies' point of view, helping to sustain British military power through arms purchases means that – though their region is unstable and their legitimacy as rulers open to challenge – they have a powerful ally in the global north (alongside the US and, to some extent, France) with both an interest in bolstering and defending them and the military capacity to do so. Arms exports therefore constitute one component of a broader system of military cooperation aimed at ensuring the survival of the conservative regional order.

This chapter will describe the political economy of UK arms sales and their strategic value to the British state, before evaluating the relative importance of British arms exports to the Gulf in the modern era. We will identify the major export deals secured by the UK, examine government policy towards controversies around corruption, and outline the various forms that UK–GCC military cooperation takes.

The political economy of British arms sales

As the security expert Mark Phythian notes, British arms sales in the post-Second World War era were not merely a commercial matter. Whitehall's policy was 'defined by the need to maintain the existing beneficial configuration of power and influence in the international system. Arms sales played a key role in cementing influence and securing the continuation of the existing order.' For states such as the UK, the US and the USSR, arms sales were an important mechanism for projecting their power worldwide.[1] Arms sales from north to south therefore increased, as newly independent states worked to build up their independent capabilities and prestige. With the capacity of the oil-producer states to pursue this policy increasing dramatically after the 1973–4 oil crisis, Britain saw an opportunity.[2]

The economic and strategic benefits of arms exports are in many ways intertwined. In his 1965 report, which laid the basis for Britain's current, state-backed, export-oriented arms industry, Whitehall official Donald Stokes encouraged the MoD to ensure that its future requirements were compatible with the export industry's needs. Longer production runs for both national use and foreign export would lower unit costs and be more efficient overall.[3] Arms exports helped Britain maintain its military industrial base, retain skills and keep relevant technologies in operation, as well as generating income.[4]

Petrodollar recycling plays an important role here. As Achcar notes, major arms purchases by the oil producers 'help finance [the exporter states'] arms industries, a contribution that is especially appreciated when economic crisis forces arms-exporting countries' governments to curtail domestic military outlays.'[5] More fundamentally, the reason that maintaining an economically viable military industrial base is important is that London has made a strategic choice to remain a global military power even in the face of its long-term decline in status as a world power.[6]

Arms sales are viewed by recipients as a seal of political approval and legitimacy.[7] Additionally, as pointed out by Nazih Ayubi, an expert on state formation in the Middle East, high military expenditure 'represents an important aspect of the growth in the "body and muscle" of the state in the Arab world' since independence.[8] For the UK to facilitate such a process is inescapably a political decision. Arms sales to friendly Arab regimes were understood to be useful, both in terms of keeping those regimes in power and, more specifically, for developing good relations with their militaries, rendering the latter more reliable as ultimate guarantors of stability.[9] As Eugene Rogan, director of the Middle East Centre at St Anthony's College, University of Oxford, put it in evidence to the House of Commons Foreign Affairs Select Committee, '[t]he sale of arms has been primarily to enable autocratic governments to stay in power. The complex weapons systems that we have sold to countries across the region . . . have primarily been used against their own people . . . with only very few exceptions.'[10]

Research by Shannon Lindsey Blanton, an academic specialising in human rights and political violence, has shown that arms sales to developing countries contribute to internal repression. In these states, the means of violence are often sought more to fend off internal threats than external ones, and the purchase of arms increases the likelihood that regimes will respond to domestic challenges with physical force. Blanton's research covered a wide range of developing countries during the 1980s, including all states of the GCC except Bahrain. She found that:

> the import of arms by developing countries is linked to the violation of personal integrity rights. Arms acquisitions appear to contribute to repression by making violent political acts more feasible. To this end, arms may play a direct instrumental role in the infliction of human rights abuse or they may represent the endpoint of a longer process of strengthening the military or fuelling a national security mentality which in turn leads to human rights repression.[11]

The choice of arms provider, from the customer state's point of view, is not purely a matter of price, specification and capability but, rather, has a political dimension as well. According to Phythian, this was certainly the case when, after the Gulf War of 1991, Kuwait decided to purchase arms from all the permanent five states of the UN Security Council except China (albeit the US was by far the favoured supplier). 'It was the political alliances created, rather than the weapons bought, which ultimately guaranteed its independence.' Within these parameters, more specific political choices could be made. Phythian attributes Kuwait's selection of BAE Sea Skua over 'reportedly less expensive' French anti-ship missiles in 1996 to the French stance on Iraq sanctions, which was softer than Britain's. When a coup in Qatar in 1995 brought to power a new emir who had been educated at Sandhurst, Britain was first country to recognise the transfer of power, and the following year it won an arms deal worth £500 million.[12]

While arms sales contribute to Britain's balance of payments, the extent of the economic benefits are less clear when various costs are considered. The industry enjoys subsidised loans and insurance cover offered by the government's Export Credit Guarantee Department, thus transferring risk from the private sector to the state.[13] The Export Credit Guarantee Department's exposure in respect of the Al Yamamah deal stood at £450 million in 1989 and rose to £1 billion in 1999.[14] This is particularly significant given that the contract was signed during the Iran–Iraq War, with all that conflict's implications for the security of the region. The vulnerability of the Saudi monarchy made the insurance of these arms exports an important consideration.

The government also provides extensive marketing services to the industry in the form of the Defence and Security Organisation, which operated as part of the larger agency UK Trade and Investment between 2003 and 2016 and is now incorporated into the new Department for International Trade. According to evidence given to the UK Parliament's Committees on Arms Export Controls by the anti-militarist NGO Campaign Against Arms Trade, 'DSO . . . [employs] just under 160 civil servants . . . while all other identified sectors have a combined total of around 140 UKTI staff devoted to them. This is despite arms accounting for less than 1.5% of UK exports.'[15] British defence attachés promote British goods and feed back market information, and a regular succession of ministerial, prime ministerial and even royal visits to prospective buyer states smooths the path for major orders.[16] British intelligence services have also reportedly lent assistance, monitoring market opportunities and the activity of competitors, particularly the French. According to Phythian, DSO was routinely in receipt of signals intelligence from the UK's Government Communications Headquarters (GCHQ), not to monitor end-use but to serve the goal of maximising sales.[17]

The ongoing administration of major UK–Saudi arms deals is overseen by the British Ministry of Defence. The MoD Saudi Armed Forces

Project (MODSAP) covers the landmark contracts to supply Tornado and Typhoon military jets and associated equipment discussed later in this chapter. The Saudi Arabian National Guard Communications Project (SANGCOM) is another state-to-state deal, under which the UK is committed to procure communications equipment for the Saudi National Guard, a force that Curtis notes is 'specifically designed to defend the royal family from social unrest and military coups from the regular forces'.[18] In each case, memoranda of understanding have been signed between the two governments, following which the MoD places contracts with manufacturers to fulfil the UK's obligations. Both MODSAP and SANGCOM are run by British military and civil personnel, although MODSAP is funded directly by Saudi Arabia.[19]

No other major British export industry enjoys quite this level of state support; while these various costs might be hard to measure, they are certainly substantial. In a research paper produced jointly for the Stockholm International Peace Research Institute and Campaign Against Arms Trade, Sam Perlo-Freeman calculates that annual total direct subsidies, including those outlined here, may add up to between £64 million and £102 million.[20] This is a reflection of the fact that arms sales are far from a purely commercial matter. They are a means of enabling Britain to maintain the military-industrial capacity and the strategic relationships necessary to continue as a global power.

UK–GCC arms sales in the modern era

Over the course of the post-Cold War era, Britain has maintained a position as one of the world's leading arms exporters, standing in fifth place overall, some distance behind the two former Cold War superpowers, who are in a separate category, but broadly alongside other permanent members of the UN Security Council, leading capitalist states and military powers.[21] During the same post-1991 period, the principal customer states of the British arms industry have also been among the leading recipients of major arms transfers worldwide. The world's top fifteen recipients of major transfers include Britain's top three customers: Saudi Arabia (third in the global list), the US (twelfth) and India (first). If the six GCC states comprised a single country market, the combined total of major inward transfers since 1991 would place it in the clear lead worldwide – remarkable when one considers that the total population of the GCC area in 2008 stood at a mere 39 million.[22]

According to the Foreign and Commonwealth Office, the Middle East and North Africa region accounts for 'over 50% of all UK defence sales by value in the past 10 years'.[23] The government treats eighteen arms export destinations as 'priority markets', of which five are GCC states: Saudi Arabia, Kuwait, Qatar, Oman and the UAE.[24] The British arms industry has a significant share in the GCC market relative to other exporters, though the US is in the lead. From the British point of view, the GCC market's importance has become even more pronounced in recent years, principally in the case of Saudi Arabia.

According to data from the Stockholm International Peace Research Institute, Saudi Arabia is the largest Gulf market for arms imports, accounting for 47 per cent of the GCC's major inward arms transfers over the post-1991 period. The UAE accounts for 32 per cent, with Kuwait, Oman, Qatar and Bahrain accounting for 10, 5, 4 and 2 per cent respectively.[25]

Among the exporters, the US, predictably, is in a category of its own, accounting for 55 per cent of major arms transfers to the GCC area since 1991. US arms exports account for 60 per cent, 72 per cent, and 81 per cent of those imported by Saudi Arabia, Kuwait and Bahrain respectively. Only in the relatively minor market of Oman is the US narrowly nudged into second place by another supplier, the UK, which takes 36 per cent to the US's 34 per cent.

The UK and France make up a second-order category of major supplier, with 14 per cent and 16 per cent respectively of the post-1991 GCC market. In the two largest country markets the Europeans have given the otherwise dominant Americans a degree of competition. France takes 30 per cent of the UAE market to the US's 45 per cent, and, while the overall post-Cold War gap in share of the Saudi market between the US and the UK is 60 per cent to 21 per cent, the British succeeded in overtaking the US in the five-year period between 2009 and 2013.[26]

Between them, the US, Britain and France have provided 85 per cent of major GCC arms imports since the Cold War. Only in the case of Kuwait (6 per cent) and the UAE (8 per cent) does another supplier, Russia, have anything more than an insignificant share. Otherwise, this major commercial and strategic market is divided up between the three leading NATO powers. This represents a change from the longer-term picture. Before 1971 the UK was virtually the sole arms supplier to the smaller Gulf states and on a par with the US in terms of exports to Saudi Arabia, and the overall value of these exports was quite low. This was a reflection of the UK's direct dominance of the Gulf at that time.[27]

The shift occurs after the 1971 British withdrawal and after the sharp rise in oil revenues for the Gulf producers from 1973–4. These two developments meant that the smaller Gulf states had more money to spend on arms, the latitude to diversify the alliances that facilitate such purchases, and the need to strengthen themselves militarily to some degree now that British protection had been downgraded. The total value of major arms purchases by the UAE, for example, was thirty-seven times higher in the period 1971 to 1991 than it had been between 1950 and 1970. Moreover, between 1971 and 1980, 61 per cent of those purchases came from France, 18 per cent came from the UK, and 6 per cent came from the US. Significant French exports began in the early 1970s, with Britain's share of what was suddenly becoming a major export market diminishing almost immediately after the 1971 withdrawal. Between 1981 and 1991, France took 40 per cent of the UAE market, the US 16 per cent and the UK 11 per cent.[28]

France, which unlike the US is a peer competitor with the UK as a second-tier global power, also made significant inroads into the Saudi market between 1971 and 1991, accounting for 22 per cent of major exports compared with the UK's 13 per cent, while 59 per cent went to the US. The UK's share here is almost entirely accounted for by the Al Yamamah contracts of the mid- to late 1980s. In the same period, France also outstripped the UK's market share in Kuwait (21 per cent to 14 per cent, with 25 per cent going to the US) and Qatar (79 per cent to 19 per cent). The 1971 withdrawal not only created a demand for arms sales to the region but also freed up the Gulf states to develop their military relationships with the UK's peers. London's ability to exploit the opportunity that petrodollars represented to its arms industry after the 1973–4 oil crisis was therefore now subject to competition.[29]

Figure 5.1 shows, in comparative and absolute terms, how the value of British arms transfers to Saudi Arabia has fluctuated in the modern era. There have been three export booms: in the early to mid-1990s, at the start of the twenty-first century, and in the final part of the time period under review. In most but not all of these instances, UK imports have accounted for a significant proportion of the total, overtaking the US in the five-year period between 2009 and 2013.

The strategic importance and commercial value of the Saudi market not only far exceeds that of its neighbours but is of world-level significance in both respects. Britain has maintained a decent market share

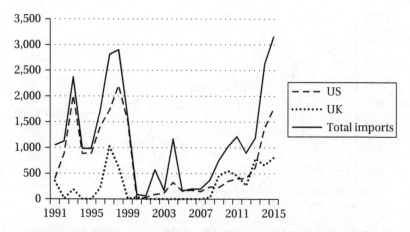

Figure 5.1 Leading sources of major arms transfers to Saudi Arabia, 1991–2015

Note: Values are SIPRI trend indicator values expressed in US$ million at constant (1990) prices. Zero on the y axis indicates that the value of deliveries is less than $0.5 million.

Source: SIPRI.[30]

despite competition from the United States. Given that the US is both a much larger arms exporter and of far more significance to the Gulf monarchies in terms of ensuring their survival, this is a considerable achievement for a declining second-tier power such as the UK.

The relative importance of UK–GCC arms sales

British arms transfers to the Gulf must also be assessed in a global context. As figure 5.2 shows, the overall linear trend since the end of the Cold War points to a clear and steady reduction in the value of major UK arms transfers to the rest of the world, compared with a rise in the value of major arms transfers to the GCC. The Gulf has become an indispensable market for the British arms industry. In the period 2006 to 2015, UK transfers to Saudi Arabia accounted for 34 per cent of the

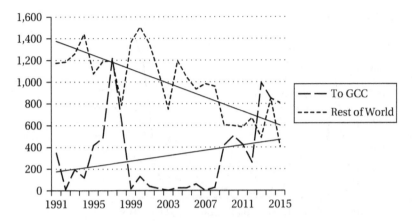

Figure 5.2 Values and overall linear trend of major arms transfers from the United Kingdom, 1991–2015

Note: Values are SIPRI trend indicator values expressed in US$ million at constant (1990) prices. Zero on the y axis indicates that the value of deliveries is less than $0.5 million.

Source: SIPRI.[31]

total value of major arms exports, and the GCC accounted for 39 per cent of the total. This compares with 15 per cent of the total going to the US and 11 per cent to India, the other two leading export destinations for the UK, over those same ten years.[32]

The GCC market has therefore become crucial to the UK, not so much in terms of allowing its arms exports industry to grow as simply in terms of maintaining that industry at its current level. The UK does have a wide array of customers for its military goods, with India and the US accounting for more of its exports than all the GCC states apart from Saudi Arabia. But the Saudi market is the largest of all, particularly since the signing of the Al Salam deal in 2007, as will be discussed later on in this chapter.

Again, the significance of these trends must be emphasised above all in terms of their implications for British power. Maintaining a domestic arms industry is crucial to the UK's key strategic aim of remaining a global military power. If the GCC market – with large capital surpluses and its monarchies desperate for protection – is not already indispensable to the UK in this regard, it is likely to become so if the trends observed since 1991 continue. Since the end of the Cold War, Gulf petrodollars (and Saudi petrodollars in particular) have become highly important to the military dimension of British power.

Major deals and inter-Western competition

A look behind the overall figures reveals an ongoing effort by the British state to win individual export contracts in the face of a range of political difficulties and in the midst of sometimes stiff competition with rival global north powers. After the Gulf War of 1991, the GCC states made a concerted effort to bolster their military capabilities, heralding a boom period for the arms exporters of the global north.

An early British success came when Oman selected Vosper Thorneycroft to supply two missile corvettes for its navy, beating French and Dutch competition. Defence Secretary Tom King hailed this, together with another deal entered into with Malaysia, as 'the largest warship export orders for 20 years'.[33] Later that year, Qatar ordered four fast attack craft from Vosper Thorneycroft in a £200 million deal that represented a rare breakthrough in what was generally a French-dominated market.[34] However, there was disappointment for the UK when Vickers lost out on a potential £500 million deal to supply Kuwait with an estimated 200 tanks, with the American M1A2 Abrams being seen as more technologically advanced.[35] Nevertheless, Whitehall estimated that Britain won 30 per cent of Kuwaiti arms contracts in 1991 and 1992, including those for mine clearance and naval base reconstruction.[36]

Following the 1995 palace coup in Qatar and the rise to power of the new Sandhurst-educated emir, London signed a wide-ranging arms contract with Doha covering the supply of armoured personnel carriers (by GKN), patrol boats (Vosper Thornycroft) and Hawk trainer aircraft (BAE). The then UK defence secretary, Michael Portillo, had offered a comprehensive Gulf security proposal to Qatar, which British diplomats described as part of a bid to find a fresh foothold in the Gulf states.[37] Nevertheless, the US and France have continued to dominate the Qatari market, accounting for 47 and 31 per cent respectively of the emirate's imports since 1991 compared with just 5 per cent for the UK.[38] Britain's rival arms suppliers have also attempted to break into the GCC markets where it has been dominant. In 2004, AgustaWestland lost out to France's NH Industries on a helicopter order for Oman worth between £720 million and £960 million.[39] However, in general, such markets tended to remain reliably secured.

Al Yamamah II

In 1992 there was some anxiety over the future of British arms sales to Saudi Arabia, given the kingdom's budget difficulties resulting from the low oil price. The Saudi government shelved a plan to build an enormous £10 billion air base, a project that BAE had been set to lead on, and for which it had invited several British construction firms to tender.[40] Defence Secretary Malcolm Rifkind flew to the kingdom to try and rescue the second phase of Al Yamamah, which had envisaged the £20 billion sale of a range of equipment over the course of a decade, under a memorandum of understanding originally signed in 1988. The final contract was due to have been signed, but Saudi budget concerns had thrown a question mark over the deal. At the time, BAE was not in good health, and it was thought that Al Yamamah II 'could account for the equivalent of nearly a quarter of [the firm's] total annual sales, and would underpin its future prosperity.'[41]

Whether a result of Rifkind's visit or not (it may be that the expressed fears had been overblown), the Saudis reaffirmed their commitment to the project,[42] and in 1993 the finalisation of the deal for 48 Tornados was announced following talks between Prime Minister John Major and Saudi King Fahd.[43] The package covered a significant military infrastructure programme in addition to the Tornados, including ground defence radars and hardened shelters for the aircraft.[44]

Although there was to be much talk in the British press over the years to come of the extent of supposed Saudi influence over the British government, a 1994 report in *The Guardian* provided an interesting insight into how the relationship was perceived by some in the Saudi kingdom. The report noted that 'it is virtually impossible to talk to an educated Saudi – in or outside government – who does not believe that both countries [the US and the UK] are bent on keeping [the Saudi kingdom] in a state of frightened dependency so as to milk it for weapons sales'. The report went on:

Such people ask a number of questions. Why do Western leaders preach budget restraint to Riyadh, yet insistently push huge arms contracts at it? Why do they say they want stability in the world's leading oil producer, yet make weaponry demands that mean robbing civil programmes and stoking the anger of Islamic hardliners at home and abroad? Why do they speak of the need for a strong Saudi Arabia, yet exert immense pressure to get every big contract, preventing the country from diversifying its economic ties and broadening its alliances? And why do they expect Riyadh to go on paying the lion's share for Western maneuvers, basing and deployments whose scale and usefulness

Saudi Arabia now questions? . . . Once the tape recorder is turned off and the notebook put away, Saudi officialdom lets rip on the subject of visiting American and British ministerial salesmen in unambiguous terms. 'Blackmailers' is the most common . . . [and also] 'bloodsuckers'.[45]

Al Salam

In 2005, it emerged that Prime Minister Tony Blair and Defence Secretary John Reid had been holding secret talks with Saudi Arabia in pursuit of a huge arms deal worth up to £40 billion. The deal related principally to Eurofighter Typhoon military jets and would be comparable in scale to Al Yamamah. However, the Saudi government was reportedly stalling negotiations while making certain demands, including the expulsion from Britain of two Saudi dissidents and the end of an investigation by the UK's Serious Fraud Office into corruption around the Al Yamamah deal.[46]

A pre-contract memorandum of understanding between the two governments, signed in 2006, covered the provision of seventy-two Typhoons to replace older aircraft, including Tornados sold under Al Yamamah. The biggest commercial beneficiary would be BAE, with its 37 per cent share in the Eurofighter consortium. *The Independent* reported that the order 'in effect amounts to the third phase of the Al Yamamah programme . . . [including] a full package of training, through life support, spares and technology transfer, which will at least double the value of the deal and perhaps increase its value by 150 per cent.' The MoD kept the agreement's full details confidential, simply saying that it 'intended to establish a greater partnership in modernising the Saudi Arabian armed forces and developing close service-to-service contacts, especially through joint training exercises.'[47]

The new contract (dubbed Al Salam) was a blow to French hopes of securing a rival deal for their own Rafale combat aircraft, for which President Jacques Chirac had been lobbying.[48]

Unlike the Al Yamamah contract, the basis for the deal was to be cash rather than oil, apparently part of a Saudi drive to reduce the scope for corruption.[49] However, these efforts did not extend to support for the SFO's ongoing enquiries. In November 2006, the Saudis suspended negotiations over the deal, reportedly in an attempt to exert pressure on the British to end the SFO investigation. An SFO decision to seek bank account information from Switzerland was apparently the trigger for the Saudi move, which France, still hoping to sell its Rafales, observed with interest.[50] Finally, after the demise of the SFO investigation (covered in detail later in this chapter), the finalisation of the £40 billion Al Salam contract was announced in September 2007.[51] The deal was described by *Jane's Defence Weekly* as signalling 'the start of an enhanced strategic alliance' between Britain and Saudi Arabia.[52]

Included in the deal was a joint venture between BAE and Alsalam Aircraft Company, the Saudis' own commercial partner, which would oversee the final assembly work, in Saudi Arabia, of many of the aircraft, as well as long-term logistical support. This would supposedly help the Saudis develop their own high-tech industrial base.[53] Subsequently, in 2009, BAE won a support service contract with Saudi Arabia to service their Typhoons, worth a reported £500 million.[54]

Questions of corruption and malfeasance

Questions of corruption around British arms sales to the GCC states, most notably Saudi Arabia, and questions of malfeasance – legal or moral wrongdoing by state officials – both in their handling of those controversies and in their involvement in military exports more generally, have been the subject of a great deal of news coverage in recent decades. No allegations of corruption or bribery, or official malfeasance in relation to those issues, have been proven in a court of law, and those accused both on the Saudi and the British side have strenuously and consistently denied them. It is plainly beyond the scope of this book to establish legal guilt, but what can be documented and analysed is the ways in which the British state has handled these controversies and what these episodes tell us about the UK's relationship with the Gulf states.

The fact that allegations of corruption have not been legally proven does not of course preclude us from noting the many indications that such activities may well have occurred. In 1989, an arms industry source told *The Observer*, '[w]hen you sell to Saudi Arabia, you are really selling to the Saudi royal family – a limited company with 200 shareholders. It is quite simple. In some countries, you pay import duties of 30 per cent, in others you pay commissions' – i.e. bribes.[55] The former UK defence secretary Ian Gilmour told BBC *Newsnight* in 2006:

> You either got the business and bribed, or you didn't bribe and didn't get the business. You either went along with how the Saudis behaved, or what they wanted, or you let the US and France have all the business . . . If you are paying bribes to high-up people in the government, the fact that it's illegal in Saudi law doesn't mean much.[56]

Aside from such individual testimonies, the overall approach of the British state on these issues gives the impression that, for whatever reason, any transparent and thorough investigation of such matters is regarded as undesirable. As will be shown below, it is the lengths to which the state is prepared to take this approach that illustrate the importance it attaches to the UK–Saudi relationship, even over and above other important considerations of government.

The most important case in which the question of corruption illuminated the nature of Britain's relationship with the GCC states, specifically Saudi Arabia, relates to the Serious Fraud Office's investigation into alleged bribes paid by BAE Systems to the Saudis to lubricate arms deals. The way this episode unfolded, and the way it was handled by the British government, tells us a great deal, not only about how highly the alliance with Riyadh is valued and the lengths to which politicians will go to protect it, but also about how that relationship is weighed in the balance against the state's other core priorities. The SFO episode showed that the British government was prepared to contradict the wishes of both Washington and major players in the City of London in order to protect commercial dealings with the Saudis from scrutiny and the relationship with Riyadh from serious damage. The episode is covered in more depth in Nicholas Gilby's excellent book on corruption allegations around UK arms sales, *Deception in High Places: A History of Bribery in Britain's Arms Trade*.[57] Here, we will pick up the key points and add some observations relevant to the wider subject of the present book.

In 2003, *The Guardian* reported that the permanent secretary (the senior civil servant) at the MoD had 'failed to follow up for two years allegations that . . . BAE Systems ran a slush fund designed to bribe Saudi officials . . . prevented the MoD's fraud squad investigating the case, and withheld the SFO's warnings [about the alleged bribery] from the defence secretary.'[58]

As noted earlier in this chapter, the Saudis suspended talks over what became the Al Salam fighter jet deal in November 2006 after the continuing SFO investigation began looking into Swiss bank accounts as part of its investigation. Meanwhile the Defence Industries Council, a body representing leading arms firms, wrote to the defence secretary, not referencing their concern over the SFO probe directly but talking in general terms about the importance to them of the Gulf market.[59] However, pressure from key constituencies was not all coming from the same direction. In December 2006, the *Independent on Sunday* reported that, in July 2002, the US assistant secretary of state for economic and business affairs, E. Anthony Wayne, had pressed MoD officials to investigate thoroughly what the Americans regarded as 'a longstanding, widespread pattern of bribery allegations involving BAE'.[60]

The key moment came on 14 December 2006, when the attorney general, Lord Goldsmith, announced in Parliament that the SFO had decided to call off the probe. He quoted the SFO's official statement, which said:

This decision has been taken following representations that have been made both to the Attorney General and to the [SFO] Director concerning the need to safeguard national and international security. It has been necessary to balance the need to maintain the rule of law against the wider public interest. No weight has been given to commercial interests or to the national economic interest.

Goldsmith went on to say that he had consulted the prime minister and the foreign and defence secretaries who

expressed the clear view that continuation of the investigation would cause serious damage to UK/Saudi security, intelligence and diplomatic co-operation, which is likely to have seriously negative consequences for the United Kingdom public interest in terms of both national security and our highest priority foreign policy objectives in the Middle East. The heads of our security and intelligence agencies and our ambassador to Saudi Arabia share this assessment.[61]

BAE shares leapt by 10 per cent at the news, a greater rise than even that seen after negotiations on the Typhoon deal were announced.[62]

The SFO had reportedly been lobbied to drop the probe by the prime minister, the foreign and defence secretaries, the heads of the security and intelligence agencies, and the British ambassador to Saudi Arabia, while BAE had been running a media and lobbying campaign warning that Saudi Arabia could pull the plug on negotiations for the Typhoon deal and instead purchase Rafale jets from France.[63] Prime Minister Blair in turn had been lobbied vigorously by the Saudi government.[64] According to *The Observer*, 'Saudi Arabia threatened to stop sharing vital intelligence – particularly intercepted communications between al-Qaeda members active there' – unless the SFO probe was called off. 'Senior Whitehall sources said the Saudis warned they would also kick out British military and intelligence personnel based in the country.'[65]

However, as noted above, not all of the pressure went in this direction. F&C Asset Management, one of Britain's biggest institutional investors, wrote to the defence procurement minister warning that the decision to halt the SFO investigation could undermine the integrity of UK financial markets. F&C at the time held more than £100 billion under management and noted that, as a BAE shareholder, it would benefit from the decision in a narrow, immediate sense. Nevertheless, it expressed serious concern at the broader implications this decision could have for the efficient functioning of financial markets as a whole:

We believe that, for long term investors, bribery and corruption distort and destabilise markets, expose companies to legal
liabilities, disadvantage non-corrupt companies and reduce
transparency for investors seeking investment opportunities . . .
There is a danger that the government's recent action will be
perceived as undermining the consistent application of the UK's
national legislation governing corrupt practices.[66]

Similar concerns were expressed by the major institutional investors, Morely Fund Management, and the UK's biggest pension fund,
Hermes, whose chief executive Mark Anson warned Blair that 'lack
of credibility in the regulation of one company can spread to the rest
of the stock market creating higher risk premiums and cost of capital
. . . bribery wastes business profits.'[67] It bears emphasising that this
opposition came not from marginal pressure groups but major players
in arguably the key sector of Britain's political economy: the financial
services industry. The fact that the government was prepared to go
against these interests, and to risk the costs to the City of London that
they described, is an indication of how much weight was given to the
relationship with Saudi Arabia and the potential effect of allowing the
SFO investigation to run its course.

It then emerged that Saudi threats to British security described in
press reports at the time the SFO probe was called off may have been
overstated. Whitehall sources told *The Guardian* that MI6 and MI5
possessed no intelligence that the Saudis intended to sever security
links. They had simply been asked hypothetically whether it would
be damaging to UK national security if such a breach did happen
and replied that, naturally, it would. The head of MI6 then reportedly
refused to sign up to a dossier stating that it 'endorsed' Blair's national
security claim, in support of the government's response to concerns

raised by the OECD on its handling of the issue.[68] If the Saudis had not in fact made these threats, this directly contradicted what the UK ambassador to Saudi Arabia had told the SFO director, according to sources who spoke to the *Financial Times*.[69]

The attorney general had said in his statement that commercial or economic interests were not the grounds for the decision to call off the SFO. If the claimed national security grounds were not the real reason either, then it may be reasonable to conclude by process of elimination that it was the strategic relationship with Saudi Arabia as it pertained to Britain's global role, not to the security of its citizens, that the government was prepared to go to such extraordinary lengths to protect.

However, there was another potential reason for the decision. The *Financial Times* reported in January 2007 that, before it was abandoned, the SFO probe 'had widened to examine whether Ministry of Defence staff were aware of commission payments to Saudi Arabian officials, according to sources familiar with the investigation.'[70] These allegedly included secret payments paid to Saudi Prince Bandar bin Sultan bin Abdulaziz Al Saud, head of the Saudi National Security Council, amounting to £30 million every quarter for at least ten years. This was done, said *The Guardian*, 'with the knowledge and authorisation of Ministry of Defence officials under the Blair government and its predecessors'. The aborted SFO inquiry was understood to have uncovered these payments. '[A]ccording to those familiar with the discussions at the time [of the decision to call off the inquiry], Lord Goldsmith had warned colleagues that British "government complicity" was in danger of being revealed unless the SFO's corruption inquiries were stopped.'[71] Bandar himself 'categorically denied' the allegation made in *The Guardian's* report.[72]

As noted earlier in this chapter, the Al Salam contract was eventually finalised once the worst of the controversy over the quashed SFO investigation had died down. However, the US embassy in London made a formal protest over the decision to drop the investigation, and, in 2007, prosecutors in Washington served subpoenas on BAE demanding full disclosure of its files on the Al Yamamah programme. The firm's announcement that the US Department of Justice had opened a criminal inquiry into its dealings with Saudi Arabia wiped more than £1 billion off its market value.[73]

In February 2008, a British high court judge hearing a legal challenge to the scrapping of the inquiry noted: 'I have seen nothing to suggest that anyone [in the British government] did anything but roll over' in response to the pressure allegedly coming from the Saudi side.[74] The court later ruled that the decision to call off the investigation was unlawful: 'There is no evidence . . . that any consideration was given as to how to persuade the Saudis to withdraw the threat, let alone any attempt made to resist the threat . . . It is obvious . . . that the decision to halt the investigation suited the objectives of the executive [the government]. Stopping the investigation avoided uncomfortable consequences, both commercial and diplomatic.'[75] Saudi Prince Bandar was named by the court as the man behind what they characterised as an attempt to pervert the course of justice by threatening the British government over intelligence sharing.[76]

However, three months later the House of Lords overturned the high court's ruling. The Law Lords, acting as the UK equivalent of a supreme court, said that the courts have no power to interfere with the SFO decision. Lord Bingham stated that 'The [SFO] director was confronted by an ugly and obviously unwelcome threat . . . The director's decision was one he was lawfully entitled to make . . . It may indeed be doubted whether a responsible decision-maker could, on the facts before the director, have decided otherwise.'[77]

Putting aside the question of whether or not the decision to abandon the SFO probe was lawful, the assessment of the high court about the British government's conduct during the episode is of more relevance to an analysis of UK–Saudi relations. The court appeared to take the view, contradicting the intelligence sources cited by *The Guardian* in an earlier report, that the security threats from the Saudis were real. But it also concluded that the government had made no challenge to those threats, effectively because they suited its own interests. If this is correct, then it is less a case of the Saudis blackmailing the British state over the security of its citizens and more one of the Saudis and the British government together placing extreme pressure on the Serious Fraud Office. What is harder to answer is the question of whether these extraordinary measures were taken to protect the UK–Saudi relationship, to protect the UK government on the question of corruption, or some balance of both these considerations. Either way, in the government's eyes, those concerns were deemed sufficiently grave to make the political fallout from the decision, and the opposition it elicited from a range of key power centres, a price worth paying.

Eventually in 2010, while not conceding the central charge of bribery, BAE pleaded guilty to charges of false accounting and making misleading statements in a settlement deal with the Department of Justice in Washington and paid a fine of US$400 million. The admissions covered the al Yamamah contract as well as smaller deals in the Czech Republic and elsewhere in central Europe.[78]

Military cooperation

British arms sales to the Gulf Arab monarchies are but one important part of an extensive system of military cooperation whose roots can be traced back to Britain's imperial heyday. A report on Anglo-American military ties with the GCC states published by the *Financial Times* on the eve of the invasion of Iraq in 2003 – which drew on information from both open sources and discussions with unnamed Western diplomats and Gulf analysts – gives a snapshot of the depth, breadth and qualitative nature of these relationships as they stand in the modern era.[79]

The report noted recent defence agreements with all the Gulf states, UK ground forces present in the UAE and Kuwait, UK air forces present in every GCC state bar Qatar, and a naval presence in every state bar Qatar and the Saudi kingdom. According to the analysts interviewed by the *Financial Times*,

> some of whom are former officials now in the private sector, the scale of the military facilities made available by the Gulf states to the US and Britain cannot be gauged by the few bland statements that accompany official announcements of 'access' or 'cooperation agreements' . . . A careful choice of words – or, better still say Gulf analysts, official silence – helps conceal the depth of the rulers' long-term dependence on the US and Britain.

The word 'dependence' should be emphasised here.

One Western diplomat was quoted describing Britain's 1996 defence cooperation agreement with the UAE as 'the UK's largest single commitment to the defence of a country outside NATO'. From the other side, a 'senior Gulf official' remarked that '[e]ach year we spend billions on defence. And each year we become more dependent on the US and the West.'

The report continued: 'US and British involvement is not confined to Gulf states' external defence, analysts point out. It includes the provision of equipment for internal security and extensive collaboration with, and training by, US and British intelligence services and law-enforcement agencies.' Of course, the term 'law enforcement' implies differing degrees of legitimacy and different functions, depending on the extent to which a state is democratic or authoritarian in nature. As Shashank Joshi, associate fellow at the Royal United Services Institute, pointed out in January 2012, '[i]t would be British arms and security forces trained by British personnel that would do much of the killing if a "Saudi Spring" ever did unfold.'[80]

The strategic value of the Gulf Arab monarchies to British capitalism and the British state has meant that securing and defending those monarchies from the threat posed by their own populations has long been a priority for London. With this overall picture in mind, we can now examine in more detail how this relationship has developed over the post-Cold War period.

Developments since the end of the Cold War

In 1995, *Jane's Defence Weekly* reported that 1,500 British officers and non-commissioned officers were serving with Oman's defence and security forces, some on loan from UK military, while others were ex-UK military under contract to Oman. UK–Omani joint manoeuvres were regularly held, and training was being provided to the Omani navy, while BAE worked on upgrading the Sultanate's air defence systems.[81]

The 1996 UK–UAE defence cooperation accord mentioned above was described to Parliament by Defence Secretary Michael Portillo as providing for

the strengthening of military co-operation between the UAE and the UK in a number of areas, including training, the conduct of combined exercises, the provision of modern defence equipment and related services to the UAE armed forces and the development of joint military plans and military deployment strategies for the defence of the UAE. Under the terms of the accord, the UK is committed to assisting the UAE in deterring threats or preventing aggression against the UAE and, in the event of such aggression taking place, to implementing the joint military plans which are judged appropriate for the defence of the UAE . . . The accord builds upon the 1971 treaty of friendship between the UK and the UAE.[82]

As far as precise details of Britain's new defence commitments were concerned, the government refused a request to place a copy of the accord in the House of Commons library, deeming Portillo's outline quoted above to be sufficient.[83]

In 1994 Bahrain experienced its most serious unrest for twenty-five years as armed protesters clashed with security forces while GCC leaders met for a regional security conference. Nine people were killed and, according to Bahraini opposition figures in exile, the British head of the Manama's state security services, Ian Henderson (mentioned in chapter 1), was denounced at the funerals of protesters.[84] In 1998, Baroness Symons, under-secretary of state at the Foreign Office, told the House of Lords that the British Ministry of Defence had been providing training to the Bahrain National Guard on the protection of key installations.[85] When the Bahraini government violently put down a popular uprising in the spring of 2011, increased media scrutiny of the relationship between Whitehall and Manama revealed a range of details regarding the support provided by the British up to that point.

In the years leading up to the uprising, Britain had been providing expertise and training in counter-terrorism and, according to *The Times*, had trained 'most of the senior-ranking military and police commanders in the kingdom' at Sandhurst, including the interior minister.[86] An enquiry made under the Freedom of Information Act by the *Evening Standard* revealed that the King of Bahrain had recently paid the MoD to teach eighty-one soldiers at various British military academies in the preceding years. Four officers had attended Shrivenham Defence Academy, at a cost of £117,000, while fifty-seven had attended Sandhurst. The king was patron of the Sandhurst Foundation (the college's charitable arm), had donated £70,000 a year, and pledged to give it £1.7 million in 2017 if it remained a 'going concern'. Britannia Royal Naval College, Dartmouth, had trained twenty Bahraini naval officers since 1997. Going back further, in 1982 the Bahraini ambassador to the UK, Sheikh Khalifa bin Ali bin Rashid Al Khalifa, had completed an officer's training course at RAF Cranwell.[87] Similar investigations by *The Guardian* revealed that over the preceding five years the MoD had helped train more than a hundred Bahraini military officers at Sandhurst and other top colleges. Places had been made available for Gulf state military personnel on junior officer training courses for the British army, the RAF, the Royal Navy and the joint services command and staff course, while teams had also been sent to Bahrain to deliver specific training courses.[88]

The Arab uprisings of early 2011 in general, and the involvement of the GCC's 'Peninsular Shield' force in putting down the protests in Bahrain in particular, drew attention to Britain's role in supporting the apparatus of coercion in the rest of the Gulf. *The Independent* reported that, before the uprisings, British police had helped to train counterparts from Bahrain, Abu Dhabi, Qatar and Saudi Arabia through the 'National Policing Improvements Agency', whose spokesman said that respect for human rights underpins all their training (which, if true, had evidently not had a substantive effect, judging by the extensive abuses documented by leading human rights NGOs during the 2011 crackdown).[89]

The *Daily Telegraph* reported that 'Britain keeps a large and secretive military training team in Saudi Arabia, where British personnel advise and teach the kingdom's forces in areas including crowd control.'[90] The 'British Military Mission' in Saudi Arabia is comprised of seconded British army personnel that train and advise the Special Security Brigade of the Saudi Arabian National Guard. There is also a small Royal Navy liaison team providing support to the King Fahd Naval Academy. In 2013, there were roughly twenty British naval personnel, forty from the army and seventy from the air force stationed in Saudi Arabia.[91]

Bahrain provided the UK military with a staging post for air communications to Afghanistan and Iraq during the occupations of those countries and contributed approximately one hundred personnel in support of NATO forces in Afghanistan. Naval facilities made available by Bahrain to the British allow operations in the Gulf, the Red Sea, the Gulf of Aden and the north-west Indian Ocean, as well as mine-hunting operations in the Strait of Hormuz.[92]

Written evidence to the Foreign Affairs Committee from the Royal United Services Institute described the military relationship with Bahrain as

crucial to the UK's pursuit of its national strategic aims. Bahrain welcomes British naval vessels into its waters and port facilities, allows the RAF to use its airfields, and routinely waives the sorts of protocols Britain would have to follow before entering the national territory of certain of its neighbours. Bahrain also supplies the UK with intelligence, in particular though not exclusively in connexion with counter-terrorism. In a sense, the kingdom is a substitute for an aircraft carrier permanently sta-tioned in the Gulf.[93]

In short, Bahrain plays a crucial role in allowing Britain to project military power into the strategically vital Gulf region, saving it the considerable expense that might be incurred if such facilities were not available.

The Qatar crisis

One of the major themes of this chapter is that British arms sales to the Gulf Arab monarchies are significant not purely in terms of the profits they generate for firms such as BAE Systems. They have an important strategic and political character as well. This is illustrated in an episode ongoing at the time of writing, where a dispute broke out between Qatar and its fellow GCC states and London responded in an interest-ing and perhaps revealing way.

Accusing Qatar of being too close to Iran – and of colluding with terrorist groups and the Muslim Brotherhood – Saudi Arabia, the UAE and Bahrain led the way in severing ties between the GCC and Doha, attempting to isolate it until it agreed to various demands (which essentially amounted to it abandoning an independent foreign policy).[94] While President Donald Trump gave vocal support to the Saudi-Emirati move,[95] it became clear that the government beneath him – specifically the State Department and the Pentagon – took a dif-ferent view, and that London was firmly in the latter camp.

Days after the crisis began, the US defense secretary, James Mattis, signed off on a $12 billion deal to supply Doha with dozens of F-15 fighter jets, and the Pentagon stated explicitly that the sale would increase US–Qatari security cooperation – a clear rejection of the

Saudi–Emirati position. More surprisingly, in September 2017, Qatar signed an initial order for twenty-four Eurofighter Typhoon jets from the UK in a potential £8.6 billion deal. The then British defence secretary, Michael Fallon, said that 'the security of the GCC, of all Gulf countries, is critical to the UK's own security' and that he hoped the Typhoon fleets of the various Gulf states would be able to operate together, helping to 'enhance security within the region across all Gulf allies'. The Typhoon deal came as a surprise to observers, partly because little had been heard of any advance negotiations, and partly because, as indicated earlier in this chapter, the Qatari market has hitherto been dominated by France and the US. This, coupled with the diplomatic language coming out of London and Washington (Trump aside), suggests that the Anglo-American allies were taking very deliberate steps to support Qatar and prevent the break-up of the GCC.[96]

This recent episode underlines the point that arms sales are never purely commercial. They constitute expressions and bonds of military cooperation and thus have a political and strategic character. Here they appear, at least in part, to have served the purpose of signalling strongly to London's Gulf allies that Qatar's isolation would not be tolerated and that the GCC states should therefore settle their differences. This polite but unambiguous rejection of a major diplomatic gambit by Riyadh also indicates where the balance of power ultimately lies in a UK–Saudi relationship characterised by asymmetric interdependence.

Conclusions

Arms exports, as well as generating billions of pounds in revenues, help Britain to maintain the military-industrial capacity required as the basis for global power projection. In this sense, Gulf wealth matters to British power for strategic reasons, not just narrowly economic ones. The GCC is a key market for UK arms exports, and sales to those states also serve as a form of political support and a way of establishing close ties between London and the various Gulf monarchies. The high degree of state support provided to the arms export industry is reflective of its fundamentally strategic value. Recall as well that these major arms deals are signed between governments, not between, say, the Saudi kingdom and BAE.

As one of the world's leading arms exporters and a power with a long-standing geopolitical interest in the Gulf region, Britain is one of three major (and competing) arms suppliers to the GCC states, in broadly equal second place alongside France, with the US clearly in the lead. However, Britain has a major stake in the strategically and economically crucial Saudi market, overtaking that of the US in a recent five-year period. The British arms export industry is becoming increasingly dependent on Saudi purchases as other global markets decline in relative terms.

UK arms sales to the GCC states, particularly Saudi Arabia, have long been surrounded by questions of corruption. Whitehall has gone to considerable lengths to avoid formal scrutiny of these issues, to the point of antagonising both the United States and important interests within the City of London. It is unclear whether this extremely defensive approach has been taken to protect the London–Riyadh alliance from damaging political and public scrutiny, to protect leading arms exporters or even Whitehall itself from allegations of involvement in corruption being legally proven, or some balance of these two considerations. To the extent that the first consideration is relevant, Whitehall's willingness to contradict both Washington and key City interests is testament to the importance it attaches to the alliance with the Saudis.

British military cooperation with the GCC states is extensive and multi-layered and runs across the entire Gulf region. Although there is much secrecy around the precise degree of commitment Britain has made to the defence of these monarchies, enough detail exists in the public realm to make clear that the GCC states are practically reliant on the UK, and to a far greater extent on the US, for their defence, even ultimately for their survival. However, the moral questions around UK arms sales to and military cooperation with the Gulf Arab monarchies have become the relationship's major point of political vulnerability, as recent developments, explored in the next chapter, have dramatically exposed.

6

The Arab Uprisings and the War in Yemen

Recent years have seen two of the most significant episodes in the history of UK–GCC relations: the popular uprisings that swept the Middle East from the winter of 2010–11 and the 2015 intervention by a Saudi-led coalition of states in the civil war in Yemen. While this book is concerned primarily with mapping the deep structures that underpin the UK–GCC relationship in the current historical epoch, these episodes are worth dwelling upon as they help us to understand in more detail how the relationship works in practice.

In this chapter we will examine Britain's response to the Arab uprisings, in so far as arms sales to and military cooperation with the Gulf Arab monarchies are concerned, and then look at the extent, nature and durability of Britain's support for the Saudi-led intervention in Yemen's civil war. What we find is that London responded to the challenge that the Arab uprisings represented to the GCC monarchies, particularly in Bahrain, with a major strategic vote of confidence in the conservative regional order. We then find that the Saudi-led intervention in Yemen enjoyed important material support from London even in the face of compelling evidence that large numbers of civilians were being killed indiscriminately and a world-leading humanitarian catastrophe was being created. These events illustrate the urgent need for academics, journalists and the general public to devote more attention and scrutiny to the UK–GCC relationship.

The Arab uprisings

The poor and sometimes extremely poor human rights record of the Gulf Arab monarchies is well known and long established. Although political systems vary from state to state, as does the degree of repression and the precise constraints on political freedom and freedom of expression, they are all fundamentally authoritarian and non-democratic. Abuses by security forces, including the use of torture, as well as unfair trials and the criminalisation of the most basic forms of dissent, are widespread across the GCC region. These systematic violations of fundamental human rights have been extensively documented over the years by world-leading NGOs such as Amnesty International and Human Rights Watch.[1]

The uprisings that swept the Middle East from the winter of 2010–11 onwards were an outpouring of many years of frustration at authoritarian government, patrimonialism, corruption, economic dysfunction and violent repression.[2] The wave reached the GCC as well, most notably in the form of massive demonstrations in Bahrain and smaller protests in Oman. The spring 2011 uprising in Bahrain was an overwhelmingly peaceful, largely non-sectarian, popular demand for constitutional government that was met with a violent response from the Bahraini domestic security services, backed up by an intervention of the Saudi-led GCC 'Peninsular Shield' force, which facilitated Manama's crushing of the uprising.[3]

Business as usual

As we saw in the last chapter (figure 5.3), the Arab uprisings and their aftermath coincided with a sharp increase (beginning in 2009) in the value of major British arms exports to the GCC states. This is accounted for mostly by transfers to the Saudi kingdom. However, in the case of Bahrain, scene of the most significant uprising in the GCC countries, we also find a rise in exports coinciding with the unrest. This pattern also holds in the case of Oman, also the site of protests, albeit smaller in scale and not fundamentally threatening the monarchy's survival.[4]

In the cases of Bahrain and Saudi Arabia, the start of the increase in British exports pre-dates the start of the Arab uprisings, but the overall rise in the supply of arms is undisturbed by those events in subsequent years. In the case of Oman, the rise comes afterwards. Overall, the data show that the British government's response to the new wave of demands for democracy region-wide was to continue a sharp increase in arms supplies to its key authoritarian allies. These arms sales were pushed for by London even when pro-democracy protesters were on the streets or being suppressed by the coercive apparatus of the Gulf states.

In February 2011 David Cameron made a hastily arranged stopover in Cairo, conducted a walkabout in Tahrir Square and spoke of how

Table 6.1 Value of export licences approved by the UK government in respect of Bahrain (£m)

	2008	2009	2010	2011	2012	2013	2014	2015	2016	Total
Military	£0.6	£0.6	£4.9	£2.2	£4.6	£18	£4.3	£18	£5.3	£59
Dual-use	£4.5	£2.3	£3.9	£11	£3.4	£16	£15	£9.3	£1.4 £3.9	£69
Total	£5.2	£2.9	£8.8	£13	£8.0	£34	£19	£27	£9.1	£128

Note: Values are not adjusted for inflation.
Source: CAAT.[5]

'inspired' he was by the recent events there, before heading to Kuwait for a pre-arranged tour of the Gulf to promote business links, and arms deals in particular, which (to his government's embarrassment) had coincided with the outbreak of pro-democracy protests across the region. A key aim of the tour was to promote the sale of Eurofighter Typhoons. Meanwhile, Gerald Howarth, a British defence minister, attended the region's largest arms fair in Abu Dhabi, where British firms sought buyers for, among other products, rubber bullets, CS gas for crowd control, and armoured riot vans. Of the 36-strong business delegation that accompanied the prime minister, nearly a quarter came from the military and aerospace sectors.[6]

These visits formed part of an arms sales drive by the 2010–15 Conservative–Liberal Democrat government, which bore considerable fruit. In May 2012, BAE Systems won a £1.6 billion order from Saudi Arabia for fifty-five Pilatus PC-21 aircraft and twenty-two Hawk trainer jets, both of which would help Saudi pilots learn to fly the Typhoons ordered in 2007.[7] In November 2012, a British–Kuwaiti agreement was announced whereby the UK government would award contracts to British firms to provide Kuwait with domestic security equipment in a deal potentially worth between £100 million and £150 million annually over seven years.[8] In December 2012, during a visit to Oman by David Cameron, BAE Systems signed a £2.5 billion contract to supply twelve Typhoon fighters and eight Hawk trainer jets, together with in-service support.[9]

Efforts were made to clinch similar deals with other Gulf states. In January 2013 the arms industry trade press reported that the Eurofighter consortium was back in contention for a combat jet order with Qatar, following a visit to Doha by the then British foreign secretary, William Hague.[10] In August 2013 the *Daily Telegraph* reported that one of the main agenda items in a Downing Street meeting between

David Cameron and King Hamad of Bahrain was a deal for the sale of Typhoons 'thought to be worth more than £1 billion and ... part of a concerted effort by Gulf countries to strengthen military ties with Britain.'[11]

Even the most strenuous sales efforts, however, were not guaranteed success. In November 2012, the UAE signalled interest in placing an order for the Eurofighter Typhoon from BAE Systems, as Cameron visited Abu Dhabi and signed a joint communiqué saying that Britain and the UAE would 'establish a defence industrial partnership that involves close collaboration around the Typhoon'.[12] In April 2013, Sheikh Khalifa bin Zayed bin Sultan Al Nahyan, president of the UAE, visited London and enjoyed a state lunch at Windsor Castle as well as meeting with the prime minister at Downing Street, where Cameron continued efforts to close the sale of sixty Typhoons and fend off French competition in the shape of Dassault's Rafale.[13] In November, Cameron was back in Dubai to push for the Typhoon deal, which was reported to be worth a potential US$10 billion.[14] However, in a blow to British efforts to achieve a crucial breakthrough into this major arms market, the UAE called off negotiations the following month.[15]

It is possible (though far from certain, especially given that Britain has not had a major share in the UAE arms export market in recent decades) that the failure of the Typhoon deal may have had a political dimension. As discussed in chapter 2, media reports indicated that there was some Emirati consternation regarding Britain's approach to the Arab uprisings, for example on the UK supposedly allowing Muslim Brotherhood figures to use London as a base and granting asylum to some Emirati activists. Although officials from both governments denied it, the *Financial Times* speculated that this could be behind moves made by the UAE government to cease using most of the British nationals that had been providing it with military training.

However, at the same time Abu Dhabi had been asking the UK to boost its direct military presence in the country, so any rumblings of displeasure at a perceived inadequacy in Britain's support for the Gulf states did not appear to represent any threat of a substantive, strategic rupture.[16]

Nevertheless, there was a palpable sense at this time that the GCC monarchs were on alert for any signals that UK support for them in the wake of the Arab uprisings might be anything less than fulsome. In October 2012, the Saudi government said that it was 'insulted' by news that the House of Commons Foreign Affairs Select Committee would conduct an inquiry into London's relationship with Saudi Arabia and Bahrain. Officials told the BBC that they were now 're-evaluating their country's historic relations with Britain' and that 'all options will be looked at'.[17] As with previous such remarks noted earlier in this book, no substantive change in the relationship appears to have taken place subsequently.

UK–GCC military cooperation continued after the spring of 2011, and even deepened in some areas, to the point where some analysts spoke of a 'Return to East of Suez',[18] recalling the 1971 cessation of British hegemony in the Gulf. Of course, this did not imply that Britain would now replace the United States and reprise its former role entirely, but clear signs were identified that a step-change would be made in the level of Britain's commitment.

In October 2012 the UK and Bahrain signed a Defence Co-operation Accord which, according to a ministerial statement, set out the 'framework for current and aspirational defence engagement activity including training and capacity building in order to enhance stability of the wider region, supporting Bahrain's ability to counter any exter- nal aggression.'[19] In December 2014, the government announced plans to build a £15 million naval base in Bahrain, with the cost of construction covered by Manama and London taking responsibility for future operational costs.[20]

This represented a clear sign of London's intent to project military power into the Gulf region for some considerable time to come. Academic observers David Roberts, Saul Kelly and Gareth Stansfield described a renewed effort to deepen military ties and cooperation in the Gulf in general, and with the UAE in particular.[21] In a report on British military involvement in the Gulf for the NGO War on Want, Sam Raphael and Jac St John endorse this conclusion (Raphael is an academic expert on state violence and also co-author of *Global Energy Security and American Hegemony*, a book discussed in chapter 2). In addition to the defence agreement with Bahrain and the announcement of a new naval base there, the authors note plans to expand the port in Duqm, Oman, to allow a permanent presence for the Royal Navy. This forms part of London's wider strategy to enhance its ability to project military power into the Gulf region, including the establishment of a new British Defence Staff dedicated to the Gulf, with a highly secretive 'Gulf Strategy Unit' playing a coordinating role for this policy across the defence and security apparatus of the British state.[22]

Whitehall's narrative

These moves, taken together with the major arms export drive to the GCC in recent years, added up to a clear strategic vote of confidence in the Gulf monarchies at a time when they were facing a new political challenge to their position and legitimacy. However, British ministers and officials would of course reject any suggestion that they were siding with anti-democratic forces and reinforcing authoritarian rule at such a moment in the region's history. By critically examining some official defences of recent British policy, it is possible to develop a more detailed understanding of the way British support for the Gulf states has been expressed (in the fullest sense of the term) at this important historical juncture.

Responding to criticism of British arms sales to repressive governments in the Middle East, David Cameron argued: '[w]e have one of the strictest regimes anywhere in the world for sales of defence equipment but we do believe that countries have a right to self-defence and we do believe that Britain has important defence industries that employ over 300,000 people so that sort of business is completely legitimate and right.'[23]

As noted previously, the net economic cost–benefit of Britain's arms export industry is hard to quantify definitively, given the extensive levels of state support for arms exporters. We must also recall that the benefits to the state are ultimately strategic in nature – in terms of maintaining Britain's military and diplomatic capacity to remain a global power – rather than relating primarily or narrowly to employment generation. Also problematic are Cameron's attempt to isolate the legitimate national self-defence needs of the UK arms industry's customers and Foreign Secretary Hague's statement that the sale of Tornados and Typhoons to Riyadh are 'not relevant' to concerns about human rights.[24] As has been demonstrated in Syria, a regime determined to preserve itself can make use of a wide range of weapons systems in crushing internal revolt, including military jets. The reportedly indiscriminate bombing carried out by Saudi-led intervention forces in Yemen (discussed in detail later on in this chapter) indicates how GCC air forces might respond in such a scenario. Additionally, as noted earlier, the sale of arms to certain states is not (and is not intended to be) an apolitical act. As noted in chapter 5, the provision of arms on a large scale is inescapably an expression of material and political support for such governments, expanding their capacity for and tendency towards physical repression both directly and indirectly.

Arms export licensing decisions are made by Whitehall on a case-by-case basis, using the Consolidated EU and National Arms Export Licensing Criteria adopted in October 2000. Among a number of conditions, these prohibit export where there is a clear risk of the equipment being used for 'internal repression' or where the export would 'provoke or prolong armed conflicts or aggravate existing tensions or conflicts'.[25] However, in practice these controls are applied narrowly and incompletely, and often in a reactive way, after the goods have already been sold, exported and likely put into use. The strong policy preference appears to be to provide the arms to the greatest extent that is politically possible and to point to the controls regime as a means to avoid embarrassment about their potential use.

Anna Stavrianakis and Neil Cooper, academic specialists on British arms sales, are both critical of government claims as to the supposed stringency of these safeguards. Cooper notes that official arms controls operate in 'a wider bureaucratic milieu that places an emphasis on maximizing arms exports' and that the real operative restriction is on sales to strategic opponents, 'pariah states', rather than being defined by possible end use.[26] Stavrianakis argues that Whitehall:

> continues to licence military equipment to states with a record of engaging in human rights violations, internal conflict and regional instability. More generally, the sale of UK arms exports and the character of its traditional major recipients – NATO allies and Middle Eastern states, in particular Saudi Arabia . . . – are such that the UK arms trade plays a significant role in maintaining the coercive backbone to the global capitalist system.[27]

Amnesty International argues that 'the UK Government's focus on arms sales to the MENA region . . . is completely at odds with its stated aim of upholding human rights' and, further, that '[e]quipment and components licensed for sale . . . to Bahrain [and] Saudi Arabia [as well as other MENA states, include] . . . types of equipment that are likely to have been used in serious human rights violations against civilians.'[28]

In February 2011, *The Guardian* reported that Whitehall had launched a review of arms exports to Bahrain, noting that, in the year leading up to the protests, Britain had licensed the sale of items that could be used for internal repression, such as shotguns, teargas canisters, 'crowd control ammunition', stun grenades, small arms ammunition and submachine guns. The report stated that, according to evidence seen by the journalists, injuries to protesters were consistent with the use of shotguns, including at close range.[29] The review resulted in a number of export licences being revoked, covering equipment which Whitehall assessed could be used for riot control by the Bahraini security forces and military.[30] Rosemary Hollis offers the view that

the British do not want to be seen – in front of the British public, Human Rights Watch and all those other NGOs that are monitoring this – to be aiding and abetting oppression of civilian population. But it is about not being seen to be doing these things as opposed to expecting to change the nature of the polity in these places fundamentally.[31]

In 2012, the House of Commons joint Committees on Arms Export Controls concluded that the revocation of licences to Bahrain and other MENA states in spring 2011 merely exposed the fact that the government had been allowing arms exports to known human rights abusers. The committees did not regard the revocation of the licences after the event as an adequate response.[32] As their report put it:

> [T]here is an inherent conflict between strongly promoting arms exports to authoritarian regimes while strongly criticising their lack of human rights at the same time. . . . [W]hilst the Government's statement that 'respect for human rights and fundamental freedoms are mandatory considerations for all export licence applications' is welcome, those considerations do not appear to have weighed sufficiently heavily on either the present Government or on its predecessor given the unprecedented scale of arms export licence revocations that the Government has made since the 'Arab Spring' – the stated reason for revocation being in every single case 'that this licence now contravenes Criteria 2 and 3'. [Criterion] 2 is headed 'The respect of human rights and fundamental freedoms in the country of final destination', and [Criterion] 3 is headed 'The internal situation in the country of final destination, as a function of the existence of tensions, or armed conflicts.' . . . [T]here were no significant changes in the repressive regimes concerned between the British Government's approval of the arms export licences in question and the start of the Arab Spring in December 2010, . . . the Arab Spring simply exposed the true nature of the repressive regimes which had been the case all along.[33]

Although forty-four arms export licences to Bahrain were revoked in February 2011, licences which remained extant a year later included those covering components for assault rifles and pistols, small arms ammunition, body armour and shotguns.[34] In 2012, *The Times* reported on how British firms had continued to supply Bahrain at the height of the 2011 crackdown, quoting data published by Whitehall recording approved sales of military equipment valued at more than £1 million, including licences for gun silencers, rifles and artillery.[35]

In their report, covering the period from 2010 to 2016, Raphael and St John note that up to a hundred licences for assault rifles, sniper rifles and other guns – weapons that have been used for internal repression – were approved for export by Whitehall. Training in the use of sniper rifles was provided to Bahraini security forces by British Royal Navy commandos in March 2016. Over the same period, crowd control ammunition, 'tear gas/irritant ammunition' and 'acoustic devices for riot control' were also approved for export to Oman, the UAE and Saudi Arabia. Meanwhile British firms such as G4S, Olive Group and Control Risks provided both consultancy and direct security services to the Gulf monarchies.[36]

The government's own conclusion was that there was no evidence of British-made equipment being used directly in the unrest of 2011,[37] but, in their evidence to the Committees on Arms Export Control, the UK Working Group on Arms (comprising NGOs such as Amnesty UK, Oxfam and Saferworld) questioned the value of this assertion. First, the government's arms control criteria are risk- rather than evidence-based, meaning that the risk of their being used for internal repression is sufficient to prevent their sale, and the government should not wait for evidence to emerge and then rescind licences after the fact. Second, even if abuses had been proven to be committed only with arms supplied by other states, that fact must inform any risk assessment with regard to the sale of UK arms. Third, it is difficult to see how British diplomatic missions could have the investigative capacity to establish meaningfully whether evidence of the use of British arms in repression really exists.[38] In terms of proper risk assessment, the chairman of the committees opined in 2011 that the government's 'judgements have been shown to be wildly over-optimistic and rose-tinted regarding the sale to authoritarian regimes of weapons that could be used for internal repression.'[39]

In 2011, it was reported that the GCC intervention force that entered Bahrain to protect key state installations while Bahraini forces crushed the protests in the spring of that year had entered the country in Tactica internal security vehicles sold to Saudi Arabia by BAE Systems.[40] In a written parliamentary answer, armed forces minister Nick Harvey admitted that, additionally, '[i]t is possible that some members of the Saudi Arabian National Guard who were deployed in Bahrain may have undertaken some training provided by the British military mission.'[41]

The government claimed that there was nothing inappropriate in this use of British-made armoured vehicles. As Foreign Minister Burt put it to the Commons Foreign Affairs Committee:

> [T]here is no connection between the work done by the Saudi authorities to protect certain places in Bahrain and the behaviour of Bahraini security forces subsequently. That the Bahraini forces were able to go off and do their job is clear, but they could have handled it in a completely different manner. . . . There is no logical connection between what the Saudi authorities were asked to do by the Government of Bahrain and the GCC, namely to come in and provide protection and do what they did – there is no connection between any of those vehicles and any human rights abuses. It would have been entirely open to the Bahraini security forces to do their job properly, so there is not the connection between the two.[42]

However, given the function of the Bahraini security forces and their human rights record, it is predictable that the 'job' they did was to violently put down the peaceful challenge to the monarchy. The arrival of GCC forces in British-made Tacticas while these events were unfolding was plainly complementary to and enabling of that violent crackdown.

To properly critique the British government's line on this episode and assess the full significance of UK-trained Saudi troops arriving in UK-supplied armoured vehicles to support the 2011 crackdown, it is important to recall the broader strategic context in which the GCC intervention took place.

First, notwithstanding rivalries and differences between the various GCC monarchies, the six states nevertheless constitute a particular system whereby the stability of all would be threatened if one were to be toppled by popular revolt. Specifically, as Sir Roger Tomkys, British ambassador to Bahrain from 1981 to 1984, remarked to the Foreign Affairs Committee, any Saudi intervention in Bahrain to help put down an uprising there would be intended 'to prevent a knock-on effect, or a modelling for what ought to happen in similar circumstances in the [Saudi] eastern province, where the oil is', and where many co-religionists of Bahrain's Shia majority reside.[43] As Tomkys put it in his written evidence to the committee, '[t]here is no way the Saudi Government would allow the Al Khalifa [Bahrain's ruling family], even if they so wished, to introduce full Western style democracy power in Bahrain; the risk of knock-on to the Eastern Province would be judged unacceptable and some form of Saudi takeover of Bahrain would almost certainly follow.'[44]

Second, the integrity of this broader system, and the threat posed to it by demands for democracy, is of concern to London and Washington as well. As the author and expert on Saudi Arabia, Robert Lacey, told the Foreign Affairs Select Committee:

The majority of the inhabitants of Bahrain are Shia Muslims whose loyalties - social, religious and political - look beyond

Bahrain to Iran and Iraq, Iran's massive new US- and UK-liberated Shia ally. There is not a single western country, including Britain, which would welcome a pro-Iranian Shia government dominating Bahrain and its crucial US naval base. So, inasmuch as Saudi Arabia is helping to suppress the undoubted political rights of the undoubted Shia majority of Bahrainis, it is doing our dirty work.[45]

One can dispute the overly sectarian emphasis of these remarks and note that the initial protests of spring 2011 were reportedly broad-based (see the quotes from Gulf expert Kristian Coates Ulrichsen later on in this chapter), while acknowledging that the Al Khalifa monarchy's external backers have a long-displayed aversion to any prospect of these states moving off in an independent direction of any kind, be it secular nationalist or pro-Iranian.

More broadly, in response to criticism of its support for the Gulf states in light of their poor human rights record and failure to democratise, the British government tends to claim that the monarchies themselves are agents of moderation and sustainable reform, and that continued friendly engagement is the key to encouraging them further down this path. This has been particularly true in respect of Bahrain since the events of 2011, where the London–Manama relationship has come under particular scrutiny. The Whitehall line has essentially been that, while aspects of the 2011 crackdown against protesters were clearly regrettable, the Al Khalifa monarchy has faced up to those problems, identified where reforms need to be made, and is now making good progress in addressing these issues, though more needs to be done.[46] The other aspect of the government line is to praise the king's 'National Dialogue' as the only mechanism available to resolve what is portrayed as primarily an issue of social or sectarian division rather than one of an authoritarian state resisting popular demands for democracy.[47]

However, the Whitehall narrative is sharply at odds with the assessment of more detached observers at the world's leading human rights NGOs. A report by Amnesty International published in November 2012,[48] a year after the Manama government's announcement of its reform programme, described the official pledges as a 'pretence' which had effectively been 'shelved' while the crackdown that began in the spring of 2011 continued. Amnesty accused London and Washington of 'satisfying themselves with the narrative of reform while ignoring the reality of repression', and of failing to match their periodic expressions of concern 'with any meaningful actions or consequences'.

In January 2014, Human Rights Watch reported that Bahrain had actually 'regressed further in key areas' of human rights over the previous year and documented continued repression and credible reports of torture in detention.[49] The NGO's deputy Middle East and North Africa director remarked that '[o]fficial talk of reform is a joke at a time when peaceful critics of the government are labelled terrorists and kept in jail.'[50] Also that month, commenting on the Duke of York's official visit to Bahrain to promote British business, Amnesty International commented that Manama had 'long ago reneged on promises to reform, and the country is now trapped in an endless circuit of protest–clampdown, further protest–further clampdown . . ., [with] protesters – including children – given very long prison sentences.'[51]

Nonetheless, a few weeks earlier, the British ambassador in Manama had told the Bahrain British Business Forum that 2013 had been 'a very good year for the UK/Bahrain bilateral relationship, [which] has a great future.'[52] When David Cameron welcomed King Hamad to Downing Street in August 2013, his spokesman announced that the prime minister had 'encouraged His Majesty to *continue to demonstrate substantive progress in all areas*' of reform.[53] Remarks such as these indicate that the health of the UK–Bahrain relationship is not connected to the trajectory of Bahrain's human rights record, be it positive or negative. Indeed, surveying the GCC states as a whole over the recent period in which British arms sales have increased, the NGO Freedom House has recorded either stagnation or, in the cases of Saudi Arabia, Bahrain, the UAE and Kuwait, a regression in terms of political rights and civil liberties.[54]

Returning to Bahrain, Whitehall described the Al Khalifa monarchy's National Dialogue as 'the only way to promote peace and stability' and urged 'all sides to remain engaged in the process'.[55] However, Human Rights Watch describes the National Dialogue as 'deeply flawed', noting that all but nine of the twenty-seven participating groups are linked to the government.[56] Kristian Coates Ulrichsen, an academic specialising in the Gulf, also noted the marked under-representation of opposition groups in the dialogue.[57] The fact that peaceful dissidents continue to be arrested and jailed,[58] and that prominent political prisoners are serving lengthy prison sentences up to and including life terms,[59] raises question marks over both the Al Khalifas' and the British government's interest in meaningful dialogue, given the latter's frequent praise of the process.

Moreover, the emphasis on dialogue is predicated on the government's view that 'the underlying reason for the unrest [in 2011] was sectarian.'[60] A different characterisation was given by Ulrichsen in his evidence to the Foreign Affairs Committee. As he noted, the Bahrain protests in spring 2011

> saw up to one-third of the population on the streets demanding their rights . . . the highest per capita involvement in any of the protests during the Arab spring . . . Significantly, the initial

protests involved individuals and groups from across the political (and sectarian) spectrum. . . . Faced with the rapid escalation of a broad and unifying social movement, the regime resorted to lethal force . . . and also worked to fragment the protest movement by ramping up sectarian rhetoric, deliberately targeting Shiite religious symbols . . . and splitting the movement in a classic tactic of 'divide and rule'.[61]

The Whitehall narrative here obscures questions of democracy, replacing them with a sectarian narrative in a way that complements both its own strategic priorities and the tactics of the authorities in Manama. The over-emphasis on sectarianism also reflects long-standing prejudices among Western elites about the supposed pathologies of Middle Eastern cultures.[62]

As Jane Kinninmont of Chatham House commented in oral evidence to the committee, '[a]ll the Gulf Governments would say that they are committed to a process of gradual reform but it is a convenient word, beloved of elites because it is vague, relativistic and has no deadlines attached.'[63] To the extent that Whitehall desires a degree of reform in the Gulf, this appears to be in the hope that such measures would shore up the established order in the GCC rather than transform it. This would be consistent with established British policy, described in chapter 1.

Foreign Minister Burt indicated as much when he told the Foreign Affairs Committee, 'we think that the best chance for stability in Bahrain lies through the successful national dialogue process by Bahrainis, which will seek their own political settlement, *which is highly likely to encompass the Al Khalifa leadership and the structure of Bahrain'.*[64] When Cameron welcomed the Crown Prince of Bahrain to 10 Downing Street on 19 May 2011, his spokesman told the media that

Britain backed efforts to 'normalise' the situation in the country and 'return Bahrain to a credible long-term process of reform'.[65] As Hollis observed in her evidence to the committee, 'you do not remove a dictatorship by gradual reform . . . dictators do not generally happily release one power after another.'[66] Neil Partrick, associate fellow at the Royal United Services Institute, probably spoke accurately for the state and military interests that his think tank represents when he told the committee in respect of Bahrain that '[d]emocratisation, broadly speaking, is not on anyone's agenda.'[67]

British support for the Saudi-led intervention in Yemen

The most significant episode that occurred during the period under review was the UK's support in 2015 for the intervention in the Yemeni civil war carried out by a coalition led by Saudi Arabia ('the Coalition') and involving, to varying degrees, all the GCC states except Oman (and later Qatar, which was expelled from the Coalition in June 2017 following the diplomatic dispute within the GCC over its foreign policy).[68] At the time of writing, the Coalition intervention and British (and American) support for it remain ongoing, so final and definitive conclusions on the entire episode cannot be drawn. However, nearly three years after the intervention began, it is clear that this represents a historic illustration of how UK military ties with the GCC states, principally the Saudi kingdom, operate in practice, and of the extent to which the British state is prepared to support these allies in times of war.

The Coalition intervention began on 26 March 2015 with the aim of restoring President Abd Rabbuh Mansour Hadi to office after he was ousted by the north Yemeni 'Houthi' rebel movement and forces loyal to former president Ali Abdullah Saleh. Hadi, formerly Saleh's deputy, had replaced him as part of a deal brokered by the Gulf monarchies and supported by the US and the UK, following unrest in 2011 in the wider context of the Arab uprisings. The GCC-brokered deal had been intended to curtail and contain any wider socio-political change resulting from the uprising and prevent civil war breaking out in a country that shares a long border with Saudi Arabia. The intervention consisted principally of aerial bombardment in support of local ground forces loyal to Hadi. It was backed by a UN Security Council resolution in whose drafting the leading Coalition monarchies were reported to be closely involved, which was heavily weighted against the Houthis, and which was supported by the UK, the US and France, with China and Russia abstaining.[69] The Coalition states frequently pointed to Iranian involvement on the Houthi side, although this was marginal, growing only after the Coalition intervention began and remaining relatively limited even then.[70]

In parallel with considerable practical backing for Coalition operations from the United States, strong UK support for the intervention was also pledged from the outset.[71] The then foreign secretary, Philip Hammond, noted that Britain has 'a significant infrastructure supporting the Saudi air force generally and if we are requested to provide them with enhanced support – spare parts, maintenance, technical advice, resupply – we will seek to do so . . . We'll support the Saudis in every practical way short of engaging in combat.'[72] Hammond pledged 'political . . . logistical and technical support' to the GCC operation and noted that '[t]he UK has a strong relationship with the Saudi Air Force. We train the Saudi Air Force, a large part of which is equipped with British aircraft: Tornadoes and Typhoons and UK munitions.'[73] It later emerged that UK military personnel were present in the Coalition command room and had access to the list of bombing targets, at which point the government downplayed the UK role, emphasising that it was not directly involved in Saudi operations.[74]

According to figures compiled by Campaign Against Arms Trade, the UK government approved military export licences for Saudi Arabia with a total value of £4.6 billion between the start of the Coalition intervention in March 2015 and June 2017, £2.8 billion worth in the first six months of the intervention alone, compared with a figure of £102 million in the whole of the preceding year. The dramatic increase was not related to any major new arms contract being signed; rather, it was accounted for by the export of items for military aircraft, particularly during the height of the Coalition offensive in the early months of the intervention.[75] The Foreign Office minister Tobias Ellwood confirmed to Parliament that '[m]unitions are supplied to the Saudi Air Force under pre-existing contractual arrangements. UK companies are providing precision guided Paveway weapons. The Royal Saudi Air Force is flying British built aircraft in the campaign over Yemen.'[76] The 'Paveway weapons' referred to are 500 lb laser-guided bombs manufactured by the British arms company Raytheon UK. *The Independent* reported that, when Saudi stockpiles of these bombs began to run low in July 2015, the British government authorised Raytheon to rearrange its production schedule to prioritise replenishment of the Saudis' stocks ahead of an order for the British Royal Air Force.[77]

Two and a half years after the start of the Saudi-led intervention, the office of the UN High Commissioner for Human Rights reported 4,980 verified civilian deaths, including 1,120 children, although 'the actual total of casualties is likely to be higher.' Out of a population of 27.4 million people, 7.3 million were on the brink of famine, and an outbreak of cholera had seen more than 500,000 cases reported between April and June 2017 alone. Coalition air strikes were 'the leading cause of civilian casualties', while as a result of the actions of all parties, but principally as a result of a Coalition blockade, 'the health care system in Yemen has disintegrated. . . . The population . . . was increasingly impoverished, hungry, displaced, sick, injured and/or dying . . . [in] the largest humanitarian crisis in the world . . . [a] catastrophe [which] is entirely man made.'[78] The International Crisis Group described the humanitarian situation as 'a direct consequence of decisions by all belligerents to weaponise the economy, coupled with indifference and at times a facilitating role played by the international community, including key members of the Security Council such as the US, UK and France.'[79]

There is a widespread consensus among humanitarian and human rights NGOs that the Coalition is guilty of indiscriminate bombing, encompassing serious violations of international humanitarian law, which in some instances may amount to war crimes. In January 2016, a report by UN investigators leaked to *The Guardian* described a pattern of 'widespread and systematic' attacks on civilian targets, which included camps for internally displaced persons and refugees, civilian gatherings such as weddings, residential areas, medical facilities, schools, food storage warehouses, and other essential civilian infrastructure such as the airport in Sana'a and the port in Hudaydah. The report specifically documented 119 Coalition operations as violations of international humanitarian law.[80]

In October 2015, Amnesty International called on the US and the UK to cease arms transfers to the Coalition, following a report in which it had investigated and identified specific 'serious violations of international humanitarian law, including war crimes', and, more broadly, 'a clear pattern of serious violations . . . over a period of several months'. Amnesty concluded that Coalition bombing was responsible for the majority of civilian deaths in the conflict. Calls for an end to arms transfers from the UK also came from Human Rights Watch and Save the Children, which agreed that the Coalition was repeatedly using indiscriminate force.[81]

It should also be noted, given claims made by many British politicians that Saudi Arabia is an important ally in the field of counter-terrorism, that the situation in Yemen quickly became a substantial gift to groups that pose a security threat to the United Kingdom. A panel of experts reporting to the UN Security Council stated in January 2017 that 'Al-Qaida in the Arabian Peninsula (AQAP) and the Islamic State in Iraq and the Levant (ISIL) affiliate in Yemen are now actively exploiting the changing political environment and governance vacuums to recruit new members and stage new attacks and are laying the foundation for terrorist networks that may last for years.'[82] The panel concurred with Amnesty International that some Coalition air strikes 'may amount to war crimes'.[83]

In addition to pressure from prominent and respected elements within civil society, the British government came under considerable pressure from within Westminster. In September 2015 a dispute on the issue of Yemen between the parliamentary select committees that make up the joint Committee on Arms Export Controls resulted in the highly unusual instance of separate reports being published on the same topic. The business and international development committees produced a joint report calling for the suspension of arms sales to Saudi Arabia pending an investigation into their use, while the Foreign Affairs Committee issued a separate report endorsing the call for an investigation but not the call for a suspension of arms sales.[84] In October 2016 the Labour opposition in the House of Commons tabled a motion (which MPs ultimately voted down) calling on the government to 'suspend its support for the Saudi Arabia-led coalition forces in Yemen until it has been determined whether they have been responsible for any . . . violations [of international humanitarian law].'[85]

It later emerged that the senior civil servant in charge of the government body overseeing arms export controls had recommended in February 2016 that transfers to Saudi Arabia be suspended, given that the law forbade arms exports in cases where there was a 'clear risk' that the equipment might be used in serious violations of international humanitarian law.[86] The government's own official conclusion remained that no such 'clear risk' could be identified and so the arms transfers and support for Coalition operations could continue.[87]

Campaign Against Arms Trade (CAAT – on whose steering committee the present author currently sits) brought a judicial review against the government's decision to continue arming Saudi Arabia during the conflict. The high court ruled against CAAT in July 2017, stating that the government was 'rationally entitled to conclude' that the Coalition was committed to complying with international humanitarian law, and that ongoing UK–Saudi dialogue, plus the UK government's own sources of intelligence (which the judges regarded as superior to the information available to NGOs and the UN), allowed it to reasonably decide that the legal prohibition on arms exports had not been breached.[88]

In her analysis of the judgement, the academic specialist on arms sales Anna Stavrianakis argued that the high court had shown excessive 'deference . . . to the executive and to UK–Saudi relations', including 'uncritical affirmation of government expertise', and the taking of official statements 'at face value', coupled with the mistaken view that human rights NGOs had not investigated and reported from Yemen itself (as they had, with considerable bravery and professionalism).[89] As a result, the high court had provided 'a stamp of approval to an arms export policy that has directly contributed to the deaths of thousands of civilians in Yemen.'[90] Whatever the merits of the court's judgement, it sets an important precedent. The government and the customers of its arms export industry may take confidence that neither official export controls nor the courts will impede the flow of arms, even in cases such as those pertaining to Yemen. Given the circumstances, this sets a high bar for any future suspension or cessation of arms transfers and, as such, represents a considerable boost for London's relations with the Gulf Arab regimes.

Indeed, events in Yemen have not interrupted the strengthening of UK–Saudi military ties. In December 2016, Theresa May pledged to the GCC leaders 'over £3 billion of defence spending in the region over the next decade, spending more on defence in the Gulf than in any other region of the world',[91] while, in September 2017, the then defence secretary, Michael Fallon, signed a new Military and Security Cooperation Agreement with the Saudi government.[92] On a visit to the region in April 2017, May defended the UK's continuing support for the Coalition and pledged to raise 'the humanitarian issue' with the Saudis, arguing that 'rather than just standing on the sidelines and sniping, it's important to engage, to talk to people, to talk about our interests and to raise, yes, difficult issues when we feel it's necessary to do so.'[93] It is impossible to know whether such issues were indeed raised on the visit, or in what terms, but NGOs continued to document cases of apparently unlawful airstrikes as the humanitarian situation continued to deteriorate over the course of the following months.[94]

Overall, the Yemen episode illustrates the extent and depth of the Saudi military's dependence on the UK for support in wartime (military and diplomatic) and the strength of the British state's commitment to support the Saudi kingdom even in the face of considerable pressure and criticism, and in spite of a large volume of evidence that Coalition operations were responsible for extensive civilian casualties and humanitarian suffering. The pressure on the executive that came from within Westminster itself may lead us to conclude that under a different government a different policy might have been pursued, but this is impossible to know with certainty. On this latter point, it should be noted that both Labour and Conservative governments have been responsible for arms sales to the GCC states for several decades, in full awareness of how they could be and have been used. For example, in 2010, under Gordon Brown's Labour government, Amnesty International assessed that UK-supplied Tornado fighter jets were 'extremely likely' to have been used by Saudi forces during bombing raids on Yemen in 2009 that had left scores of Yemeni civilians dead, and demanded (to no avail) that such arms exports be suspended pending an investigation.[95]

Conclusions

The Arab uprisings and Whitehall's response to them has been a revealing episode in terms of the UK–GCC relationship. A pre-existing increase in the level of major arms transfers from Britain to the Gulf states, particularly Saudi Arabia, was not disturbed by the new challenge to those regimes' position and legitimacy represented by the various popular protests. Indeed, the post-2011 period coincided with a major arms export drive to the Gulf on the part of the 2010–15 Coalition government, which met with some success. A few arms export licences were revoked when news emerged of abuses, particularly with respect to the crackdown in Bahrain in spring 2011, but the overall picture, before and after, was of a steady, ongoing supply of the means of physical coercion to the various regimes, including Bahrain and Saudi Arabia. Whitehall's policy on arms export control effectively permitted this, while British diplomats adopted a narrative on events in Bahrain which essentially defended the government there and complemented monarchical efforts to maintain the status quo. This shows that the historical trends observed in chapter 1, namely Britain's commitment to the survival of the GCC monarchies and its treatment of any challenge to their authority as a strategic threat, have continued up until the present day.

It is particularly important to bear these historical dynamics in mind in light of the ongoing tendency, previously noted, to attribute the persistence of authoritarian rule in the Gulf to the culture and values of the region, as juxtaposed with the supposedly liberal, democratic values of the UK. These simple binaries cannot adequately explain a complex reality where thousands of people in Bahrain peacefully calling for constitutional democracy were met with a violent response from forces including those who had received arms and training from Britain. Gulf societies have been and continue to be sites of internal political contestation. Given its historical role, and more recent record, Britain can hardly approach the question of who has prevailed in these contests from a position of detached innocence.

British support for the Saudi-led Coalition during the war in Yemen is ongoing at the time of writing. However, on the basis of what evidence was available nearly three years after that intervention started, it was clear that the episode had shown the extent to which the Saudi military is dependent during wartime on the UK for munitions supply and other forms of practical military support, as well as diplomatic backing. The episode also demonstrated that the British state, in maintaining its commitment to support the Saudi kingdom in such circumstances, was prepared to withstand significant criticism from respected elements within civil society and from within Westminster itself, and to accept a high level of civilian casualties and humanitarian costs.

Phythian has argued that, '[r]ather than bringing influence, arms sales have made Britain dependent apologists for insecure governments', because 'the supplier's reaction to events involving a purchaser is taken as a gauge of the supplier's reliability – that most valued quality from the point of view of the purchaser.'[96] Following this logic, one might conclude that the British state and leading UK weapons manufacturers have supported and continued to arm the Gulf states during the post-2011 period because the UK is dependent upon the GCC states as arms purchasers, but this appears too narrow an interpretation. In fact, the relationship is one of interdependence rather than of UK dependence on its GCC customers, and, further-more, it is an interdependence in which the balance of power lies ultimately with the UK. Sir Alan Munro, British ambassador to Saudi Arabia from 1989 to 1993, recently told the Foreign Affairs Committee that, if arms sales to the kingdom were stopped or severely restricted,

> it would have a major impact on our broader relationship, it would have a major impact on our own defence manufacturing sector and it would have a major impact on the military com-petence of certain elements of the Saudi armed forces, notably their air force. Remember that it is also the training – engineering training, pilot training and so on – that comes, and has done ever since the late 1960s. . . . It is a treasured element in the minds of the Saudi military establishment. We are very important to them, and they are very important to us.[97]

Although the balance of power between the two sides in this inter-dependent relationship cannot ultimately be quantified or measured precisely, there is considerable reason to conclude that the balance of power lies in the UK's favour. Britain is one of five permanent mem-bers of the UN Security Council and one of an even smaller number of states with a real capacity both to project military power worldwide and to produce and provide long-term maintenance for the kind of major weapons systems with which the Gulf states wish to equip themselves. In terms of potential allies capable of adequately arming them and of coming directly to their defence, the Gulf monarchs have limited options, which narrow further when one considers the extent to which dependence on current allies and providers of major weapons systems can become hardwired (as Munro describes above).

Perhaps the most important difference is in the relative importance of the relationship to the two sides. Maintaining the alliance with Saudi Arabia in particular and the Gulf states in general is plainly crucial to Britain's continuing status as a global power, but, for a prosperous democracy in the global north, retaining that status, in the final analysis, is a choice, not a necessity. For monarchical regimes with questionable popular legitimacy and residing in a particularly unstable region, by contrast, remaining under a security umbrella provided by an international military power is a priority that carries rather more existential dimensions.

Conclusion

This book has attempted to map the deep underlying structures of UK relations with the Gulf Arab monarchies. Gulf hydrocarbons and the petrodollar riches that are generated by their production are important to the UK not only for narrow commercial reasons but also because they play a vital role in addressing some of Britain's specific and fundamental needs as a major capitalist power. London built its relationships with the GCC monarchies through a century and a half of imperial dominance of the Gulf region and another half-century of developing and maintaining those ties beyond the end of formal empire.

This book's analysis took as its starting point the view that today's international political economy is defined chiefly by its capitalist nature and by the leading role played by states such as the US, the UK, France and China. Within this global system, Britain seeks to maximise its state power and the opportunities for capital accumulation of its key industries and corporations.

The primary significance of the Gulf lies in its vast energy reserves, first because the stability of the global economy depends on the reliable flow of oil and gas from the region, second because control over those resources constitutes a major source of geostrategic power for any state or states interested in global hegemony, and third because the revenues generated by Gulf hydrocarbon production can be 'recycled' to the leading capitalist states in a number of advantageous ways.

London therefore seeks to support and complement the projection of US military power into the region, protect the Gulf monarchies from internal and external challenges, and maximise petrodollar recycling in various forms that benefit British capitalism and the UK's status as an international power, from capital inflows to the City of London to major arms purchases. Against this background, what have we learned about the specific ways in which, and the extent to which, Gulf wealth, Gulf oil and gas, and the survival of the Gulf Arab monarchies are important to British power in the modern era?

Britain is not directly energy-dependent on the Gulf, although disruptions in the region's hydrocarbon exports would have a damaging indirect effect on the UK economy. There is a 'dual logic' shaping British and American energy strategies relating to security of Gulf energy flows and US control over them, based on the increasing importance of Gulf oil and gas in meeting global demand and on the growing dependence of emerging Asian powers – China in particular – on Gulf energy imports. The UK also has a major commercial interest in Gulf hydrocarbons given that two of its largest corporations – BP and Shell – are among the leading international energy firms. The Gulf has always been important to those firms, and is becoming increasingly so. While they have had to absorb some setbacks in recent years, they have also enjoyed notable successes and remain in a fairly strong position in a region that, overall, remains economically dependent on energy production.

Gulf petrodollars recycled through UK–GCC trade and investment play an important role in addressing the key macroeconomic challenges facing the British economy and in maintaining Britain's status as a leading capitalist power. This has been particularly true in the period following the sharp rise in oil prices around the turn of the millennium. The region has become a key export market relative to others in the developing world. UK-based banks were more successful in attracting Gulf capital than those in other financial centres, and those inflows were highly significant by the standards of the global south, if not the global north. The Gulf bailout of Barclays Bank in 2008 demonstrated that GCC capital could play a highly significant stabilising role in certain circumstances.

Perhaps the most important role played by Gulf capital, especially Saudi petrodollars, is in financing Britain's large current account deficit, thus also indirectly helping to maintain the status of the pound sterling. In this regard, these net capital inflows are significant compared with those from any other source, whether in the developing or the developed world.

British arms exports to the GCC states help the UK to maintain the military-industrial capacity required as the basis for global power projection. Exports to the rest of the world are in steady long-term decline while those to the Gulf market have steadily risen in parallel. When questions of corruption have arisen over these arms deals, Whitehall has gone to considerable lengths to avoid formal scrutiny, going so far as to defy the wishes of Washington and some major City investors in the process.

British commitments to the protection of the Gulf monarchies, while plainly of less significance than those of the US, are nonetheless wide-ranging, extensive and multi-layered. The UK's continuing support for Bahrain in the wake of its violent crackdown on pro-democracy demonstrations in 2011 amounted to a major strategic vote of confidence in the Al Khalifa monarchy, just as the wider deepening of military ties with the GCC states against the background of the Arab uprisings was a clear expression of support for the conservative regional order.

Meanwhile, the large-scale material and practical assistance London provided to the Saudi-led military intervention in Yemen – despite numerous credible reports of indiscriminate bombing, the unfolding of a major humanitarian disaster, and considerable consequent pressure on the British government to suspend arms sales – demonstrated both the extent of Whitehall's commitment to military cooperation with the Saudis and the extent of the latter's dependence on the UK (not only the US) in wartime.

This complex and multidimensional Anglo-Arabian relationship therefore holds great significance for British capitalism and British foreign relations. It is strategically significant in respect of oil and gas, economically significant in terms of petrodollar recycling, and militarily significant in sustaining the UK's arms industry. Anglo-Arabian relations are also of real consequence to those who find themselves on the wrong side of this nexus of power and interests, from pro-democracy dissidents in Bahrain to civilians caught in the ravages of the war in Yemen.

Some wider lessons

From these specific findings we can draw a few broader conclusions about the balance and nature of power relations between the two sides. As noted previously, this can be characterised as asymmetrical interdependence, whereby both sides rely on each other to some extent and have a degree of bargaining power within the relationship but where one side is stronger on balance than the other.

The states of the GCC are highly important to Britain's global power and status in all the various respects mentioned above. However, the UK is also highly important to these monarchical regimes in several ways. Britain is part of a small group of second-tier global powers (far behind the US) alongside Germany, France, Russia and (for now) China. The Gulf states are not in, and indeed are nowhere near, this category, whether judged by their military power (for which they depend entirely on the US, the UK and France) or by their level and quality of economic development (as distinct from sheer wealth). The UK by contrast is one of five permanent members of the UN Security Council, one of a small club of nuclear-armed states, one of a tiny handful of the world's nations capable of projecting military power internationally, and home to a world-leading financial centre and to some of the largest multinational corporations in the world. Britain's relative status has been sharply reduced by the recent loss of empire, and there is little evidence that Brexit will do anything other than erode that status further. But it remains far more powerful and wealthy than the vast majority of the world's nations.

While the significance of the US role in arming and defending the Gulf states is unrivalled, Britain's role is also important, and behind Britain the Gulf states do not have a large number of alternative options in terms of major states credibly capable of committing to ensuring their survival and sustaining such commitments in the long term. In addition, as the Yemen conflict has shown, British arms contracts with the Saudis involve extensive ongoing support, indicating a degree of Saudi dependence on the UK in a highly integrated relationship that cannot be easily disentangled.

On the economic side, the City of London's capacity productively to process and reinvest Gulf petrodollars is world-leading. States with large current account surpluses are in need of financial services, just as states dependent on oil and gas exports are also dependent on the secure flow of those exports at a broadly stable price if they are to retain the confidence of their customers. In addition, while the Gulf is not a significant destination for British FDI, Britain is a significant source of FDI for the Gulf, at a time when such investment is being sought as part of regional governments' plans for diversification away from reliance on oil and gas exports.

When evaluating the extent to which each side needs the other in the relationship, we should also consider what each side needs the other for. London needs to support American domination of the Gulf as part of its commitment to supporting US global hegemony, but this commitment is ultimately a choice. London needs the GCC states to spend their petrodollars on major arms purchases to sustain its domestic military industry, but only because it has chosen to attempt to preserve its status as an international military power. The social wellbeing of the British population is not necessarily dependent on London retaining this status (many prosperous societies manage very well without it).[1] In economic terms, Britain needs Gulf capital inflows to help finance its current account deficit, but that deficit is in no small part the product of a choice to balance the UK economy away from visible exports and towards financial services as part of the move to neoliberalism in the 1980s.

By contrast, the Gulf monarchies' need for support from the leading capitalist powers is of a more existential nature. The United States is their main protector, but the UK's complementary role and its own state-to-state defence agreements with the Gulf states are not insignificant. Seeking such protection, for monarchical governments with uncertain levels of domestic legitimacy and support, is less of a choice and more of a necessity.

For the UK, while the difficulty of effecting a departure from long-established geopolitical and economic strategies should certainly not be underplayed, it remains the case that Britain's close relationship with the Gulf states is based on a series of choices, each of which have possible alternatives. To give some examples, Britain could choose to swap its support for Washington's global hegemony for a more neutral and peaceful position. It could abandon attempts to maintain a capacity for international power projection, restrict its military posture to direct self-defence, and recalibrate its high-technology manufacturing base away from arms production. This could involve increased focus on the development of renewable energy technology, which in turn could help lower the importance of imported oil and gas in the UK's energy consumption mix. A government commitment to strengthening British industry along these lines could provide a boost to visible exports, narrow the current account deficit, and reduce the dependence on capital inflows from abroad.

The difficulty of making such changes should not be underplayed, but nor should it be overstated. The desirability of making such changes can be debated as well, but, in terms of analysing the balance of power in the UK–GCC relationship, this is in a way beside the point. The point is that the nature of these questions is *qualitatively different* from those facing the Gulf monarchs when they contemplate their relations with the UK, the US and France. Gulf wealth matters to British power and the maintenance of a specific economic model. The question for Britain is whether it can ensure its national prosperity with a different economic model and without wielding global power in the way that it is used to. The question for the Gulf monarchies, by contrast, is how best to ensure their *survival* into the twenty-first century. UK–GCC relations are characterised by asymmetric interdependence in many senses, but the asymmetry lies in this context perhaps above all.

To the extent that the relationship between the UK and the GCC states is one of asymmetrical interdependence, with the balance of power falling broadly on the British side, and to the extent that the basis of the relationship on the British side is a set of strategic choices that are open to reasonable contestation, this then has implications in terms of Britain's responsibility for the consequences of its decision to support the Gulf monarchies. It would plainly be excessive to assert that, were it not for Britain's 200-year-long involvement in the area, the Arab Gulf region would now be democratic, with human rights protected by law and respected by governments. This would be to obscure the variety of domestic forces that have competed for power in the Gulf historically and the more significant role of the United States in supporting the regional monarchies in recent decades. One cannot assert with any confidence what alternative historical outcome there might have been had British imperialism not been part of the causal mix. However, while we cannot engage substantively with a speculative counterfactual, we can document Britain's actual record of responsibility.

Britain has consistently provided material support to the autocratic rulers of the Gulf, including arms and training for internal security forces with an extensive record of human rights violations, such as the violent suppression of democratic activists and movements. It has been a significant external provider of these forms of assistance to all the Gulf Arab monarchies from their creation and was the leading such provider to all Gulf states except Saudi Arabia through the majority of the twentieth century. Throughout those crucial years of state formation, British imperial power weighed consistently on the side of monarchical rule, including (and especially) when that rule was contested by popular forces. London reaffirmed its strategic commitment to the support of these monarchies in more recent years, notwithstanding the violent repression of pro-democracy protests in 2011, particularly in Bahrain, and the ongoing repression and abuse of dissidents throughout the GCC region.

On the economic side, Britain has taken a leading role in providing financial services to Gulf elites that have often run their nations' finances in a way that resembles a family business. Britain's priority has been to ensure that Gulf petrodollars flow in its direction, in so far as is possible, while also strengthening monarchical rule. Any support for reform – economic or political – appears to have been aimed principally at buttressing the conservative regional order.

The question of whether British support has been decisive in maintaining the rule of the various royal families of the GCC states is beyond the scope of this book. For now, it can at least be said that the marginal effect of British support for the Gulf monarchs over the past two centuries, up to and including the present era, has been a significant factor in their survival. That being the case, the persistence of authoritarianism in the region should be understood not by simplistic reference to cultural differences but, rather, as the current product of ongoing processes of socio-political contestation and change in which British power has played an important role on the side of the regional elites.

Britain faces many formidable challenges as it approaches the third decade of the twenty-first century, from the threat of climate change to the difficulties of Brexit and the dysfunctionalities of its present economic model. As this book has hopefully demonstrated – particularly with regard to the ongoing humanitarian catastrophe in Yemen – the relationship between the UK and the Gulf Arab monarchies is also a matter that urgently demands the attention of scholarship, the media and civil society. In addition, looking closely at Anglo-Arabian relations can help us to answer larger questions concerning the nature of British power and British capitalism and their role and position in the modern world.

Notes

Introduction

1 E. W. Said, *Orientalism* (4th edn, London: Penguin, 2003).

2 Foreign Affairs Committee (House of Commons), *The UK's Relations with Saudi Arabia and Bahrain: Fifth Report of Session 2013–14*, Vol. 1: *Report, together with Formal Minutes, Oral and Written Evidence*, HC 88 (London: The Stationery Office, 2013), Ev 80.

3 Ibid., Ev 48.

4 House of Commons, Business, Innovation and Skills and International Development Committees, *The Use of UK-Manufactured Arms in Yemen: Fifth Report of the Business, Innovation and Skills Committee of Session 2016–17, Third Report of the International Development Committee of Session 2016–17: Report, together with Formal Minutes Relating to the Report*, HC 679 (London: The Stationery Office, 2016), p. 23.

5 Amnesty International, 'Saudi Arabia: first human rights defenders sentenced under leadership of "reformer" Crown Prince Mohammad Bin Salman', 25 January 2018, www.amnesty.org/en/latest/news/2018/01/saudi-arabia-first-human-rights-defenders-sentenced-under-leadership-of-reformer-crown-prince-mohammad-bin-salman/; Amnesty International, 'Bahrain: human rights activist who tore up photo imprisoned', 14 March 2016, www.amnesty.org/en/press-releases/2016/03/bahrain-human-rights-activist-who-tore-up-photo-imprisoned/; Amnesty International, 'Saudi Arabia: release blogger Raif Badawi, still behind bars after five years', 16 June 2017, www.amnesty.org/en/latest/news/2017/06/saudi-arabia-release-blogger-raif-badawi-still-behind

-bars-after-five-years/; S. Alwadaei, 'We are human rights defenders, but Bahrain says we're terrorists', *The Guardian*, 9 February 2015, www.theguardian.com/commentisfree/2015/feb/09/human-rights-defenders-bahrain-says-terrorists.

6 R. Hinnebusch, 'The Middle East in the world hierarchy: imperialism and resistance', *Journal of International Relations and Development*, 14 (2011): 213–46.

7 Ibid., p. 215.

8 For an elaboration of this argument, see D. Wearing, 'Critical perspectives on the concept of the "national interest": American imperialism, British foreign policy and the Middle East', in T. Edmunds, J. Gaskarth and R. Porter, eds, *British Foreign Policy and the National Interest* (Basingstoke: Palgrave Macmillan, 2014), pp 102–19.

9 For a UK-specific analysis, see R. Miliband, *The State in Capitalist Society* (London: Quartet, 1969) and *Capitalist Democracy in Britain* (Oxford: Oxford University Press, 1982).

10 B. Jessop, *The State: Past, Present, Future* (Cambridge: Polity, 2016), pp. 101, 210.

11 Ibid., pp. 192, 195.

12 Ibid., pp. 198, 193, 209.

13 G. Achcar, *The People Want: A Radical Exploration of the Arab Uprising* (London: Saqi Books, 2013), pp. 103–6.

14 M. Curtis, *Web of Deceit: Britain's Real Role in the World* (London: Vintage, 2003), pp. 101–19, 180–206.

Chapter 1 Empire's Legacy

1 R. Hollis, *Britain and the Middle East in the 9/11 Era* (Chichester: Wiley Blackwell, 2010), pp. 6–7.

2 J. B. Kelly, *Britain and the Persian Gulf, 1795–1880* (2nd edn, Oxford: Clarendon Press, 1968), pp. 62–3.

3 D. Holden, 'The Persian Gulf: after the British Raj', *Foreign Affairs*, 49/4 (1971): 721; J. Onley, 'Britain's informal empire in the Gulf, 1820–1971', *Journal of Social Affairs*, 22/87 (2005): 39–40.

4 P. Sluglett, 'Formal and informal empire in the Middle East', in R. W. Winks, ed., *The Oxford History of the British Empire*, Vol. V: *Historiography* (Oxford: Oxford University Press, 1999), pp. 417–18.

5 Onley, 'Britain's informal empire', p. 42.

6 Kelly, *Britain and the Persian Gulf*, pp. 358, 367, 407.

7 Ibid., pp. 825–6, 834–6; B. C. Busch, *Britain and the Persian Gulf, 1894–1914* (Cambridge: Cambridge University Press, 1967), pp. 27, 346, 369.

8 Busch, *Britain and the Persian Gulf*, p. 6.

9 M. Kent, *Moguls and Mandarins: Oil, Imperialism and the Middle East in British Foreign Policy, 1900–1940* (London: Frank Cass, 1993), p. 11.

10 R. Adelson, *London and the Invention of the Middle East: Money, Power and War, 1902–1922* (London: Yale University Press, 1995), p. 7.

11 Kent, *Moguls and Mandarins*, pp. 34–59; A. Sampson, *The Seven Sisters: The Great Oil Companies and the World They Shaped* (London: Hodder & Stoughton, 1975), p. 72.

12 Kent, *Moguls and Mandarins*, p. 10; Adelson, *London and the Invention of the Middle East*, p. 103; G. Balfour-Paul, 'Britain's informal empire in the Middle East', in J. M. Brown and W. R. Louis, eds, *The Oxford History of the British Empire*, Vol. IV: *The Twentieth Century* (Oxford: Oxford University Press, 2001), pp. 494, 496; Busch, *Britain and the Persian Gulf*, p. 383.

13 W. L. Cleveland and M. Bunton, *A History of the Modern Middle East* (Boulder, CO: Westview Press, 2009), pp. 149–73, 193–271.

14 J. Darwin, *The Empire Project: The Rise and Fall of the British World System, 1830–1970* (Cambridge: Cambridge University Press, 2009), p. 470.

15 Adelson, *London and the Invention of the Middle East*, pp. 183, 212–13; Sampson, *The Seven Sisters*, p. 77.

16 G. Troeller, *The Birth of Saudi Arabia: Britain and the Rise of the House of Sa'ud* (London: Frank Cass, 1976), p. 13.

17 Ibid., pp. 65, 75–6; J. Goldberg, 'The origins of British–Saudi

relations: the 1915 Anglo-Saudi treaty revisited', *Historical Journal*, 28/3 (1985): 703.

18 Troeller, *The Birth of Saudi Arabia*, pp. 216–31, 236; D. Silverfarb, 'Great Britain, Iraq, and Saudi Arabia: The Revolt of the Ikhwan, 1927–1930', *International History Review*, 4/2 (1982): 222; J. R. Macris, *The Politics and Security of the Gulf: Anglo-American Hegemony and the Shaping of a Region* (Abingdon: Routledge, 2010), p. 27.

19 F. Halliday, *Arabia without Sultans* (2nd edn, London: Saqi Books, 2001), p. 51.

20 Macris, *The Politics and Security of the Gulf*, p. 33; D. Silverfarb, 'Britain and Saudi Arabia on the eve of the Second World War', *Middle Eastern Studies*, 19/4 (1983): 403–7; D. Yergin, *The Prize: The Epic Quest for Oil, Money, and Power* (New York: Touchstone, 1992), pp. 334–50.

21 Onley, 'Britain's informal empire', p. 38; O. Almog, *Britain, Israel and the United States, 1955–1958: Beyond Suez* (London: Frank Cass, 2005), pp. 7–8.

22 Yergin, *The Prize*, pp. 204–5, 410, 413–19.

23 M. Curtis, *The Great Deception: Anglo-American Power and World Order* (London: Pluto Press, 1998), p. 25.

24 N. J. White, 'Reconstructing Europe through rejuvenating empire: the British, French and Dutch experiences compared', *Past and Present*, 210: suppl. 6 (2011): 214–19.

25 Curtis, *The Great Deception*, p. 18.

26 M. Curtis, *Secret Affairs* (London: Serpent's Tail, 2010), p. 27.

27 Almog, *Britain, Israel and the United States, 1955–1958*, pp. 13–14.

28 Darwin, *The Empire Project*, pp. 536, 555.

29 M. Sedgwick, 'Britain and the Middle East: In Pursuit of Eternal Interests', in J. Covarrubias and T. Lansford, eds, *Strategic Interests in the Middle East* (Aldershot: Ashgate, 2007), p. 6.

30 Macris, *The Politics and Security of the Gulf*, p. 91; W. R. Louis, 'The British withdrawal from the Gulf', *Journal of Imperial and Commonwealth History*, 31/1 (2003): I am grateful to the

anonymous academic reviewer of the manuscript for this book for encouraging me to emphasise the crucial point about the loss of the Indian empire.

31 Curtis, *The Great Deception*, pp. 20, 119.
32 Sampson, *The Seven Sisters*, p. 167; U. Rabi, 'Britain's "special position" in the Gulf: its origins, dynamics and legacy', *Middle Eastern Studies*, 42/3 (2006): 356.
33 Sampson, *The Seven Sisters*, p. 61.
34 Almog, *Britain, Israel and the United States, 1955–1958*, p. 3.
35 S. G. Galpern, *Money, Oil and Empire in the Middle East: Sterling and Postwar Imperialism, 1944–1971* (Cambridge: Cambridge University Press, 2009).
36 Ibid., pp. 16, 72; Sampson, *The Seven Sisters*, p. 151.
37 Adelson, *London and the Invention of the Middle East*, p. 72.
38 A. Anievas, 'The international political economy of appeasement: the social sources of British foreign policy during the 1930s', *Review of International Studies*, 37/2 (2011): 608.
39 P. J. Cain and A. G. Hopkins, *British Imperialism,1688–2000* (2nd edn, London: Pearson Education, 2002), pp. 43–63, 619–22.
40 Ibid., p. 619.
41 Adelson, *London and the Invention of the Middle East*, p. 6.
42 A. Hourani, 'The decline of the West in the Middle East – I', *International Affairs*, 29/1 (1953): 22, 30.
43 A. Hourani, 'The decline of the West in the Middle East – II', *International Affairs*, 29/2 (1953): 156.
44 Hourani, 'The decline of the West in the Middle East – I', p. 30.
45 Rabi, 'Britain's "special position" in the Gulf', p. 356.
46 Anievas, 'The international political economy of appeasement', pp. 605, 616.
47 M. Curtis, *Web of Deceit: Britain's Real Role in the World* (London: Vintage, 2003), pp. 237–8, 256–7.
48 Almog, *Britain, Israel and the United States, 1955*–1958, p. 8; Darwin, *The Empire Project*, p. 557.
49 Galpern, *Money, Oil and Empire in the Middle East*, pp. 81–2, 106–8; T. T. Petersen, 'Review article: transfer of power in the

Middle East', *International History Review*, 19/4 (1997): 854; Curtis, *Web of Deceit*, p. 306; Sampson, *The Seven Sisters*, p. 135.

50 Curtis, *Web of Deceit*, p. 312.

51 Curtis, *Web of Deceit*, pp. 303-15; Galpern, *Money, Oil and Empire in the Middle East*, pp. 131, 138.

52 T. T. Petersen, 'Anglo-American rivalry in the Middle East: the struggle for the Buraimi oasis, 1952-1957', *International History Review*, 14/1 (1992); Petersen, 'Review article: transfer of power in the Middle East'; Balfour-Paul, 'Britain's informal empire in the Middle East', p. 511.

53 Darwin, *The Empire Project*, pp. 597-602.

54 Galpern, *Money, Oil and Empire in the Middle East*, pp. 142, 148-9, 167.

55 Ibid., pp. 144-5, 158.

56 Darwin, *The Empire Project*, p. 603; A. von Tunzelmann, *Blood and Sand: Suez, Hungary and the Crisis That Shook the World* (London: Simon & Schuster, 2016).

57 Von Tunzelmann, *Blood and Sand*, p. 369.

58 Petersen, 'Review article: transfer of power in the Middle East', pp. 864-5.

59 Macris, *The Politics and Security of the Gulf*, pp. 108-12.

60 Ibid., p. 125.

61 Ibid., pp. 130-9.

62 Halliday, *Arabia without Sultans*, pp. 59-61.

63 Curtis, *Secret Affairs*, pp. 86-7.

64 Macris, *The Politics and Security of the Gulf*, pp. 122-3.

65 Galpern, *Money, Oil and Empire in the Middle East*, pp. 260-1, 230.

66 Rabi, 'Britain's "special position" in the Gulf', p. 359.

67 Macris, *The Politics and Security of the Gulf*, pp. 127, 129.

68 Curtis, *Web of Deceit*, pp. 271-6; C. Tripp, *A History of Iraq* (3rd edn, Cambridge: Cambridge University Press, 2007), p. 160.

69 A. Hanieh, *Lineages of Revolt: Issues of Contemporary Capitalism in the Middle East* (Chicago: Haymarket Books, 2013), pp. 24, 27.

70 Rabi, 'Britain's "special position" in the Gulf', p. 357.

71 Curtis, *The Great Deception*, p. 147.

72 H. von Bismarck, "'A watershed in our relations with the Trucial States": Great Britain's policy to prevent the opening of an Arab League Office in the Persian Gulf in 1965', *Middle Eastern Studies*, 47/1 (2011).

73 Sluglett, 'Formal and informal empire in the Middle East', p. 434.

74 Halliday, *Arabia without Sultans*, p. 456; Darwin, *The Empire Project*, pp. 643–4.

75 Galpern, *Money, Oil and Empire in the Middle East*, pp. 255, 268–71, 280.

76 Ibid., pp. 274–6.

77 Louis, 'The British withdrawal from the Gulf', pp. 92–3; Macris, *The Politics and Security of the Gulf*, pp. 157–8.

78 Louis, 'The British withdrawal from the Gulf', pp. 96–102.

79 Ibid., p. 91.

80 Macris, *The Politics and Security of the Gulf*, pp. 172–5.

81 Curtis, *Secret Affairs*, p. 95.

82 Louis, 'The British withdrawal from the Gulf', pp. 101–2; Curtis, *The Great Deception*, pp. 127, 267.

83 Curtis, *The Great Deception*, p. 144; D. Commins, *The Gulf States: A Modern History* (London: I. B. Tauris, 2012), p. 209; Macris, *The Politics and Security of the Gulf*, p. 197.

84 Curtis, *Secret Affairs*, p. 120.

85 A. Parsons, 'The Middle East', in P. Byrd, ed., *British Foreign Policy under Thatcher* (Oxford: Philip Allan, 1988), pp. 83–4.

86 Curtis, *Web of Deceit*, pp. 267–8.

87 Commins, *The Gulf States*, pp. 212–14.

88 A. R. Takriti, *Monsoon Revolution: Republicans, Sultans and Empires in Oman, 1965–1976* (Oxford: Oxford University Press, 2013), pp. 171–81; Halliday, *Arabia without Sultans*, p. 333; Macris, *The Politics and Security of the Gulf*, pp. 167–9; Curtis, *The Great Deception*, p. 166.

89 Halliday, *Arabia without Sultans*, p. 345.

90 Ibid., pp. 313, 317, 322, 330–2, 345–6.

91 Ibid., pp. 327, 343, 351.

92 Commins, *The Gulf States*, pp. 204–5.

93 Sampson, *The Seven Sisters*, p. 174; Commins, *The Gulf States*, p. 200; Halliday, *Arabia without Sultans*, p. 408.

94 Sampson, *The Seven Sisters*, pp. 265, 271; Halliday, *Arabia without Sultans*, p. 395; Curtis, *Secret Affairs*, p. 114.

95 Halliday, *Arabia without Sultans*, pp. 72–3; Curtis, *Secret Affairs*, p. 115.

96 Commins, *The Gulf States*, p. 202.

97 Curtis, *Secret Affairs*, p. 115.

98 Ibid., p. 118; Parsons, 'The Middle East', pp. 81–3.

99 Sampson, *The Seven Sisters*, pp. 289, 318, 331.

100 Parsons, 'The Middle East', p. 83; Hollis, *Britain and the Middle East in the 9/11 Era*, p. 24.

101 Commins, *The Gulf States*, p. 198; Macris, *The Politics and Security of the Gulf*, pp. 205–19.

102 Curtis, *The Great Deception*, p. 155; G. Nonneman, 'Constants and variations in Gulf–British relations', in J. A. Kechichian, ed., *Iran, Iraq and the Arab Gulf States* (Basingstoke: Palgrave, 2001), pp. 329, 346.

103 M. Phythian, *The Politics of British Arms Sales since 1964* (Manchester: Manchester University Press, 2000), pp. 20–7, 218–26; Parsons, 'The Middle East', p. 83.

104 N. Gilby, *Deception in High Places: A History of Bribery in Britain's Arms Trade* (London: Pluto Press, 2014), p. 134.

105 Hollis, *Britain and the Middle East in the 9/11 Era*, pp. 168–9, 171.

106 Nonneman, 'Constants and variations in Gulf–British relations', pp. 333–4.

107 Curtis, *The Great Deception*, pp. 161, 201.

108 Macris, *The Politics and Security of the Gulf*, pp. 212–13.

109 Commins, *The Gulf States*, pp. 234–9.

110 Parsons, 'The Middle East', p. 83; J. Hippler, 'NATO goes to the Persian Gulf', *Middle East Report*, 155 (1988): 18–21; Curtis, *Web of Deceit*, pp. 33–6, 187.

111 R. Hollis, 'At stake in the Iraqi invasion of Kuwait: borders, oil and money', *RUSI Journal*, 135/4 (1990): 17–24.

112 Nonneman, 'Constants and variations in Gulf–British relations', p. 345.
113 Curtis, *Secret Affairs*, p. 174.
114 Commins, *The Gulf States*, p. 247; Macris, *The Politics and Security of the Gulf*, p. 228.

Chapter 2 Oil and Gas

1 Yergin, *The Prize: The Epic Quest for Oil, Money, and Power* (New York: Touchstone, 1992), pp. 652, 665.
2 Ibid., pp. 685, 702, 713–14.
3 G. Bridge and P. Le Billion, *Oil* (Cambridge: Polity, 2013), p. 15.
4 P. Stevens, 'National oil companies and international oil companies in the Middle East: under the shadow of government and the resource nationalism cycle', *Journal of World Energy Law and Business*, 1/1 (2008): 21.
5 J. Carter, 'State of the Union Address', 23 January 1980, www.jimmycarterlibrary.gov/research/selected_speeches.
6 Foreign Affairs Committee (House of Commons), *The Middle East after the Gulf War: Third Report of Session 1990–91*, HC 143-I (London: The Stationery Office, 1991), p. xxvi.
7 G. Muttitt, *Fuel on the Fire: Oil and Politics in Occupied Iraq* (London: Vintage, 2012), p. 23; D. Stokes and S. Raphael, *Global Energy Security and American Hegemony* (Baltimore: Johns Hopkins University Press, 2010), p. 92.
8 US Energy Information Administration, 'Country analysis brief: United Kingdom', 9 March 2016.
9 P. Bolton, *Energy Imports and Exports*, House of Commons Library, 30 August 2013, http://researchbriefings.parliament.uk/ResearchBriefing/Summary/SN04046.
10 Department of Energy and Climate Change, 'Crude oil and petroleum products: imports by product 1920 to 2014', 30 July 2015, www.gov.uk/government/statistical-data-sets/crude-oil-and-petroleum-products-imports-by-product-1920-to-2011.

11 US Energy Information Administration, 'County analysis brief: United Kindgdom', 9 March 2016.

12 Ibid.

13 *BP Statistical Review of World Energy*, 2002, pp. 7, 22; *BP Statistical Review of World Energy*, 2016, pp. 8, 22.

14 E. R. Wald, 'Venezuela is drowning in its own oil', *Forbes*, 11 August 2016, www.forbes.com/sites/ellenrwald/2016/08/11/ven ezuela-is-drowning-in-its-own-oil/#32b4caef7da9.

15 US Energy Information Administration, 'Energy and financial markets: what drives crude oil prices', www.eia.gov/finance/ markets/crudeoil/supply-opec.php.

16 Bridge and Le Billion, *Oil*, p. 42; D. Yergin, *The Quest: Energy, Security and the Remaking of the Modern World* (London: Allen Lane, 2011), p. 287.

17 A. Evans-Pritchard, 'Texas shale oil has fought Saudi Arabia to a standstill', *Daily Telegraph*, 31 July 2016.

18 *BP Statistical Review of World Energy*, 2016.

19 Ibid.

20 US Energy Information Administration, 'World oil transit choke-points', 10 November 2014.

21 International Energy Agency, 'World energy outlook 2015 fact sheet: global energy trends to 2040', 2015, www.worldenergyout-look.org/media/weowebsite/2015/WEO2015_Factsheets.pdf.

22 US Energy Information Administration, 'International energy out-look 2016', May 2016.

23 Yergin, *The Quest*, pp. 340–1.

24 A. Goldthau, 'Challenges in global oil governance', in R. E. Looney, ed., *Handbook of Oil Politics* (London: Routledge, 2012), pp. 354–5.

25 Yergin, *The Quest*, pp. 770, 162, 173.

26 M. Klare, *Rising Powers, Shrinking Planet: How Scarce Energy is Creating a New World Order* (Oxford: Oneworld, 2008), p. 14; Bridge and Le Billion, *Oil*, pp. 5, 10–12.

27 US Energy Information Administration, 'Country analysis brief: China', 14 May 2015.

28 US Energy Information Administration, 'Country analysis brief: Saudi Arabia', 10 September 2014; 'Country analysis brief: Kuwait', 24 October 2014; 'Country analysis brief: Qatar', 20 October 2015; 'Country analysis brief: UAE', 18 May 2015.

29 Stokes and Raphael, *Global Energy Security and American Hegemony*, pp. 16–17.

30 Ibid., p. 40.

31 Ibid., p. 44.

32 Ibid., pp. 1–2.

33 Ibid., pp. 16–17, 19.

34 A. Zinni, 'Avoid a military showdown with Iraq', *Middle East Quarterly*, 5/3 (1998): 57–65.

35 K. Pollack, 'Securing the Gulf', *Foreign Affairs*, 82/4 (2003): 3–4.

36 Ibid., pp. 4, 8.

37 North Atlantic Council, 'Bucharest Summit declaration', 3 April 2008, www.nato.int/cps/en/natolive/official_texts_8443.htm.

38 H. R. Clinton, 'Remarks at the NATO strategic concept seminar', US State Department, 22 February 2010, https://2009-2017.state.gov/secretary/20092013clinton/rm/2010/02/137118.htm.

39 'Kissinger warns of energy conflict', *Financial Times*, 2 June 2005.

40 National Intelligence Council, *Mapping the Global Future*, December 2004, www.futurebrief.com/project2020.pdf.

41 Z. Khalilzad, 'The United States and the Persian Gulf: preventing regional hegemony', *Survival*, 37/2 (1995): 95–6.

42 Pollack, 'Securing the Gulf', p. 4.

43 J. Straw, 'Strategic priorities for British foreign policy', *The Guardian*, 6 January 2003, www.theguardian.com/politics/2003/jan/06/foreignpolicy.uk1.

44 Department for Trade and Industry, *Our Energy Future – Creating a Low Carbon Economy*, Cm 5761 (London: The Stationery Office, 2003), p. 83, http://webarchive.nationalarchives.gov.uk/+/http:/www.berr.gov.uk/files/file10719.pdf.

45 'Private Secretary to C', 'Letter from Richard Dearlove's private secretary to Sir David Manning', April 2011, www.iraqinquiry.

org.uk/media/173629/2001-12-03-Letter-Dearloves-Private-Sec retary-to-Manning-Iraq-attaching-SIS4-papers.pdf.

46 HM Government, *A Strong Britain in an Age of Uncertainty: The National Security Strategy*, Cm 7953 (London: The Stationery Office, 2010), www.gov.uk/government/uploads/system/uploads /attachment_data/file/61936/national-security-strategy.pdf.

47 Foreign Affairs Committee (House of Commons), *The UK's Relations with Saudi Arabia and Bahrain, Fifth Report of Session 2013–14: Report, together with Formal Minutes, Oral and Written Evidence*, HC 88 (London: The Stationery Office, 2013).

48 Ibid., Ev 133–4.

49 Foreign Affairs Committee (House of Commons), *British Foreign Policy and the 'Arab Spring', Second Report of Session 2012–13: Report, together with Formal Minutes, Oral and Written Evidence*, HC 80 (London: The Stationery Office, 2012), Ev 63.

50 Foreign Affairs Committee, *The UK's Relations with Saudi Arabia and Bahrain*, p. 19.

51 Ibid., Ev 136.

52 Ibid., Ev 138.

53 Ibid., p. 70.

54 G. Brown, 'Lord mayor's banquet speech', 12 November 2007, http://webarchive.nationalarchives.gov.uk/+/http:/www. number10.gov.uk/Page13736.

55 Cabinet Office, *The National Security Strategy of the United Kingdom – Security in an Interdependent World*, Cm 7291 (London: The Stationery Office, 2008), pp. 19, 44.

56 HM Government, *A Strong Britain in an Age of Uncertainty*, p. 18.

57 Klare, *Rising Powers, Shrinking Planet*, pp. 182–92; Stokes and Raphael, *Global Energy Security and American Hegemony*, p. 2.

58 Yergin, *The Quest*, p. 322.

59 G. Achcar, *Eastern Cauldron: Islam, Afghanistan, Palestine and Iraq in a Marxist Mirror* (London: Pluto Press, 2004).

60 FCO Iraq Policy Unit, 'UK energy strategy for Iraq', September 2004, cited in Muttitt, *Fuel on the Fire*, p. 34.

61 Royal Dutch Shell, *Annual Report and Form 20-F 2015*, p. 13, http://reports.shell.com/annual-report/2015/.

62 BP, *Annual Report and Form 20-F 2015*, p. ii, www.bp.com/content/dam/bp/pdf/investors/bp-annual-report-and-form-20f-2015.pdf.

63 P. Stevens, *International Oil Companies: The Death of the Old Business Model* (London: Royal Institute for International Affairs, 2016), pp. 4, 12.

64 Bridge and Le Billion, *Oil*, p. 54; Klare, *Rising Powers, Shrinking Planet*, p. 19.

65 Stevens, *International Oil Companies*, p. 21.

66 Stevens, 'National oil companies and international oil companies in the Middle East', p. 22.

67 Yergin, *The Quest*, pp. 89–94.

68 Stevens, *International Oil Companies*, p. 16.

69 Bridge and Le Billion, *Oil*, p. 49.

70 Klare, *Rising Powers, Shrinking Planet*, p. 192.

71 Bridge and Le Billion, *Oil*, p. 56.

72 Stevens, *International Oil Companies*, p. 7.

73 Ibid., p. 18.

74 Energy Intelligence, 'National oil companies hold top spots in Energy Intelligence's ranking of top oil firms', www.energyintel.com/pages/pr-piw-top-50-2015.aspx.

75 PricewaterhouseCoopers LLP, *Global Top 100 Companies by Market Capitalisation: 31 March 2016 Update*, www.pwc.com/gx/en/audit-services/publications/assets/global-top-100-companies-2016.pdf.

76 T. Macalister, 'BP makes record loss and axes 7,000 jobs', *The Guardian*, 2 February 2016; S. Reed, 'Shell says quarterly earnings will fall 48%', *New York Times*, 17 January 2014.

77 A. Sampson, *Who Runs This Place? The Anatomy of Britain in the 21st Century* (London: John Murray, 2005), pp. 306–7.

78 A. Critchlow, 'BP hires former MI6 spy master to beef up board', *Daily Telegraph*, 14 May 2015.

79 Royal Dutch Shell, *Annual Report and Form 20-F 2015*, p. 63.

80 Hollis, *Britain and the Middle East in the 9/11 Era*, p. 187.
81 A Barnett, 'Firms reap the benefit of Whitehall insiders', *The Observer*, 12 March 2000.
82 Sampson, *Who Runs This Place?*, p. 307.
83 Muttitt, *Fuel on the Fire*, pp. 29–30, xxix.
84 Ibid., pp. 350, 5.
85 Bridge and Le Billion, *Oil*, p. 169; Muttitt, *Fuel on the Fire*; J.-F. Seznec, 'Politics of oil supply: national oil companies vs international oil companies', in R. E. Looney, ed., *Handbook of Oil Politics* (London: Routledge, 2012), p. 55.
86 A. Hanieh, *Lineages of Revolt: Issues of Contemporary Capitalism in the Middle East* (Chicago: Haymarket, 2013), pp. 132, 254.
87 Secretary of State for Foreign and Commonwealth Affairs, *Government Response to the House of Commons Foreign Affairs Committee's Fifth Report of Session 2013–14 (HC88): The UK's relations with Saudi Arabia and Bahrain*, Cm 8780 (London: The Stationery Office, 2014), pp. 6–7.
88 R. Allen, 'Oil companies kept waiting at Saudi door', *Financial Times*, 1 May 2002.
89 Ibid.
90 J. Chung and C. Hoyos, 'Collapse of Saudi gas talks reveals gap in understanding', *Financial Times*, 7 June 2003; J. Chung and C. Hoyos, 'Saudi Arabia strikes big natural gas deal with Shell and Total', *Financial Times*, 17 July 2003.
91 E. Crooks, 'Shell and Saudi Aramco put $7bn into US refinery', *Financial Times*, 21 September 2007; US Energy Information Administration, 'Country analysis brief: Saudi Arabia', 10 September 2014.
92 E. Crooks, 'Royal Dutch Shell and Saudi Aramco unwind US joint venture', *Financial Times*, 17 March 2016.
93 A. England, 'Kuwait ties oil deals to output targets', *Financial Times*, 21 May 2008.
94 G. Chazan, 'Bottlenecks impede the development of supplies', *Financial Times*, 17 April 2012; V. Ratcliffe, 'Hopes for sufficient power pinned on Subiya expansion', *Financial Times*, 24 April 2013.

95 US Energy Information Administration, 'Country analysis brief: Kuwait', 24 October 2014.

96 R. Allen, 'Kuwait opens oilfields to foreign companies', *Financial Times*, 4 January 2001.

97 C. Hoyos, 'Kuwait's rulers ponder a new pact with big oil', *Financial Times*, 23 January 2006.

98 'BP and Kuwait seek China investments', *Financial Times*, 15 March 2005; 'Shell is following BP with Kuwait Petroleum venture', *Financial Times*, 23 March 2005; E. Crooks, 'Shell pulls out of $9bn refinery plan in China', *Financial Times*, 4 December 2009.

99 Royal Dutch Shell, *Annual Report and Form 20-F 2015*, p. E12; US Energy Information Administration, 'Country analysis brief: Oman', 28 January 2016.

100 'Shell hopes loss of Omani field is just a warning', *Financial Times*, 4 May 2005.

101 E. Crooks, 'Companies UK: BP chief-designate "delighted" with $700m gas production deal with Oman', *Financial Times*, 23 January 2007.

102 US Energy Information Administration, 'Country analysis brief: Qatar', 20 October 2015.

103 Ibid.

104 E. Crooks, 'Shell shapes $3bn production boost', *Financial Times*, 18 March 2009; E. Crooks, 'Exxon cancels gas-to-liquids project in Qatar', *Financial Times*, 20 February 2007; E. Crooks, 'Shell set to unveil job cuts', *Financial Times*, 5 September 2009; E. Crooks, 'Shell chief says oil at $80 will halt rising debt', *Financial Times*, 25 November 2009.

105 S. Pfeifer, 'Pearl crowns Shell's Qatari gasoil hopes', *Financial Times*, 6 June 2011.

106 M. Peel, 'Shell GTL: masterstroke or a wrong turn', *Financial Times*, 17 December 2011.

107 C. Adams and M. Kavanagh, 'Shell abandons $6.5bn venture as oil majors move to slash costs', *Financial Times*, 15 January 2015.

108 A. Barker and W. MacNamara, 'Centrica signs £2bn gas deal with Qatar', *Financial Times*, 24 February 2011.

109 G. Chazan and P. Clark, 'Centrica offered equity for Qatar's gas', *Financial Times*, 30 April 2012.

110 G. Chazan, 'Centrica in £4.4bn gas deal', *Financial Times*, 7 November 2013.

111 US Energy Information Administration, 'Country analysis brief: UAE', 18 May 2015.

112 Ibid.

113 J. Drummond, 'Abu Dhabi set to exploit gas from Shah field', *Financial Times*, 9 July 2008; J. Drummond, 'Occidental wins contract to develop Shah sour gas project', *Financial Times*, 21 January 2011.

114 M. Peel, C. Hall and G. Chazan, 'BP stake in Abu Dhabi concession in doubt', *Financial Times*, 16 July 2012.

115 M. Peel, C. Hall and J. Blitz, 'New volatility in UK relations with UAE', *Financial Times*, 23 October 2012.

116 S. Kerr and M. Peel, 'BP back in Abu Dhabi oil race', *Financial Times*, 13 December 2012.

117 R. Ramesh, 'UAE told UK: crack down on Muslim Brotherhood or lose arms deals', *The Guardian*, 6 November 2015.

118 Kerr and Peel, 'BP back in Abu Dhabi oil race'.

119 A. Travis and R. Ramesh, 'Muslim Brotherhood are possible extremists, David Cameron says', *The Guardian*, 17 December 2015.

120 C. Adams and S. Kerr, 'Shell and BP balk over signing-on fee for big Abu Dhabi fields', *Financial Times*, 12 February 2015.

Chapter 3 British Neoliberalism and Gulf Capitalism

1 C. Hall, N. Draper, K. McClelland, K. Donington and R. Lang, *Legacies of British Slave-Ownership: Colonial Slavery and the Formation of Victorian Britain* (Cambridge: Cambridge University Press, 2014); B. Chandra, *History of Modern India* (Hyderabad: Orient BlackSwan, 2009).

2 K. Coutts and R. Rowthorn, 'The UK balance of payments: structure and prospects', *Oxford Review of Economic Policy*, 29/2 (2013): 307.

3 M. C. Sawyer, 'The structure of the economy', in M. C. Sawyer, ed., *The UK Economy* (16th edn, Oxford: Oxford University Press, 2005), pp. 31–2; C. J. Green, 'The balance of payments', in M. J. Artis, ed., *The UK Economy: A Manual of Applied Economics* (13th edn, London: Weidenfeld & Nicolson, 1992), p. 200.

4 J. Foreman-Peck, 'Trade and the balance of payments', in N. F. R. Crafts and N. W. C. Woodward, eds, *The British Economy since 1945* (Oxford: Oxford University Press, 1991), pp. 150, 141.

5 Ibid., p. 169.

6 Ibid., p. 176.

7 R. Roberts and D. Kynaston, *City State: A Contemporary History of the City of London and How Money Triumphed* (London: Profile Books, 2002), p. 89.

8 P. J. Cain and A. G. Hopkins, *British Imperialism, 1688–2000* (2nd edn, London: Pearson Education, 2002), p. 642.

9 Green, 'The balance of payments', p. 221; R. Harrington, 'Money and finance: public expenditure and taxation', in M. J. Artis, ed., *The UK Economy: A Manual of Applied Economics* (13th edn, London: Weidenfeld & Nicolson, 1992), pp. 108–11.

10 T. Norfield, *The City: London and the Global Power of Finance* (London: Verso, 2016), pp. 54, 69–70.

11 Green, 'The balance of payments', pp. 165–6.

12 F. Brenchley, *Britain and the Middle East: An Economic History, 1945–87* (London: Lester Crook Academic, 1989), pp. 121–2, 185, 272–4, 280.

13 Ibid., pp. 316–20, 325, 328.

14 A. Hanieh, *Capitalism and Class in the Gulf Arab States* (Basingstoke: Palgrave Macmillan, 2011), pp. 78–81; Brenchley, *Britain and the Middle East*, pp. 49, 187.

15 G. Bahgat, 'Sovereign wealth funds in the Gulf: opportunities and challenges', in R. E. Looney, ed., *Handbook of Oil Politics* (London: Routledge, 2012), p. 366; S. Bazoobandi, *The Political Economy of the Gulf Sovereign Wealth Funds: A Case Study of Iran, Kuwait, Saudi Arabia and the United Arab Emirates* (Abingdon: Routledge, 2013), pp. 37, 73.

16 Brenchley, *Britain and the Middle East*, pp. 265-7.

17 M. W. Khouja and P. G. Sadler, *The Economy of Kuwait: Development and Role in International Finance* (London: Macmillan, 1979), pp. 200-1, 206.

18 Bazoobandi, *The Political Economy of the Gulf Sovereign Wealth Funds*, pp. 40, 50-1.

19 Interview with the author, September 2016.

20 D. Gowland, 'Balance of payments', in M. C. Sawyer, ed., *The UK Economy* (16th edn, Oxford: Oxford University Press, 2005), pp. 146-7.

21 'World Bank open data', http://data.worldbank.org/.

22 Norfield, *The City*, p. 189.

23 Coutts and Rowthorn, 'The UK balance of payments', p. 320.

24 Norfield, *The City*, p. 199.

25 Ibid., 200-3; T. Norfield, 'UK foreign direct investment profits', *Economics of Imperialism*, 22 March 2013, http://economicsofim perialism.blogspot.co.uk/2013/03/uk-foreign-direct-investment -profits.html.

26 Norfield, *The City*, p. 37.

27 Ibid., pp. 71-2.

28 J. Froud, M. Moran, A. Nilsson and K. Williams, 'Wasting a crisis? Democracy and markets in Britain after 2007', *Political Quarterly*, 81/1 (2010): 30-1.

29 Coutts and Rowthorn, 'The UK balance of payments', pp. 313, 308.

30 Ibid., pp. 319-20.

31 G. Luciani, 'Oil and political economy in the international relations of the Middle East', in L. Fawcett, ed., *International Relations of the Middle East* (Oxford: Oxford University Press, 2009), pp. 91-3.

32 Hanieh, *Capitalism and Class in the Gulf Arab States*, pp. 12-13, 16.

33 Ibid., pp. 54-5, 76.

34 G. Achcar, *The People Want: A Radical Exploration of the Arab Uprising* (London: Saqi Books, 2013), p. 86.

35 Hanieh, *Capitalism and Class in the Gulf Arab States*, pp. 43-8.

36 Ibid.

37 Ibid., p. 53.

38 Ibid., p. 90.

39 E. Woertz, 'Oil, the dollar, and the stability of the international financial system', in R. E. Looney, ed., *Handbook of Oil Politics* (London: Routledge, 2012), p. 381.

40 UNCTAD (United Nations Conference on Trade and Development) Data Center, http://unctadstat.unctad.org/wds/ReportFolders/ reportFolders.aspx?sCS_ChosenLang=en (data in constant prices not available).

41 M. Sturm, J. Strasky, P. Adolf and D. Peschel, *The Gulf Cooperation Council Countries: Economic Structures, Recent Developments and Role in the Global Economy*, European Central Bank Occasional Paper Series no. 92, July 2008, p. 40.

42 Ibid.

43 Ibid., pp. 39, 6.

44 Hanieh, *Capitalism and Class in the Gulf Arab States*, p. 98.

45 J. Gieve, 'Sovereign wealth funds and global imbalances', *Bank of England Quarterly Bulletin 2008 Q2*, 14 March 2008, https:// papers.ssrn.com/sol3/papers.cfm?abstract_id=1147064.

46 S. Nsouli, 'Petrodollar recycling and global imbalances', *International Monetary Fund*, 23 March 2006.

47 Ibid.

48 Bazoobandi, *The Political Economy of the Gulf Sovereign Wealth Funds*, p. 1.

49 Bahgat, 'Sovereign wealth funds in the Gulf', p. 364; see also Bazoobandi, *The Political Economy of the Gulf Sovereign Wealth Funds*, p. 7.

50 Sturm, Strasky, Adolf and Peschel, *The Gulf Cooperation Council Countries*, pp. 30, 50.

51 Bazoobandi, *The Political Economy of the Gulf Sovereign Wealth Funds*, p. 55.

52 Bahgat, 'Sovereign wealth funds in the Gulf', p. 370; Bazoobandi, *The Political Economy of the Gulf Sovereign Wealth Funds*, p. 19; Woertz, 'Oil, the dollar, and the stability of the international financial system', p. 387.

53 Sturm, Strasky, Adolf and Peschel, *The Gulf Cooperation Council Countries*, p. 7.

54 SWFI (Sovereign Wealth Fund Institute), 'Sovereign wealth fund rankings', June 2016. www.swfinstitute.org/sovereign-wea lth-fund-rankings/.

55 Bazoobandi, *The Political Economy of the Gulf Sovereign Wealth Funds*, pp. 30–1.

56 SWFI, 'Sovereign wealth fund rankings'.

57 Ibid., p. 2; Gieve, 'Sovereign wealth funds and global imbalances'.

58 Hanieh, *Capitalism and Class in the Gulf Arab States*, p. 95.

59 Bahgat, 'Sovereign wealth funds in the Gulf, p. 365.

60 Ibid., p. 372; Bazoobandi, *The Political Economy of the Gulf Sovereign Wealth Funds*, p. 27; C. Davidson, *After the Sheikhs: The Coming Collapse of the Gulf Monarchies* (London: Hurst, 2012), p. 43.

61 Bazoobandi, *The Political Economy of the Gulf Sovereign Wealth Funds*, pp. 87–8, 167.

62 Hanieh, *Capitalism and Class in the Gulf Arab States*, p. 97; Bazoobandi, *The Political Economy of the Gulf Sovereign Wealth Funds*, p. 24.

63 Ibid., p. 28.

64 Ibid., pp. 11, 145.

65 Ibid., p. 62.

66 Ibid., pp. 164–5.

67 Hanieh, *Capitalism and Class in the Gulf Arab States*, pp. 106, 110.

68 Sturm, Strasky, Adolf and Peschel, *The Gulf Cooperation Council Countries*, p. 67.

69 Hanieh, *Capitalism and Class in the Gulf Arab States*, p. 174.

70 M. Al Asoomi, 'Oman and Bahrain have a lot to gain from GCC plan', *Gulf News*, 19 June 2013.

71 Hanieh, *Capitalism and Class in the Gulf Arab States*, pp. 1, 64–5.

72 Davidson, *After the Sheikhs*, p. 44; Hanieh, *Capitalism and Class in the Gulf Arab States*, pp. 120–1.

73 Hanieh, *Capitalism and Class in the Gulf Arab States*, pp. 133, 139; Economist Intelligence Unit, *GCC Trade and Investment Flows:*

The Emerging-Market Surge (London: Economist Intelligence Unit, 2011), p. 4.

74 Hanieh, *Capitalism and Class in the Gulf Arab States*, pp. 125–7.

Chapter 4 How Important is Gulf Wealth to British Capitalism?

1 T. Norfield, *The City: London and the Global Power of Finance* (London: Verso, 2016).

2 Ibid., p. 123.

3 Ibid., pp. 123–6.

4 Ibid., pp. 7, 173–5, 6, 2.

5 Ibid., pp. 97–8.

6 Ibid., pp. 106–8.

7 Ibid., pp. 110–11.

8 J. Sassoon, 'Speech by the commercial secretary to the Treasury, Lord Sassoon, to the Middle East Association's City and GCC Financial Services Summit', 19 July 2010, www.gov.uk/government/speeches/speech-by-the-commercial-secretary-to-the-treasury-lord-sassoon-to-the-middle-east-associations-city-gcc-financial-services-summit.

9 A. Burt, 'Minister for the Middle East addresses Abu Dhabi Investment Forum', 20 October 2010, www.gov.uk/government/speeches/minister-for-the-middle-east-addresses-abu-dhabi-investment-forum.

10 Foreign Affairs Committee (House of Commons), *The UK's Relations with Saudi Arabia and Bahrain, Fifth Report of Session 2013–14: Report, together with Formal Minutes, Oral and Written Evidence*, HC 88 (London: The Stationery Office, 2013), p. 19.

11 D. Howell, 'UK relations with the GCC region: a broadening partnership', 20 June 2012, www.gov.uk/government/speeches/uk-relations-with-the-gcc-region-a-broadening-partnership.

12 Office of National Statistics, 'Time series: BoP-consistent: Saudi Arabia: exports: SA', 9 December 2016, www.ons.gov.uk/economy/nationalaccounts / balanceofpayments / timeseries / erdi / mret;

Office of National Statistics, 'Time series: BoP-consistent: residual Gulf Arabian (R5): exports NSA', 29 July 2016, www.ons.gov. uk/economy/nationalaccounts/balanceofpayments/timeseries/ boqw/pb (data in constant prices is not made available by the Office of National Statistics).

13 Office of National Statistics, 'Dataset: geographical breakdown of thecurrentaccount,thePinkBook:2016',29July2016,www.ons.gov. uk/economy/nationalaccounts/balanceofpayments/datasets/9g eographicalbreakdownofthecurrentaccountthepinkbook2016.

14 CAAT (Campaign Against Arms Trade), 'UK arms export licences', www.caat.org.uk/resources/export-licences (data generated by CAAT from the Strategic Export Controls database of the UK Department for Business, Innovation and Skills).

15 Ibid.

16 Burt, 'Minister for the Middle East addresses Abu Dhabi Investment Forum'.

17 Foreign Affairs Committee, *The UK's Relations with Saudi Arabia and Bahrain*, pp. 36–7.

18 Department for International Trade, 'Doing business in the United Arab Emirates: UAE trade and export guide', 21 December 2015.

19 Department for International Trade, 'Doing business in Saudi Arabia: Saudi Arabia trade and export guide', 15 February 2016.

20 Department for International Trade, 'Doing business in Qatar: Qatar trade and export guide', 16 September 2015.

21 Department for International Trade, 'Doing business in Kuwait: Kuwait trade and export guide', 6 February 2015; Department for International Trade, 'Doing business in Oman: Oman trade and export guide', 11 May 2015.

22 Foreign Affairs Committee, *The UK's Relations with Saudi Arabia and Bahrain*, p. 20.

23 Hansard, House of Commons, 17 November 2008, Col. 41W.

24 Prime Minister's Office, 'David Cameron welcomes UAE Airbus deal', 17 November 2013, www.gov.uk/government/news/david-cameron-welcomes-uae-airbus-deal.

25 J. Sassoon, 'Speech by the commercial secretary to the Treasury,

Lord Sassoon, to the Middle East Association', 25 October 2012, www.gov.uk/government/speeches/speech-by-the-commercial-secretary-to-the-treasury-lord-sassoon-to-the-middle-east-asso ciation.

26 C. Hendry, 'Charles Hendry's speech at the Middle East and North Africa Energy conference: Chatham House, London', 31 January 2011, www.gov.uk/government/speeches/charles-hendrys-spee ch-at-the-middle-east-and-north-africa-energy-conference-chat ham-house-london.

27 Sassoon, 'Speech by the commercial secretary to the Treasury, Lord Sassoon, to the Middle East Association's City and GCC Financial Services Summit'.

28 L. Saigol, 'Saudis keen to boost trade with UK', *Financial Times*, 13 October 2011.

29 M. Foster, 'Civil service moves special: who's who at Liam Fox's Department for International Trade?', *Civil Service World*, 24 August 2016, www.civilserviceworld.com/articles/news/civil-ser vice-moves-special-whos-who-liam-foxs-department-internatio nal-trade.

30 Foreign Affairs Committee, *The UK's Relations with Saudi Arabia and Bahrain*, Ev 141.

31 Department for International Trade, 'Serco's partnership with UK government helps secure UAE wins', 19 March 2014, www.gov.uk/ government/case-studies/sercos-partnership-with-ukti-helps-sec ure-uae-wins.

32 UK Export Finance, 'We helped Carillion with the first ever government loan to an overseas buyer', 21 July 2015.

33 UK Export Finance, 'UK Export Finance support to British export-ers at 12-year high', 20 June 2013, www.gov.uk/government/news/ uk-export-finance-support-to-british-exporters-at-12-year-high.

34 UK Export Finance, 'Massive boost to British industry in biggest ever petrochemical project', 21 June 2013, www.gov.uk/government/ news/massive-boost-to-british-industry-in-biggest-ever-petroche mical-project.

35 Norfield, *The City*, p. 107.

36 Office of National Statistics, 'Time series: IIP: assets: total: Saudi Arabia', 29 July 2016. www.ons.gov.uk/economy/nationalacco unts/balanceofpayments/timeseries/hfiz; Office of National Stat istics, 'Time series: IIP: assets: total: residual Gulf & Arab coun tries', 29 July 2016, www.ons.gov.uk/economy/nationalaccounts/ balanceofpayments/timeseries/hfis/pb.

37 L. Saigol and S. Pfeifer, 'UK plays catch-up on Iraq investment', *Financial Times*, 22 November 2011.

38 Office of National Statistics, 'Dataset: 10 geographical break down of the UK international investment position, the Pink Book: 2016', 29 July 2016, www.ons.gov.uk/economy/nationalaccounts/ balanceofpayments/datasets/10geographicalbreakdownoftheuk internationalinvestmentpositionthepinkbook2016.

39 S. Hamroush, 'International perspective on UK foreign direct investment (FDI): 2014', 30 August 2016, www.ons.gov.uk/econ omy/nationalaccounts/balanceofpayments/articles/international perspectiveonukforeigndirectinvestmentfdi/2014.

40 United Nations Conference on Trade and Development, *Bilateral FDI Statistics 2014*, http://unctad.org/en/Pages/DIAE/FDI%20 Statistics/FDI-Statistics-Bilateral.aspx.

41 Department for International Trade, 'Doing business in Saudi Arabia: Saudi Arabia trade and export guide', 15 February 2016.

42 Department for International Trade, 'Doing business in Oman: Oman trade and export guide', 11 May 2015.

43 British Offset, www.britishoffset.com.

44 J. Gieve, 'Sovereign wealth funds and global imbalances', *Bank of England Quarterly Bulletin 2008 Q2*, 14 March 2008, https:// papers.ssrn.com/sol3/papers.cfm?abstract_id=1147064.

45 Foreign Affairs Committee, *The UK's Relations with Saudi Arabia and Bahrain*, p. 37.

46 'UK's Brown backs Islamic finance', 13 June 2006, http://news.bbc. co.uk/1/hi/business/5074068.stm; 'Cameron unveils Islamic bond plan', 29 October 2013, www.bbc.co.uk/news/business-24722440.

47 W. Hague, 'UK economy is open for business and determined to go from strength to strength', 22 September 2010, www.gov.uk/

government/speeches/uk-economy-is-open-for-business-and-determined-to-go-from-strength-to-strength.

48 HM Treasury, 'Group founded to boost London's growing Islamic finance market', 30 October 2013, www.gov.uk/government/news/group-founded-to-boost-londons-growing-islamic-finance-market.

49 M. Sturm, J. Strasky, P. Adolf and D. Peschel, *The Gulf Cooperation Council Countries: Economic Structures, Recent Developments and Role in the Global Economy*, European Central Bank Occasional Paper Series no. 92, July 2008, p. 52.

50 Gieve, 'Sovereign wealth funds and global imbalances'.

51 G. Bahgat, 'Sovereign wealth funds in the Gulf: opportunities and challenges', in R. E. Looney, ed., *Handbook of Oil Politics* (London: Routledge, 2012), pp. 362–3.

52 E. Dash, 'Citi to announce big cuts and new investors', *New York Times*, 15 January 2008, www.nytimes.com/2008/01/15/business/15citi.html.

53 J. Eaglesham, 'Brown flies to Gulf in quest for petrodollars', *Financial Times*, 1 November 2008.

54 R. Dean, T. Griggs and W. Wallis, 'UK becomes the place to do business for "the most important investor in the world"', *Financial Times*, 7 October 2006.

55 Bahgat, 'Sovereign wealth funds in the Gulf', p. 366.

56 A. Hanieh, *Capitalism and Class in the Gulf Arab States* (Basingstoke: Palgrave Macmillan, 2011), p. 96.

57 D. Lubin, 'Petrodollars, emerging markets and vulnerability', *Citigroup Economic & Market Analysis*, 19 March 2007, p. 2.

58 Bank of International Settlements, 'Locational banking statistics', 11 December 2016, www.bis.org/statistics/bankstats.htm (data are for June 2016).

59 Bank of England, 'External business of monetary financial institutions operating in the UK – 2016 Q2', 2 September 2016, http://www.bankofengland.co.uk/statistics/Pages/ebb/2016/sep.aspx (data are for 2015, quarter 4).

60 Ibid.

61 J. Croft and P. Thal Larsen, 'Barclays seeks to put investors' minds

at ease', *Financial Times*, 26 June 2008; P. Thal Larsen and J. Croft, 'Qataris take up to 10% of Barclays', *Financial Times*, 25 June 2008; S. Kerr, 'Sums add up for Qataris', *Financial Times*, 25 June 2008.

62 P. Thal Larsen, 'Barclays turns to Middle East for cash boost', *Financial Times*, 31 October 2008.

63 K. Stacey and P. Thal Larsen, 'Barclays feared bail-out could undermine confidence', *Financial Times*, 4 November 2008.

64 A. Darling, *Back From the Brink: 1,000 Days at Number 11* (London: Atlantic Books, 2011), p. 173; C. Binham, D. Schafer and P. Jenkins, 'Qatar connection adds to Barclays' woes', *Financial Times*, 1 February 2013.

65 K. Burgess and P. Thal Larsen, 'Barclays practises appease-ment', *Financial Times*, 18 November 2008; P. Thal Larsen and G. Parker, 'Chancellor warns over bail-out terms', *Financial Times*, 18 November 2008; K. Burgess, 'L&G retreats on Barclays vote', *Financial Times*, 21 November 2008.

66 K. Burgess, P. Thal Larsen and N. Hume, 'Gulf investor sells Barclays stake', *Financial Times*, 1 June 2009; P. Jenkins, J. O'Doherty, A. Felsted and S. Kerr, 'Qataris sell Barclays stake for £615m profit', *Financial Times*, 21 October 2009.

67 S. Goff and P. Jenkins, 'Barclays faces probe into capital raising fees – bank reveals inquiry into Mideast deal', *Financial Times*, 28 July 2012; C. Binham, 'Barclays at risk of US scrutiny in Qatar probe', *Financial Times*, 30 August 2012; J. Guthrie, 'Barclays case could rattle bigwigs', *Financial Times*, 21 January 2013; C. Binham, 'Stakes are high for Barclays and SFO over Qatar investors probe', *Financial Times*, 24 September 2016; E. Dunkley and C. Binham, 'Secretive deal involved Qatari clients', *Financial Times*, 26 November 2015; Serious Fraud Office, 'SFO charges in Barclays Qatar capital raising case', 20 June 2017, www.sfo.gov.uk/2017/06/20/sfo-charges-in-barclays-qatar-capital-raising-case/; J. Treanor 'Barclays bank and former bosses to stand trial in January 2019', *The Guardian*, 17 July 2017; M. Arnold, J. Croft and C. Binham, 'UK court dismisses charges against Barclays over Qatar deal', *Financial Times*, 21 May 2018.

68 Norfield, *The City*, pp. 216–17.
69 R. Khalaf, '"We created a lot of jealousy" – lunch with the FT: Sheikh Hamad bin Jaber Al Thani', *Financial Times*, 16 April 2016.
70 J. Chung, 'Gulf finance: boom brings strong demand', *Financial Times*, 27 November 2006; R. Wigglesworth, 'RBS vows to keep lending in Middle East', *Financial Times*, 11 March 2009.
71 L. Saigol, 'Gulf finance: an exciting opportunity for international banks', *Financial Times*, 27 November 2006.
72 M. Caruana Galizia, R. Carvajal, M. Cabra, E. Díaz-Struck, M. Garcia Rey and W. Fitzgibbon, 'Explore the Swiss leaks data', *International Consortium of Investigative Journalists*, 8 February 2015, www.icij.org/project/swiss-leaks/explore-swiss-leaks-data.
73 Gieve, 'Sovereign wealth funds and global imbalances'.
74 Office of National Statistics, 'Time series: BoP: current account: balance: Saudi Arabia', 29 July 2016, www.ons.gov.uk/economy/nationalaccounts/balanceofpayments/timeseries/bftb/pb; Office of National Statistics, 'Time series: BPM5 current account balance with Gulf Arabian countries', 29 July 2016, www.ons.gov.uk/economy/nationalaccounts/balanceofpayments/timeseries/jitv/pb.
75 Office of National Statistics, 'Dataset: geographical breakdown of thecurrentaccount,thePinkBook:2016',29July2016,www.ons.gov.uk/economy/nationalaccounts/balanceofpayments/datasets/9geographicalbreakdownofthecurrentaccountthepinkbook2016.
76 Ibid.
77 Office of National Statistics, 'Time series: IIP: liabilities: total: Saudi Arabia', 29 July 2016, www.ons.gov.uk/economy/nationalaccounts/balanceofpayments/timeseries/hfqd/pb; Office of National Statistics, 'Time series: IIP: liabilities: total: res Gulf and Arab countries', 29 July 2016, www.ons.gov.uk/economy/nationalaccounts/balanceofpayments/timeseries/hfpw/pb.
78 Office of National Statistics, 'Dataset: 10 geographical breakdown of the UK international investment position, the Pink Book: 2016', 29 July 2016, www.ons.gov.uk/economy/nationalaccounts/balanceofpayments/datasets/10geographicalbreakdownoftheukinternationalinvestmentpositionthepinkbook2016.

79 Sassoon, 'Speech by the commercial secretary to the Treasury, Lord Sassoon, to the Middle East Association's City and GCC Financial Services Summit'.

80 Howell, 'UK relations with the GCC region: a broadening partnership'.

81 Ibid.

82 UK Trade and Investment, 'Business secretary beats the drum for UK business in the UAE', 19 January 2014, www.gov.uk/government/news/business-secretary-beats-the-drum-for-uk-business-in-the-uae.

83 UK Trade and Investment, 'Fund management in the UK: the destination of choice for investment management', January 2015, pp.7–8, www.slideshare.net/mackles/ukti-asset-managementbrochure.

84 Ibid., pp. 24, 29, 31.

85 Ibid., pp. 19, 8.

86 R. Ramesh, 'UK set up secret group of top officials to enable UAE investment', *The Guardian*, 9 November 2015.

87 Davidson, *After the Sheikhs*, pp. 92–4.

88 R. Booth, 'London's Shard: a "tower of power and riches" looking down on poverty', *The Guardian*, 30 December 2011, www.theguardian.com/artanddesign/2011/dec/30/shard-of-glass-london.

89 Department for International Trade, 'Doing business in Qatar: Qatar trade and export guide', 16 September 2015.

90 S. Kerr, 'Gulf money adopting high-octane new profile', *Financial Times*, 22 May 2007.

91 Hendry, 'Charles Hendry's speech at the Middle East and North Africa Energy conference: Chatham House, London'; J. Kollewe, 'Canary Wharf owners reject £2.2bn Qatar bid', *The Guardian*, 7 November 2014.

92 Department for International Trade, 'Doing business in Kuwait: Kuwait trade and export guide', 6 February 2015.

93 C. Krauss, 'OPEC took aim at U.S. oil producers, but hurt itself, too', *New York Times*, 15 June 2017.

94 J. Kinninmont, 'Vision 2030 and Saudi Arabia's social contract: austerity and transformation', Royal Institute of International Affairs, 20

July 2017, www.chathamhouse.org/publication/vision-2030-and-saudi-arabias-social-contract-austerity-and-transformation.

95 R. Cox, 'A big question in Riyadh: the status of Aramco's I.P.O.', *New York Times*, 24 October 2017.

96 A. Monaghan, 'London's reputation at risk from watering down City rules, IoD warns', *The Guardian*, 2 August 2017.

97 T. May, 'Prime minister's speech to the Gulf Co-operation Council 2016', 7 December 2016, www.gov.uk/government/speeches/prime-ministers-speech-to-the-gulf-co-operation-council-2016.

98 Prime Minister's Office, 'Gulf Co-operation Council – United Kingdom, first summit 6 to 7 December 2016, Kingdom of Bahrain: joint communiqué', 7 December 2016, www.gov.uk/government/publications/gulf-co-operation-council-united-kingdom-first-su mmit-joint-communique/gulf-co-operation-council-united-king dom-first-summit-6-to-7-december-2016-kingdom-of-bahrain-joint-communique.

99 K. Ahmed, 'Qatar announces £5bn UK investment', 27 March 2017, www.bbc.co.uk/news/business-39410075.

Chapter 5 Arming Authoritarianism

1 M. Phythian, *The Politics of British Arms Sales since 1964* (Manchester: Manchester University Press, 2000), p. 2.

2 Ibid., p. 10.

3 Ibid., pp. 1–3; Perlo-Freeman disputes elements of the economic logic expressed here, while sharing the fundamental view that the government supports the UK's arms export industry in 'the belief that possessing domestic military industrial capabilities is necessary for national security . . . [and] the view that military power is a . . . "public good".' See S. Perlo-Freeman, *Special Treatment: UK Government Support for the Arms Industry and Trade*, SIPRI and Campaign Against Arms Trade, November 2016, www.sipri.org/sites/default/files/Special-treatment-report.pdf.

4 N. Cooper, *The Business of Death: Britain's Arms Trade at Home and Abroad* (London: I. B. Tauris, 1997), p. 138.

5 G. Achcar, *The People Want: A Radical Exploration of the Arab Uprising* (London: Saqi Books, 2013), p. 106.

6 Phythian, *The Politics of British Arms Sales since 1964*, pp. 32, 40.

7 Ibid., p. 40.

8 N. Ayubi, *Over-Stating the Arab State: Politics and Society in the Middle East* (London: I. B. Tauris, 1995), p. 256.

9 Phythian, *The Politics of British Arms Sales since 1964*, pp. 227, 273.

10 Foreign Affairs Committee (House of Commons), *British Foreign Policy and the 'Arab Spring', Second Report of Session 2012–13: Report, together with Formal Minutes, Oral and Written Evidence*, HC 80 (London: The Stationery Office, 2012), Ev 8.

11 S. L. Blanton, 'Instruments of security or tools of repression? Arms imports and human rights conditions in developing countries', *Journal of Peace Research*, 36/2 (1999), p. 241.

12 Phythian, *The Politics of British Arms Sales since 1964*, pp. 273, 274, 278.

13 Cooper, *The Business of Death*, pp. 138–45.

14 Hansard, House of Commons, 2 April 2008, Col. 1072W.

15 Committees on Arms Export Controls, *Scrutiny of Arms Exports (2012): UK Strategic Export Controls Annual Report 2010, Quarterly Reports for July to December 2010 and January to September 2011, the Government's Review of Arms Exports to the Middle East and North Africa, and Wider Arms Control Issues* (HC 419-II, First Joint Report of Session 2012–13), Vol. II: *Oral and Written Evidence and the Committees' Correspondence with Ministers* (London: The Stationery Office, 2012), Ev 37.

16 Cooper, *The Business of Death*, pp. 138–45.

17 Phythian, *The Politics of British Arms Sales since 1964*, p. 25.

18 M. Curtis, *Web of Deceit: Britain's Real Role in the World* (London: Vintage, 2003), p. 261.

19 N. Gilby, *Deception in High Places: A History of Bribery in Britain's Arms Trade* (London: Pluto Press, 2014), p. 175; Hansard, House of Commons, 27 June 2007, Col. 795W; Foreign Affairs Committee, *The UK's Relations with Saudi Arabia and Bahrain*, pp. 46–7.

20 Perlo-Freeman, *Special Treatment*, p. 21.

21 SIPRI (Stockholm International Peace Research Institute), *Arms Transfers Database*, www.sipri.org/databases/armstransfers/.

22 Ibid.; National Geographic, *Atlas of the Middle East* (2nd edn, Washington, DC: National Geographic Society, 2008).

23 Foreign Affairs Committee, *British Foreign Policy and the 'Arab Spring'*, Ev 63.

24 Committees on Arms Export Controls, *Scrutiny of Arms Exports (2012): UK Strategic Export Controls Annual Report 2010, Quarterly Reports for July to December 2010 and January to September 2011, the Government's Review of Arms Exports to the Middle East and North Africa, and Wider Arms Control Issues* (HC 419-I, First Joint Report of Session 2012–13), Vol. I: *Report, together with Formal Minutes* (London: The Stationery Office, 2012), p. 65.

25 SIPRI, *Arms Transfers Database*.

26 Ibid.

27 Ibid.

28 Ibid.

29 Ibid.

30 Ibid.

31 Ibid.

32 Ibid.

33 'Oman, Malaysia sign UK deals', *Jane's Defence Weekly*, 7 September 1991.

34 'UK firm lands Qatari deal', *Jane's Defence Weekly*, 13 June 1992; D. White, 'Vosper Thorneycroft clinches £200m deal', *Financial Times*, 5 June 1992.

35 C. Bellamy and A. Glinecki, 'Vickers loses £500m Kuwait order for tanks', *The Independent*, 12 October 1992.

36 Hansard, House of Commons, 18 May 1993, Cols 140, 141.

37 'Qatar weapons deal for UK', *Financial Times*, 18 November 1996.

38 SIPRI, *Arms Transfers Database*.

39 J. Lewis, 'Oman air force selects NH90', *Jane's Defence Weekly*, 4 August 2004.

40 J. Renton, 'BAE: Saudis shelve air base', *The Observer*, 23 August 1992.

41 R. Norton-Taylor and S. Beavis, 'Rifkind tries to rescue Saudi deal', *The Guardian*, 19 September 1992.

42 D. Pallister, 'Saudis confirm £40bn arms deal after pull-out fear', *The Guardian*, 29 October 1992.

43 P. Webster, '£5bn Tornado order from Saudis saves 19,000 jobs', *The Times*, 29 January 1993.

44 R. Atkins and D. White, 'UK wins £4bn defence deal', *Financial Times*, 29 January 1993.

45 L. Plommer, 'Weapon-toting West bleeds Saudis dry', *The Guardian*, 17 December 1994.

46 D. Leigh and E. MacAskill, 'Blair in secret Saudi mission', *The Guardian*, 27 September 2005.

47 M. Harrison, 'Britain secures £10bn contract from Saudis for Eurofighter', *The Independent*, 22 December 2005.

48 R. Beeston, 'Saudis scupper French hopes of fighter deal', *The Times*, 20 April 2006.

49 R. Gribben, 'BAE lands arms deal for a new generation', *Daily Telegraph*, 19 August 2006; J. Boxell, 'Eurofighter agreement puts Saudis on straighter flight path', *Financial Times*, 18 August 2006.

50 J. Boxell, R. Khalaf, M. Peel and P. Hollinger, 'Saudis suspend £10bn jet talks over fraud case', *Financial Times*, 28 November 2006.

51 R. Wachman, 'BAE lands Saudi plane deal', *The Observer*, 16 September 2007.

52 T. Ripley, 'Typhoon: deal of the decade', *Jane's Defence Weekly*, 26 September 2007.

53 Ibid.

54 G. Jennings and L. Gelfand, 'Saudi Arabia and UK agree RSAF Typhoon support deal', *Jane's Defence Weekly*, 21 October 2009.

55 Quoted by *The Observer*, 19 March 1989; cited in Phythian, *The Politics of British Arms Sales since 1964*, p. 224.

56 N. Tweedie, 'We bribed Saudis, says ex-minister', *Daily Telegraph*, 17 June 2006.

57 Gilby, *Deception in High Places*, pp. 154–78.

58 D. Leigh and R. Evans, 'MoD chief in fraud cover-up row', *The Guardian*, 13 October 2003.

59 D. O'Connell, 'UK defence industry chiefs fear Saudi backlash', *Sunday Times*, 3 December 2006.

60 F. Elliot, 'US pressured Blair into arms bribery inquiry', *Independent on Sunday*, 3 December 2006.

61 Hansard, House of Lords, 14 December 2006, Cols 1711–12.

62 'BAE shares soar after bribe probe is abandoned', *The Independent*, 17 December 2006.

63 C. Adams and J. Boxell, 'SFO drops probe into BAE bribe allegations', *Financial Times*, 15 December 2006.

64 S. Fidler, 'Saudis piled pressure on Blair', *Financial Times*, 15 December 2006.

65 G. Hinsliff and A. Barnett, 'Al-Qaeda spy threat killed Saudi jets probe', *The Observer*, 17 December 2006.

66 Quoted in M. Milner, 'Fund manager raises alarm over dropping of BAE inquiry', *The Guardian*, 23 December 2006.

67 K. Burgess and J. Eaglesham, 'City fuels row over BAE probe', *Financial Times*, 23 December 2006.

68 D. Leigh, R. Norton-Taylor and R. Evans, 'MI6 and Blair at odds over Saudi deals', *The Guardian*, 16 January 2007.

69 M. Peel, '"People could die": how the inquiry into BAE's Saudi deals was brought to earth', *Financial Times*, 26 February 2007.

70 M. Peel and J. Burns, 'BAE probe "had widened to MoD staff"', *Financial Times*, 16 January 2007.

71 D. Leigh and R. Evans, 'BAE accused of secretly paying £1bn to Saudi prince', *The Guardian*, 7 June 2007.

72 'Prince Bandar's statement: "This is an extremely serious allegation"', *The Guardian*, 8 June 2007.

73 R. Beeston, 'US embassy protested to Britain over Blair's decision to halt BAE inquiry', *The Times*, 28 April 2007; D. Leigh and R. Evans, 'Shares plunge as US justice department launches inquiry into arms firm's Saudi deals', *The Guardian*, 27 June 2007.

74 C. Buckley, 'Court told of Blair's pressure on SFO over Saudi inquiry', *The Times*, 15 February 2008; D. Leigh and R. Evans, 'A cover-up laid bare: court hears how SFO inquiry was halted', *The Guardian*, 15 February 2008.

75 F. Gibb and P. Webster, '"An unlawful, abject surrender and a threat to British justice"', *The Times*, 11 April 2008.

76 D. Leigh, 'Ministers under pressure to reopen BAE corruption probe', *The Guardian*, 11 April 2008.

77 D. Leigh, 'Law lords: fraud office right to end bribery investigation', *The Guardian*, 31 July 2008.

78 D. Leigh and R. Evans, 'BAE admits guilt over corrupt arms deals', *The Guardian*, 6 February 2010.

79 R. Allen, 'Gulf states keep lid on extent of defence ties', *Financial Times*, 18 February 2003.

80 S. Joshi, 'A relationship with strategic – and business – motives', *The Independent*, 14 January 2012.

81 J. de Lestapis, 'Oman's armed forces keep up the standard', *Jane's Defence Weekly*, 30 September 1995.

82 Hansard, House of Commons, 28 November 1996, Col. 388.

83 Hansard, House of Commons 20 March 1997, Col. 867.

84 M. Sheridan, 'Violent Shia protests embarrass Bahrain', *The Independent*, 20 December 1994.

85 Hansard, House of Lords, 2 March 1998, Col. WA125.

86 M. Savage, L. Pitel and D. Haynes, 'Arms trade at heart of close ties with old ally', *The Times*, 18 February 2011.

87 T. Harper and C. Woodhouse, 'Monarchy pays UK government to train its officers at Sandhurst', *Evening Standard*, 18 February 2011.

88 B. Quinn and R. Booth, 'Britain cancels Bahrain and Libya arms export licences', *The Guardian*, 18 February 2011.

89 J. Taylor, 'How Britain taught Arab police forces all they know', *The Independent*, 19 February 2011; Amnesty International, *Year of Rebellion: The State of Human Rights in the Middle East and North Africa*, 9 January 2012, pp. 32–6, www.amnesty.org/en/documents/MDE01/001/2012/en/; Human Rights Watch, *Targets of Retribution: Attacks against Medics, Injured Protesters, and Health Facilities*, 18 July 2011, www.hrw.org/report/2011/07/18/targets-retribution/attacks-against-medics-injured-protesters-and-health.

90 J. Kirkup, 'British "may have trained Bahrain force"', *Daily Telegraph*, 26 May 2011.

91 Foreign Affairs Committee, *The UK's Relations with Saudi Arabia and Bahrain*, pp. 46–7.

92 Ibid., Ev 100, 85.

93 Ibid., Ev 108.

94 P. Wintour, 'Qatar given 10 days to meet 13 sweeping demands by Saudi Arabia', *The Guardian*, 23 June 2017.

95 D. Smith, S. Siddiqui and P. Beaumont, 'Gulf crisis: Trump escalates row by accusing Qatar of sponsoring terror', *The Guardian*, 9 June 2017.

96 P. Beaumont, 'US signs deal to supply F-15 jets to Qatar after Trump terror claims', *The Guardian*, 15 June 2017; T. Seal, 'BAE gains surprise win for Typhoon fighter jet with Qatar deal', *Bloomberg*, 18 September 2017, www.bloomberg.com/news/articles/2017-09-18/qatar-to-buy-24-typhoon-jets-to-beef-up-u-k-defense-partnership; Foreign and Commonwealth Office, 'Foreign secretary welcomes Qatar's commitment to combat terrorism', 23 July 2017, www.gov.uk/government/news/foreign-secretary-welcomes-qatars-commitment-to-combat-terrorism; N. Wadhams, 'Tillerson faults Saudi-led bloc for failing to end Qatar crisis', *Bloomberg*, 19 October 2017, www.bloomberg.com/news/articles/2017-10-19/tillerson-faults-saudi-led-bloc-for-failing-to-end-qatar-crisis-j8yqqibp.

Chapter 6 The Arab Uprisings and the War in Yemen

1 Human Rights Watch, *World Report 2017*, pp. 107–11, 385–9, 462–8, 491–3, 510–18, 629–32, www.hrw.org/sites/default/files/world_report_download/wr2017-web.pdf.

2 For two indispensible reviews of the political-economic roots of the uprisings, see G. Achcar, *The People Want: A Radical Exploration of the Arab Uprising* (London: Saqi Books, 2013), and A. Hanieh, *Lineages of Revolt: Issues of Contemporary Capitalism in the Middle East* (Chicago: Haymarket Books, 2013).

3 Amnesty International, *Year of Rebellion: The State of Human Rights in the Middle East and North Africa*, 9 January 2012, pp. 32–6, www.

amnesty.org/en/documents/MDE01/001/2012/en/; M. Slackman and N. Audi, 'Bahrain police use force to crack down on protests', *New York Times*, 16 February 2011; E. Bronner and M. Slackman, 'Saudi troops enter Bahrain to help put down unrest', *New York Times*, 14 March 2011; Human Rights Watch, *Targets of Retribution: Attacks Against Medics, Injured Protesters, and Health Facilities*, 18 July 2011, www.hrw.org/report/2011/07/18/targets-retribution/attacks-against-medics-injured-protesters-and-health.

4 CAAT (Campaign Against Arms Trade), 'UK arms export licences', www.caat.org.uk/resources/export-licences; SIPRI (Stockholm International Peace Research Institute), *Arms Transfers Database*, www.sipri.org/databases/armstransfers/; 'Fresh protests break out in Oman', *Al Jazeera*, 1 March 2011, www.aljazeera.com/news/middleeast/2011/03/201131101527815578.html.

5 CAAT, 'UK arms export licences'.

6 N. Watt and R. Booth, 'David Cameron's Cairo visit overshadowed by defence tour', *The Guardian*, 21 February 2011.

7 A. Clark, 'Saudi Arabia rides to the rescue of BAE aircraft workers', *The Times*, 24 May 2012.

8 A. Monaghan, 'Kuwait deal to boost security firms', *Daily Telegraph*, 30 November 2012.

9 R. Cooper, 'BAE Systems strikes £2.5bn deal to sell jets to Oman', *Daily Telegraph*, 22 December 2012.

10 A. Chuter, 'Typhoon may be back in Qatari fighter competition', *Defense News*, 4 January 2013.

11 B. Farmer, 'Britain to sell Typhoon jets to Bahrain, despite human rights record', *Daily Telegraph*, 9 August 2013.

12 C. Hoyos and K. Stacey, 'UAE signals interest in Typhoon', *Financial Times*, 7 November 2012.

13 'UAE and Bahrain: credibility gulf', *The Guardian*, 29 April 2013.

14 C. Hoyos, K. Stacey and J. Pickard, 'Cameron pushes to seal Typhoon deal in Dubai', *Financial Times*, 13 November 2013.

15 A. Osborne and A. Tovey, 'Blow for BAE as its £6bn Typhoon deal collapses', *Daily Telegraph*, 20 December 2013.

16 S. Kerr, 'UAE calls end on contracts for some British military trainers', *Financial Times*, 23 May 2014.

17 F. Gardner, 'Saudi Arabia "insulted" by UK inquiry', 15 October 2012, www.bbc.co.uk/news/uk-politics-19943865.

18 G. Stansfield and S. Kelly, *A Return to East of Suez? UK Military Deployment to the Gulf*, Royal United Services Institute briefing paper, April 2013.

19 Hansard, House of Commons, 31 October 2012, Col. 289W.

20 'UK to establish £15m permanent Mid East military base', 6 December 2014, www.bbc.co.uk/news/uk-30355953.

21 D. B. Roberts, 'British national interest in the Gulf: rediscovering a role?', *International Affairs*, 90/3 (2014); S. Kelly and G. Stansfield, 'Britain, the United Arab Emirates and the defence of the Gulf revisited', *International Affairs*, 89/5 (2013).

22 S. Raphael and J. St John, *Arming Repression: The New British Imperialism in the Persian Gulf*, September 2016, pp. 5–6, www.waronwant.org/resources/arming-repression-new-british-imperialism-persian-gulf.

23 'David Cameron in the Gulf: defence sales "legitimate"', 5 November 2012, www.bbc.co.uk/news/uk-politics-20202058.

24 Committees on Arms Export Controls, *Scrutiny of Arms Exports (2012): UK Strategic Export Controls Annual Report 2010, Quarterly Reports for July to December 2010 and January to September 2011, the Government's Review of Arms Exports to the Middle East and North Africa, and Wider Arms Control Issues* (HC 419-II, First Joint Report of Session 2012-13), Vol. II: *Oral and Written Evidence and the Committees' Correspondence with Ministers* (London: The Stationery Office, 2012), Ev 25–6.

25 Department for Business, Innovation and Skills, 'Consolidated EU and national arms export licensing criteria', 21 November 2012.

26 N. Cooper, 'Arms exports, new labour and the pariah agenda', *Contemporary Security Policy*, 21/3 (2000): 62, 73.

27 A. Stavrianakis, 'Licenced to kill: the United Kingdom's arms export licencing process', *Economics of Peace and Security Journal*, 3/1 (2008): 31.

28 Foreign Affairs Committee (House of Commons), *British Foreign Policy and the 'Arab Spring', Second Report of Session 2012–13: Report, together with Formal Minutes, Oral and Written Evidence,* HC 80 (London: The Stationery Office, 2012), Ev 164, 167.

29 P. Beaumont and R. Booth, 'UK supplied weapons used in Bahrain crackdown', *The Guardian,* 18 February 2011; A. Dawber, 'Britain under fire for selling arms to Bahrain', *The Independent,* 18 February 2011.

30 Foreign Affairs Committee (House of Commons), *The UK's Relations with Saudi Arabia and Bahrain, Fifth Report of Session 2013–14: Report, together with Formal Minutes, Oral and Written Evidence,* HC 88 (London: The Stationery Office, 2013), pp. 82–3.

31 Ibid., Ev 24.

32 Committees on Arms Export Controls, *Scrutiny of Arms Exports (2012): UK Strategic Export Controls Annual Report 2010, Quarterly Reports for July to December 2010 and January to September 2011, the Government's Review of Arms Exports to the Middle East and North Africa, and Wider Arms Control Issues* (HC 419-I, First Joint Report of Session 2012–13), Vol. I: *Report, together with Formal Minutes* (London: The Stationery Office, 2012), pp. 117–18.

33 Ibid., pp. 20, 22.

34 Ibid., pp. 126–8.

35 K. Eason, 'Show will go on, Formula One chief says as violence flares up', *The Times,* 15 February 2012.

36 Raphael and St John, *Arming Repression,* pp. 15, 10, 13, 9.

37 Committees on Arms Export Controls, Vol. I: *Report, together with Formal Minutes,* pp. 109, 113.

38 Committees on Arms Export Controls, Vol. II: *Oral and Written Evidence and the Committees' Correspondence with Ministers,* Ev 48.

39 Committees on Arms Export Controls, Vol. I: *Report, together with Formal Minutes,* p. 115.

40 L. Gelfand, 'Saudi-led force arrives in Bahrain to quell protests', *Jane's Defence Weekly,* 23 March 2011.

41 J. Kirkup, 'British "may have trained Bahrain force"', *Daily Telegraph*, 26 May 2011.

42 Foreign Affairs Committee, *The UK's Relations with Saudi Arabia and Bahrain*, Ev 93.

43 Ibid., Ev 14.

44 Ibid., Ev 98.

45 Ibid., p. 60.

46 Hansard, House of Commons, 19 March 2012, Col. 471W; Foreign Affairs Committee, *British Foreign Policy and the 'Arab Spring'*, Ev 41.

47 Ibid., Ev 41, 81.

48 Amnesty International, 'Bahrain: reform shelved, repression unleashed', 21 November 2012, www.amnesty.org/en/articles/news/2012/11/bahrain-promises-reform-broken-repression-unleashed/.

49 Human Rights Watch, 'World report 2014: Bahrain', January 2014, www.hrw.org/world-report/2014/country-chapters/bahrain.

50 Human Rights Watch, 'Bahrain: prospects of reform remain dim', 21 January 2014, www.hrw.org/news/2014/01/21/bahrain-prospects-reform-remain-dim.

51 'Prince Andrew to promote Britain in Bahrain visit', 13 January 2014, www.bbc.co.uk/news/uk-25723020.

52 I. Lindsay, 'HM ambassador's speech to the Bahrain British Business Forum', Foreign and Commonwealth Office, 13 December 2013, www.gov.uk/government/speeches/hm-ambassadors-speech-to-the-bahrain-british-business-forum.

53 N. Morris, 'David Cameron entertains Bahrain's dictator King Hamad al-Khalif', *The Independent*, 6 August 2013 (emphasis added).

54 Cited in Foreign Affairs Committee, *The UK's Relations with Saudi Arabia and Bahrain*, p. 24.

55 Foreign and Commonwealth Office, 'Country case study: Bahrain – progress on reform implementation', 10 April 2014, www.gov.uk/government/case-studies/country-case-study-bahrain-progress-on-reform-implementation; British Embassy Manama, 'UK

supports His Majesty King Hamad's initiative on dialogue', 15 January 2014, www.gov.uk/government/world-location-news/uk-supports-his-majesty-king-hamads-initiative-on-dialogue; Secretary of State for Foreign and Commonwealth Affairs, *Government Response to the House of Commons Foreign Affairs Committee's Fifth Report of Session 2013–14 (HC88) – The UK's relations with Saudi Arabia and Bahrain*, Cm 8780 (London: The Stationery Office, 2014).

56 Human Rights Watch, 'World report 2014: Bahrain'.

57 K. C. Ulrichsen, 'Written evidence from Dr Kristian Coates Ulrichsen', 12 December 2012, https://publications.parliament.uk/pa/cm201314/cmselect/cmfaff/88/88vw39.htm.

58 Amnesty International, 'Bahrain: Nabeel Rajab jail sentence shows authorities will not tolerate peaceful critics', 14 May 2015, www.amnesty.org/en/articles/news/2015/05/bahrain-nabeel-rajab-jail-sentence-shows-authorities-will-not-tolerate-peaceful-critics/.

59 L. Leicht, 'Bahrain: why Abdulhadi al-Khawaja should be free', Human Rights Watch, 10 April 2012.

60 Foreign Affairs Committee, *British Foreign Policy and the 'Arab Spring'*, Ev 81.

61 Ulrichsen, 'Written evidence from Dr Kristian Coates Ulrichsen'.

62 E. W. Said, *Orientalism* (4th edn, London: Penguin, 2003).

63 Foreign Affairs Committee, *The UK's Relations with Saudi Arabia and Bahrain*, Ev 7.

64 Ibid., p. 92 (emphasis added).

65 N. Watt, 'Anger at Cameron's invitation to Bahraini prince to No 10', *The Guardian*, 20 May 2011.

66 Foreign Affairs Committee, *The UK's Relations with Saudi Arabia and Bahrain*, Ev 26.

67 Ibid., Ev 4.

68 P. Wintour, 'Gulf plunged into diplomatic crisis as countries cut ties with Qatar', *The Guardian*, 5 June 2017.

69 Achcar, *The People Want*, pp. 189–95; International Crisis Group, *Yemen: Is Peace Possible?*, Middle East Report No. 167, 9 February 2016, pp. 1–4, 21–2.

70 T. Juneau, 'Iran's policy towards the Houthis in Yemen: a limited return on a modest investment', *International Affairs*, 92/3 (2016).

71 J. Borger, 'US military members could be prosecuted for war crimes in Yemen', *TheGuardian*, 3 November 2016, www.theguardian.com/world/2016/nov/03/us-military-members-war-crimes-yemen.

72 P. Foster, L. Loveluck and A. Mojalli, 'UK "will support Saudi-led assault on Yemeni rebels – but not engaging in combat"', *Daily Telegraph*, 27 March 2015.

73 'British technical support for Saudi op in Yemen: Hammond', 27 March 2015, http://news.yahoo.com/british-technical-support-saudi-op-yemen-hammond-210205762.html.

74 E. Graham-Harrison, 'British and US military "in command room" for Saudi strikes on Yemen', *The Guardian*, 15 January 2016.

75 CAAT, 'UK arms export licences'.

76 Hansard, House of Commons, 19 October 2015, Written question – 11948.

77 J. Cusick, 'UK could be prosecuted for war crimes over missiles sold to Saudi Arabia that were used to kill civilians in Yemen', *The Independent*, 27 November 2015.

78 United Nations High Commissioner for Human Rights, *The Situation of Human Rights in Yemen, including Violations and Abuses since September 2014*, pp. 4, 6, 7, 9, 10, 12, 15, 16, https://reliefweb.int/sites/reliefweb.int/files/resources/A_HRC_36_33_EN.pdf.

79 International Crisis Group, *Instruments of Pain (I): Conflict and Famine in Yemen*, 13 April 2017, www.crisisgroup.org/middle-east-north-africa/gulf-and-arabian-peninsula/yemen/b052-instruments-pain-i-conflict-and-famine-yemen.

80 E. MacAskill, 'UN report into Saudi-led strikes in Yemen raises questions over UK role', *The Guardian*, 27 January 2016.

81 Amnesty International, *Yemen: 'Bombs Fall From the Sky Day and Night' – Civilians Under Fire in Northern Yemen*, 7 October 2015, www.amnesty.org/en/documents/mde31/2548/2015/en/; Human Rights Watch, 'Yemen: Coalition used UK cruise missile in unlawful airstrike', 25 November 2015, www.hrw.org/news/2015/11/25/yemen-coalition-used-uk-cruise-missile-unlawful-airstrike; Save

the Children, *Nowhere Safe for Yemen's Children: The Deadly Impact of Explosive Weapons in Yemen*, November 2015, www.savethechildren.org.uk/resources/online-library/nowhere-safe-yemens-children.

82 Panel of Experts on Yemen, *Final Report of the Panel of Experts on Yemen*, 31 January 2017, p. 3, https://reliefweb.int/sites/reliefweb.int/files/resources/N1700601_0.pdf.

83 Ibid., p. 52.

84 P. Wintour, 'Shelve UK arms sales to Saudis over Yemen, say two MPs' committees', *The Guardian*, 15 September 2016.

85 Hansard, House of Commons, 26 October 2016, Col. 337.

86 A. Ross and R. Evans, 'UK minister ignored official warning over Saudi weapons exports, court hears', *The Guardian*, 7 February 2017.

87 P. Wintour, 'Saudis have not breached humanitarian law in Yemen, concludes Foreign Office', *The Guardian*, 14 November 2016.

88 *The Queen* (on the application of Campaign Against Arms Trade) v *The Secretary of State for International Trade* (2017), case no: CO/1306/2016, Approved Judgement, 10 July 2017, www.judiciary.gov.uk/wp-content/uploads/2017/07/r-oao-campaign-against-arms-trade-v-ssfit-and-others1.pdf.

89 For one notable example in addition to the many others cited in this chapter, see R. Mohamed, 'The ugly truths of Yemen's war must not stay buried in the rubble', *Amnesty International*, 25 September 2015, www.amnesty.org/en/latest/news/2015/09/the-ugly-truths-of-yemens-war-must-not-stay-buried-in-the-rubble/.

90 A. Stavrianakis, 'When "anxious scrutiny" of arms exports facilitates humanitarian disaster', *Political Quarterly*, 5 October 2017, pp. 1, 2, 6, 7.

91 T. May, 'Prime minister's speech to the Gulf Co-operation Council 2016', 7 December 2016, www.gov.uk/government/speeches/prime-ministers-speech-to-the-gulf-co-operation-council-2016.

92 Ministry of Defence, 'New agreement strengthens UK–Saudi Arabia

defence relationship', 19 September 2017, www.gov.uk/govern
ment/news/new-agreement-strengthens-uk-saudi-arabia-defence-
relationship.

93 'Theresa May defends UK ties with Saudi Arabia', 4 April 2017,
www.bbc.co.uk/news/uk-politics-39485083.

94 Human Rights Watch, 'Yemen: Coalition airstrikes deadly for
children', 12 September 2017, www.hrw.org/news/2017/09/12/ye
men-coalition-airstrikes-deadly-children; Amnesty International,
'Yemen: USA, UK and France risk complicity in collective punishment of civilians', 17 November 2017, www.amnesty.org/en/latest/
news/2017/11/yemen-usa-uk-and-france-risk-complicity-in-col
lective-punishment-of-civilians/.

95 'Amnesty links British jets to Saudi attacks in Yemen', *The Guardian*,
24 August 2010, www.theguardian.com/world/2010/aug/24/brit
ish-jets-saudi-yemen-attacks.

96 M. Phythian, *The Politics of British Arms Sales since 1964*
(Manchester: Manchester University Press, 2000), p. 323.

97 Foreign Affairs Committee, *The UK's Relations with Saudi Arabia
and Bahrain*, Ev 28.

Conclusion

1 R. Wilkinson and K. Pickett, *The Spirit Level: Why Equality is Better
for Everyone* (London: Penguin, 2010). In fact, as Wilkinson and
Pickett show, the global north countries with the highest levels
of social wellbeing are the Nordic nations and Japan, whereas on
most relevant measures the UK and the US are to be found at the
opposite end of the scale.

Index

North Sea oil 39, 51, 52, 89
Nsouli, S. 100-1

The Observer 72, 170, 173
offshore wealth, GCC 138
oil
  crisis (1973-4) 37, 86-7, 155, 161
  and gas 9-10, 47-50, 81-3, 216-8
    strategic importance 50-67
    UK commercial interests 67-81
  post-2000 boom
    and current account balances
      97-101
    domestic growth 106-7
    sovereign wealth funds (SWFs)
      101-6
  and sterling 20-2, 24, 26
  supply routes 55-6
  see also British Empire;
    petrodollars; *specific countries*
Oman
  arms deals 165, 190
  Dhofar rebellion 28, 35-6
  foreign direct investment (FDI),
    UK 127
  military cooperation 179, 193
  oil 74
    British IOCs in 77
    and Saudi Arabia 25
  uprisings (2010-11) 188, 189
OPEC 37-8, 39, 43, 48, 55-6, 150-1
Ottoman Empire 15, 16, 29

Partrick, N. 205
'Peninsula Shield' force 181, 188
petrodollars 89-91, 97, 99, 130-1,
    156, 165
  crisis and opportunity, US 37-40
  recycling 86-7, 100-1, 156,
    217-8
Phillips, T. 5
Phythian, M. 155, 157, 158, 213-14
police and military training 180-2
political violence *see* human rights
    and political violence
Pollack, K. 59-60, 61
Portillo, M. 166, 179-80
private security firms, UK 198

Qatar
  arms deals 157, 165, 166, 183-4,
    190
  Barclays and financial crisis (2008)
    135-7
  coup 157, 166
  crisis 183-4
  gas (LNG) 52, 53, 57, 77-8,
    79
  investments in UK 146-7, 149-50,
    152
    foreign direct investment (FDI)
    127
  oil: British IOCs in 77-9
  UK export market and investment
    121, 122, 123
Qatar Investment Authority (QIA)
    102, 105, 130, 135, 146,
    149-50

Rabi, U. 29
Raphael, S. 58, 193, 198
Rayner, C. 124
'Red Line Agreement' 18
'Red Sea Oil and Gas' project, Saudi
    Arabia 75
'rentier state' paradigm 95-6
Rifkind, M. 166-7
Roberts, D. 193
Rogan, E. 156
Rolls-Royce 89, 122, 123, 127
Rowthorn, R. 92, 95
Royal Dutch Shell *see* Shell
Royal United Services Institute 179,
    182-3, 205

Saddam Hussein 42, 43-4, 62
Said, E. 5
Al Said, Qaboos (sultan of Oman) 35,
    36, 138
St John, J. 193, 198
Al Salam arms deal, Saudi Arabia
    168-9, 171-2, 175-6
Sampson, A. 20
Sassoon, Lord 115, 122-3,
    146
Saud, King (Ibn Saud) 15, 16, 17,
    28